Andonia Reynolds

Angela H. Robinette

Anita Adrain

Ann M. B. McIntyre

Brenda Gerling

Chantelle McFarland

Cheryl Viczko

Christine Lang

Ciara Caston Finley

Claire Valiquette

Dave August

Dee Taggart

Doreen Kilbreath

Elaine Valerie Thompson

Janice Gallant

Jennifer Pascoa

Jessica Sinclair

Joe Kavanagh

Karla VandenBerg

Kerstin Pelletier

Kimberly E. Beaudoin

Lady JB Owen

Lynda L Sullivan

Marion Andrews

Matthew A. Swierk

Melody J. Carberry

Mickey Forsyth

Peter Giesin

Summer Bozohora

Yun Rhee

IGNITE IMPACT

TRANSFORMATIONAL STORIES THAT WILL INSPIRE YOU TO MAKE A POSITIVE DIFFERENCE IN YOUR LIFE

INTRODUCTION BY

Lady JB Owen

Founder and CEO of Ignite Publishing, JBO Global Inc, World-class Speaker,
International Best Selling Author, and Knighted Lady

FOREWORD BY

Forbes Riley

Award Winning Motivational Speaker, Creator of SpinGym, Award Winning TV Host

PROJECT COORDINATOR

Elaine Valerie Thompson

International Best Selling Author
Founder of The Wellwishers Haven and Yes You Can
Certified FlowCode Coach™, Reiki Master Teacher, Intuitive Healer, Cell Health Coach

PROJECT LEADERS

Ciara Caston Finley

International Best Selling Author, Founder & CEO of Desiderata Kitchen,
Chef Extraordinaire, Heart-Centered Creative & Love Activator

Andonia Reynolds

International Best-Selling Author
Founder of Mustang Wisdom & The Many Hats We Wear
Equine-Assisted Transformational Coach | Entrepreneur | Creator of Inspire-O-Neer
International Speaker

OTHER FEATURED AUTHORS

Angela H. Robinette • Anita Adrain • Ann M. B. McIntyre
Brenda Gerling • Chantelle McFarland • Cheryl Viczko
Christine Lang • Claire Valiquette • Dave August • Dee Taggart
Doreen Kilbreath • Janice Gallant • Jennifer Pascoa
Jessica Sinclair • Joe Kavanagh • Karla VandenBerg • Kerstin Pelletier
Kimberly E. Beaudoin • Lynda L Sullivan • Marion Andrews
Matthew A. Swierk • Melody J. Carberry • Mickey Forsyth
Peter Giesin • Summer Bozohora • Yun Rhee

PUBLISHED BY IGNITE PUBLISHING™

Dedication

To the dreamers who dare, the doers who rise, and the souls who know deep down that they are here to make an *impact*.

This book is for those who refuse to sit on the sidelines of life and who believe that their actions, no matter how small, have the power to create transformation. *Impact* is not reserved for the few. It is found in every choice, every connection, and every moment we decide to show up with intention, courage, and purpose.

To every author in this book, you have shared your stories, ignited conversations, and sparked waves of change that will expand far beyond these pages. Your words will reach hearts you may never meet, uplift minds you may never know, and inspire lives in ways you cannot yet imagine. That is the true power of *impact*, legacy, and expansion.

And, to you, the reader, this book is your invitation to step into your own greatness, purpose, and *impact*. May these stories awaken something deep within you, strengthen your belief in what is possible, and remind you that your presence on this planet impacts all of us.

Start a wave of *impact*; Ignite what's possible. Inspire action. Leave your indelible mark.

Dedicate yourself to making a global *impact* by starting within yourself.

Being a contributing author to "Ignite Impact" has been an incredible experience. From the beginning, the Ignite team has provided unwavering support, encouragement, and expert guidance, making the journey of sharing my story seamless and empowering. This process has deepened my growth as a writer and allowed me to connect with an inspiring community of authors. I am beyond grateful for this opportunity and for saying yes to a project that has truly made an impact on my life.

—Brenda Gerling

Writing with Ignite has been one of the most impactful experiences of my life. The journey called me deep within myself to connect to the heart of my story while inviting me to share my heart within the Ignite community. I find myself wanting to continue this journey to share new chapters of my life in this compilation book series. This is more than a publishing business; this is a tribe of creators impacting one another and the world as we express our truths and write vulnerable stories to Ignite something new within ourselves.

—Chantelle McFarland

Everyone at Ignite has been incredibly supportive and encouraging. From trying to figure out what story I could write that was going to be impactful to the editing process, I could feel that their sole purpose was to help me be successful. I have learned so much, and as a result, I have become a much stronger writer! Thank you to the entire Ignite team!!

—Christine Lang

As a chef and entrepreneur, I've always believed in the power of connection, whether through food or shared experiences. But putting my heart into words was a different kind of transformation. It allowed me to embrace my own story with newfound confidence and courage.

Ignite provided a platform and a community of visionaries who uplift and inspire. Through this process, I discovered that my voice matters, that my experiences can spark change, and that telling my story is one of the most powerful ways to connect and empower others. Seeing my words in print has been an indescribable gift, knowing they have the potential to impact someone's life.

To anyone considering writing their story: Do it. Your voice, your journey, and your truth have the power to inspire, heal, and ignite impactful change. The world needs your story.

—Ciara Caston Finley

This was a profound experience of writing with Ignite. I jumped in with both feet, had no expectations, and trusted the process. The magic that unfolded was divine, and the connections that were made will last a lifetime. Becoming a published author has definitely helped me grow and is propelling me forward in ways I could not have imagined.

As I embark on this new journey, I look forward to amazing things to come, including my next story with Ignite. Thank you for making this powerful experience comfortable and with ease. I am deeply grateful.

—Claire Valiquette

Everyone is at the top of their game, easy to work with, considerate, and professional, and they get the job done promptly and efficiently. Hats off to them! This Company has been phenomenal to work with.

—Dave August

I never realized the emotions I still had pent up after 22 years. Putting your feelings and memories into words can help lighten your heart's load. I am grateful for the opportunity to share my Impact moment with others and work with the amazing people at Ignite.

—Doreen Kilbreath

Writing in Ignite Impact has been a transformative journey, helping me heal and grow in ways I never imagined. It has advanced my career and personal life and connected me to an empowering and supportive community that fuels my flow.

—Elaine Valerie Thompson

Writing with Ignite has been an inspirational experience! The guided support and community are unlike what I've ever experienced. I LOVED being a part of the global movement to bring more joy to everyone and support the building of schools in the world! I highly recommend this journey to anyone who would love to contribute.

—Janice Gallant

Writing a book has been on my bucket list for about 30 years, and having the opportunity to write a small part of my story is very profound. Our stories are meant to be told! I've been inspired and deeply impacted by the stories of so many others, and I am so grateful to be a part of this book. Thank you for inviting me in. It's been a life-changing experience.

—Jennifer Pascoa

This experience was very healing and brought a lot of clarity, peace, and expansion. Celebrating my journey and inspiring others with my story was a beautiful opportunity. Thank you for the opportunity to be a part of something much bigger than myself!

—Jessica Sinclair

For years, friends and family have encouraged me to share my journey in a book, though I struggled to see the starting point or focus for such an endeavor. It was a challenge to envision! As fate would have it, my path crossed with JB and Peter at Ignite Publishing, and their incredible support and understanding made all the difference. They opened my eyes to the simple truth: with proper guidance, anything is possible.

—Joe Kavanagh

For years, friends and family have encouraged me to share my journey in a book, though I struggled to see the starting point or focus for such an endeavor. It was a challenge to envisage! However, my path crossed with JB and Peter at Ignite Publishing, and their incredible support and understanding made all the difference. They opened my eyes to the simple truth: with proper guidance, anything is possible. Their proposal to contribute a chapter to the upcoming "Ignite Impact" book inspired me to take this leap. The community and collaboration made the process not only feasible but genuinely rewarding. With their nurturing approach and expert advice, I'm embarking on this exciting adventure, knowing it's a structured path towards achieving something truly meaningful.

—Karla VandenBerg

Working with Ignite Publishing has been a transformative journey for me. Writing my story allowed me to experience deeper healing and helped me embrace my voice in a way I hadn't before. I have felt truly acknowledged and heard through sharing my story, which has been incredibly empowering.

—Kerstin Pelletier

This experience of writing my story had brought possibilities beyond my comprehension! I have jumped through fear and leaped over challenges. I have ignited roots deep within my soul. I have broken through barricades that I thought were not possible. I have courage that I thought was lost forever. I believe in myself and have found my worth in life again. I am so drunk on self that I feel so high on life, and the Magic that has been brought to my attention is beyond belief. My life is changed forever from the inside out. I have never experienced support, kindness, encouragement, and the most positive community to make all this magic possible! Biggest shout out to Lady JB and the Ignite Team. I could have never done it without you. Many blessings with much Love

—Kimberly E. Beaudoin

I have contributed to other compilation books, and this is the first time I have felt totally supported and appreciated.

—Matthew A. Swierk

It once again has been an honor to write with Ignite Publishing. This is my second compilation book. It has given me great insight into the magical world of Ignite and the precious process and care they take with the writers. From uncovering your story to editing and printing, these gracious experts take you on your own journey. One that will bring you out, the other side more confident. Surprising even yourself. Allowing your truth and submissions to come forth and light the way for the readers to connect and engage. Someone needs your story. Someone needs to hear how you overcame adversity. Be brave; the benefits of knowing someone is not alone can spark such great joy. Discovering that they, too, can overcome their current reality. The impact of your story can create such a beautiful ripple in the world for which so many are searching. Shine your magnificent light so someone else can find their way.

—Melody J. Carberry

Writing with Ignite has been wonderful. New and experienced authors are treated with respect, kindness, and amazing support. I highly recommend working with the Ignite team!

—Mickey Forsyth

Working with Ignite has been such an amazing experience. The entire process was seamless, and I absolutely love all the systems in place. Having multiple editors and allowing so many opportunities to meet with the entire group was an abundance of support. I can't say enough about Lady JB and her expertise and attention to every detail. Her knowledge of words and being able to help

—Yun Rhee

Contents

IGNITE IMPACT AUTHORS — 3

DEDICATION — 5

TESTIMONIALS FROM AUTHORS — 6

WHAT IS AN IGNITE BOOK? — 14

INTRODUCTION — 20

FOREWORD BY FORBES RILEY — 25

LADY JB OWEN - We All Make Impact — 29

ELAINE VALERIE THOMPSON - Beyond The Mirror — 39

CIARA CASTON FINLEY - Peace in the Pieces — 47

ANDONIA REYNOLDS - Blackheart's Gift — 55

PETER GIESIN - The Power of Almost — 63

MELODY J CARBERRY - Good Graces — 71

CHRISTINE LANG, BA(ECON), CPA, CGA, CCS -
The Journey of a Resilient High School Dropout — 81

DEE TAGGART - The Impact of One Decision — 89

JESSICA SINCLAIR - The Rainbows After the Storms — 99

YUN RHEE - Keys To The Kingdom — 107

KIMBERLY E. BEAUDOIN - Rising Up — 115

ANGELA H. ROBINETTE - A Gift — 123

MATTHEW A. SWIERK - The Journey Back to Me — 131

MICKEY FORSYTH - Lessons Of Care — 139

JOE KAVANAGH - The Exposure! — 147

KARLA VANDENBERG - Chasing Sparkles and Dreams — 155

Doreen Kilbreath - My Everything ... 165

Chantelle McFarland - My Heart Whispers ... 173

Dave August - The Door of Opportunity ... 183

Lynda L. Sullivan - The Journey Back to the True Me ... 191

Brenda Gerling - Preserving Wisdom ... 199

Kerstin Pelletier - Breathing the Light of Spirit ... 207

Ann M. B. McIntyre - It Will Make Me Feel Better ... 215

Jennifer Pascoa - A Mosaic of Threads ... 223

Summer Bozohora - Relationships Are Assignments ... 231

Marion Andrews - A Spiritual Journey of
Survival and Transformation ... 239

Claire Valiquette - Angel Voices ... 247

Janice Gallant - Clearing Debris Through Forgiveness ... 255

Anita Adrain & Cheryl Viczko - Divinely Guided Encounters:
How One Moment Changed Everything ... 265

Impactful Affirmations for you to use in your life ... 280

Impactful Books Recommendations ... 284

Resources ... 287

Project Leaders ... 290

Photo Credits ... 292

Thank You ... 293

WHAT IS AN IGNITE BOOK?

Ignite Publishing™ is not just a publishing company. It is a movement—a call to action, a beacon for others, and a force for transformation. For almost a decade, we have been leading the way in *Empowerment Publishing*, bringing together voices from all over the world to share powerful, life-changing stories. With almost 800 authors published and now our twenty-fourth compilation book complete, we continue to witness the unstoppable 'igniting' effect of authentic storytelling.

At Ignite, we do not just produce books. We design literature of inspiration that ignites possibility, fuels passion, and awakens purpose. Our books remind us that stories matter, that our experiences hold wisdom, and that one voice, one message, and one act of sharing can shift the trajectory of where we are headed in the future.

The stories in this book show that impact is not about status, wealth, or influence. It is found in the small moments, the courageous decisions, and the everyday choices that define how we show up in the world. True impact is not measured by what we accomplish for ourselves but by how we lift others, the conversations we spark, and the change we ignite through our presence and purpose.

When you pick up this book, you're experiencing more than just reading words on a page. You are stepping into a vision, engaging in a profound desire to awaken the world to unlimited new possibilities. These stories are here to expand your perspective, fuel your passion, and infuse within you the realization that you, too, are here to make a dynamic and beloved impact.

The Structure of Each Story

The name "Ignite" was chosen with intention. It represents the moment when a spark catches fire, when an idea takes flight, and when a single shift in perspective forever changes a life. Every Ignite book is filled with vulnerable, unfiltered, and deeply heartfelt stories that move, propel, and inspire. These books remind you that impact is not reserved for the few—it is universally within all of us.

Every Ignite book follows a structured journey designed to take the reader through an experience of inspiration, reflection, and action. Each section is crafted with intention, guiding you to absorb the story and apply its lessons to your own life.

Power Quotes: Ignite Your Thinking

Each story begins with an Ignite *Power Quote*. These are not just words on a page. They are powerful statements that challenge perspectives, spark curiosity, and encourage deep thought. They serve as a catalyst for reflection, offering insight into the themes that follow and setting the tone for the story ahead.

A well-written Power Quote has the ability to shift the way we see the world. It can encourage us to take action, remind us of forgotten truths, or give us the courage to step forward boldly. Each Ignite *Power Quote* has been carefully crafted to inspire a sense of purpose and highlight the immense impact one thought, idea, or decision can have.

As you read these quotes, take a moment to let them settle within you. Consider how they apply to your life and might challenge you to think differently about your influence in the world. Use them whenever you need to encourage and motivate you.

Personal Intention: The Heart of the Story

Before the story begins, each author shares their *Personal Intention*. This is an honest reflection from their heart, an opportunity to connect with the deeper meaning behind their words. Their intention is not just to tell you about their story but to ignite something greater within you.

Through this section, the author expresses what they hope you will take away from their experience. Some intentions are deeply personal, revealing lessons learned through pain, struggle, or triumph. Others are focused on encouragement and support, offering wisdom and guidance for you in your life.

These *Personal Intentions* remind us that stories are not just meant to be told. Their purpose is to be felt, lived, and passed on. They hold the power to awaken something dormant within us, shifting our perceptions and guiding us toward new intentions. Each author has chosen to share a piece of their journey, hoping it will resonate with someone who needs it most. Their words serve as a bridge, connecting lived experiences. They are blueprints for what is possible, invitations to rise, and proof that the human spirit is capable of extraordinary transformation.

As you read these sections, reflect on what speaks to you the most. Notice where their words resonate and how their experiences might mirror your own.

THE IGNITE MOMENT: A DEFINING SHIFT

We believe that everyone has had an *Ignite Moment*™, a pivotal experience that changed their life and reshaped their understanding of what is achievable. These moments often arise from unexpected obstacles, moments of deep retrospection, or events that force a shift in our perspective.

The Ignite Moment is the heartbeat of each author's story. It is the moment of realization that something has changed, and there is no going back. Some moments come as whispers, a subtle but profound shift in awareness. While others arrive like a lightning bolt, bringing immediate and undeniable truth. Yet, each one produces the same result: it ignites the soul.

Each chapter in this book reveals an *Ignite Moment* that led the author to a new way of thinking, living, or contributing to the world. These moments remind us that growth often comes from discomfort, that knowledge is born from circumstances, and that impact is created when we choose to take what we have learned and use it to better ourselves.

As you read each narrative, reflect on your own *Ignite Moments*. Think about the times in your life when something shifted, when a challenge became a lesson, or when you realized you had more strength than you thought you had. Consider how those moments have shaped you and how they might be the key to the impact you are meant to create going forward.

IGNITE ACTION STEPS: MAKING IMPACT REAL

All the stories are designed to do more than just inspire thought. They are meant to encourage action. That is why each chapter ends with *Ignite Action Steps*, practical insights, and strategies that allow you to apply what you have learned to your own life.

True impact happens when we turn inspiration into action. These steps offer a clear pathway for integrating new perspectives, shifting limiting beliefs, and making tangible changes. They are not just ideas but real, proven methods and techniques the authors have used to transform their own lives into something greater.

The great thing is you don't need big, dramatic actions to make an impact. It often starts with small, intentional choices that lead to something greater over time. These *Ignite Action Steps* are designed to help you take the next step, whether big or small. Try each one and see how they help you in making a bigger impact on your trajectory.

REFLECTION QUESTIONS: TURNING INSIGHT INTO ACTION

Woven throughout the chapters, you will find insightful *Reflection Questions* designed to deepen your connection to the stories and help you explore your own experience. These prompts invite you to pause, reflect, and consider how the themes within the chapters relate to your life. Some will encourage introspection, guiding you to look back at pivotal moments that have shaped you. Others will prompt you to think forward, envisioning the impact you want to create and the steps you are ready to take.

True transformation happens when we go beyond inspiration and engage with what we have learned. These reflection sections are a space for you to slow down, absorb the shared learning, and apply it in a meaningful way. Use them as a personal journal, a guide for deeper exploration, or even a conversation starter with those around you. The more you engage with these questions, the more you will uncover about your path, purpose, and the impact you are here to make.

READ THE BOOK YOUR WAY

Every reader engages with an Ignite book differently. Some will move through the chapters in order, absorbing each story as part of a greater journey. Others will flip to a random page, trusting that the story they land on holds the message they need to hear.

However you choose to read this book, trust that the stories within it will meet you exactly where you are. There is no right or wrong way to take in these lessons, only the way that resonates most with you. Some stories may awaken you. Others may reaffirm what you already know deep within. Some may bring clarity to a situation you are facing, while others may light a spark you did not even realize you needed.

Take your time with these stories. Reflect on the words that stand out to you. Let them guide your thoughts and inspire your next steps. Read with an open heart, and be willing to see yourself in the awareness of others. The impact of this book is not just in the reading. It is in what you do with the lessons, perspectives, and truths that unfold throughout these pages.

Your Story is Part of This Journey

As you turn these pages, remember that this book is more than a collection of stories. It is an invitation that encourages you to see yourself in these experiences, recognize your defining moments, and reflect on the path that has shaped you. These narratives are not just here to inspire. They are here to remind you that your life holds meaning in ways you may not yet fully realize.

You are an essential part of this world. The lessons, insights, and revelations within these chapters are meant to stir something in you, to remind you that *your* journey carries wisdom, depth, and the potential to leave a lasting impression on others. As you engage with these stories, allow them to guide you inward. Consider how your experiences have shaped you, how your challenges have strengthened you, and how your voice has the power to create influence in ways far beyond what you can see.

Share Your Ignite Moment

Stories create an impact when they are shared. If a story in this book touches you, we encourage you to reach out to the author and let them know. Every author has chosen to share their journey with the hope that it will inspire someone else, and your response is part of that exchange.

We also encourage you to share your own *Ignite Moments*. Speak about them with those around you, write them down, or find a way to bring them into the world. Your story has the power to Ignite lives, just as the stories in this book are igniting yours.

Perhaps you have already had an *Ignite Moment*, one that shifted your path or changed your perspective. Or maybe your *Ignite Moment* is still unfolding, and this book will be the catalyst that brings it into focus. Whatever your journey, remember that your impact happens when you both give and receive. It grows when shared, reflected upon, and passed on for others to grow from.

By sharing your story, you create a continuous positive effect that reaches far beyond what you can see. Your experience may be the very thing that helps someone else find their inner knowing, embrace their truth, or take action toward their own transformation. Never underestimate the power of your story, your voice, or the message that you have to share.

Welcome to the Ignite Family

As you enjoy each story written in, *Ignite Impact*, know that you are now part of something much bigger. You are connected to a community of people who believe in the power of storytelling, the strength of human connection, and the potential within each of us to create lasting change.

The *Ignite Family* is built on the belief that every story has value, every experience carries wisdom, and every person holds the ability to make an impact. Whether you are an author, a reader, a dreamer, or a changemaker, you belong here. You are part of a movement that is dedicated to inspiring, uplifting, and transforming lives, one *Ignite Moment* at a time.

These stories will challenge you, inspire you, and empower you to create the impact you desire, not just in your own life but in the world around you. Your role in this movement is just as important as the stories on these pages.

So embrace this journey. Step into your *Ignite Moment*. Recognize the impact you are already making, and let it expand in ways you never imagined.

The world is waiting for the impact only you can create. Let this book be the spark that ignites it.

Introduction

The Smallest Gesture Can Create the Greatest Impact

Impact is not just something we create. It is something we embody. It begins as a spark within, fueled by our thoughts, shaped by our desires, and guided by the mindset we cultivate. Before it ripples outward to shift perspectives, transform communities, and change the world, it starts in the quiet spaces of our own awareness.

We all long to make a difference, leave a mark that outlasts us, and know that our presence in this world holds meaning. Too often, we believe *impact* requires something external—money, influence, or a platform large enough to be seen. The truth is *impact* begins the moment we decide to live with intention. It is present in the energy we bring to a conversation, the kindness we extend to a stranger, and the encouragement we offer when someone needs it most. These seemingly small actions create ripples that build into something far greater than we could ever imagine.

The authors in this book did not set out to create a global *impact*. They were simply navigating their own journeys, facing struggles, embracing transformation, and learning to rise in the face of adversity. Some endured loss that reshaped their world. Others found themselves at a crossroads, forced to choose between staying where they were or stepping into something greater. In those moments, *impact* was not yet a movement. It was a choice, a realization, a shift in perspective that led them to a higher calling.

What transforms us inevitably transforms those around us. The strength gained through struggle, the wisdom uncovered through hardship, and the purpose discovered in our darkest hours do not stay contained. They expand outward, shaping how we lead, uplift others, and inspire change, often without even realizing it.

Some of the most extraordinary moments of *impact* begin with the simplest gesture. The smile you exchange with a stranger may be the compassion they need that day. A kind word you speak may alter the course of someone's confidence. That heartfelt conversation you shared to plant a seed of hope can grow into something life-changing. You see, the greatest shifts do not always come from grand actions. They materialize from the small, intentional moments that make someone feel seen, heard, and valued.

This book is a testament to that truth.

THE DEEP HUMAN NEED FOR IMPACT

Many of us were not raised to seek *impact*. Instead, we were taught to be small, polite, and fit into the mold created for us. Society often rewards those who blend in, follow the rules, and remain quiet instead of disrupting the status quo. From a young age, we are conditioned to dim our light. *Ignite Publishing*™ exists to change that.

Ignite is about owning the fullness of who you are. It is about recognizing that your story, truth, and experiences hold infinite value. When you allow yourself to be fully seen, you permit others to do the same. *Impact* is not just about what you do. It is about how you radiate your energy, stand in your power, and inspire others to rise alongside you.

These authors have lived through moments that broke them open and forced them to rebuild. They have endured experiences that tested their resilience, their faith, and their belief in what is possible. They have chosen to share those moments, not because it is easy, but because it is necessary. These stories are filled with determination, courage, and transformation. They remind us that *impact* is not measured solely by achievement but by how we rise, carry our lessons forward, and use them to elevate those around us.

Impact creates movement. When one person makes a shift, that shift influences another. That influence expands into families, communities, industries, and entire generations. Some of the most influential movements in history began with one individual who refused to stay silent, turned pain into purpose, and allowed their personal transformation to ignite something greater.

Your Hardships Hold the Seeds of Impact

There comes a moment in life when we are faced with a choice. We can allow hardship to break us or let it refine us into the person we are destined to be. The moments that shake us to our core and leave us questioning everything we once knew are often the moments that hold the most extraordinary power.

Some people take their pain and carry it quietly, never allowing it to become more than a personal burden. Others take that same pain and turn it into purpose, using their experience to create something meaningful. A struggle can remain a private chapter or become the catalyst for transformation.

Impact does not come from avoiding challenges. It comes from what we choose to do with them. Those who create real change are not always the ones with the loudest voices or the largest platforms. They are the ones who decide that their story matters, recognizing that what they have endured can serve as a guiding light for someone else and taking a step forward, not because it is easy, but because they know their journey has meaning.

Think about a time in your own life when you faced adversity. Maybe it was a moment of profound loss, a setback that felt impossible to overcome, or a challenge that pushed you beyond what you thought you could handle. In that moment, you had a choice. You could shrink, or you could rise. You could remain in the struggle or turn it into something that served a greater purpose.

The greatest *impact* often comes from those who take their most difficult moments and allow them to fuel something larger than themselves. How we respond to life's hardships has the power to shape not only our future but the future of those around us.

Making an Impact and Sparking Change

Throughout history, ordinary people have taken their most challenging moments and turned them into something extraordinary. *Impact* does not happen by accident. It happens when we take the lessons life has given us and use them as fuel to create something meaningful.

The stories in this book carry that same intention.

Within these pages, you will read about people who have faced unimaginable challenges and emerged stronger, wiser, and more determined to make a difference. Each story holds a lesson, an insight, and a message meant to reach you exactly where you are.

As you reflect on the stories in this book, consider how your own journey has shaped you. Think about the ways you have already impacted others, perhaps without even realizing it. Your presence, words, and actions create waves in ways you may never fully see.

Impact does not begin with changing the world. It starts with changing the way we see ourselves. The moment we decide to rise after falling, it begins. The moment we recognize that our experiences and our presence carry significance, it begins. And when we decide to stop waiting for permission and start living with the intention of making a difference.

The choice to make an impact is always yours.

You are not just reading a book. You are stepping into a moment of expansion, a shift in awareness, and a deeper understanding of the influence you hold. The world is waiting for the *impact* only you can make. As you turn these pages, ask yourself.

What am I here to ignite?

With passion, purpose, and possibility,

Lady JB Owen

Forbes Riley

Foreword

Forbes Riley

"Be somebody no one thought you could be."

Impact is not just a word. It is an energy, a force, a ripple that extends far beyond what we can see. It's the lasting imprint we leave on the world, the legacy that outlives us, and the undeniable proof that our lives matter. We all seek it in some way. We want to know that we are making a difference, that our time on this earth has meaning, and that the struggles we have endured and the victories we have celebrated were not just random events but part of something bigger.

I have spent my entire life obsessed with the concept of *impact*. As an entrepreneur, a speaker, a mother, and a woman who has navigated every possible twist and turn life could throw at me, I have learned one undeniable truth: *impact* is not accidental. It is intentional. We create, shape, and build *impact* through our choices, the stories we share, and the courage we show in standing up and saying, "I have something valuable to offer this world."

I remember the first time I truly understood the power of *impact*. It wasn't in a high-stakes business deal, a significant pitch, or even a financial break-through. It was in the quiet space of personal loss, a moment that shattered me and forced me to search for meaning.

I was fifteen years old when my father—an engineer, my rock, and my greatest supporter had a devastating accident at work. In an instant, life changed. He caught his hand in a printing press, an injury that would lead to fifteen surgeries over three years and leave my once-strong father struggling in ways I never could have imagined. As the sole provider for our family, his accident left us financially broken. And though he remained present, something fundamental had shifted.

That was my first Ignite Moment, the realization that life is unpredictable and fragile, but our response to it is what defines us. I had a choice: let that moment break me or let it shape me.

I chose to rise.

I used my pain as fuel. I took everything my father had instilled in me, his resilience and his ingenuity, and built something greater. His *impact* on me did not fade because his circumstances changed. It *evolved*. It became the foundation for the *impact* I would one day create for others.

That is the truth about *impact*. It is not just about what we do; it is about how we make people feel, the way we show up in the world, and how we transform even the most painful experiences into something meaningful.

Over the years, I have built businesses, coached thousands of entrepreneurs, and mastered the art of the pitch. But the greatest *impact* I have ever made has come through the power of my story.

This book is about people who have chosen to own their experiences, embraced their truths, and stepped forward to share their journeys. Their stories are not just words on a page but blueprints for transformation. They prove that *impact* is not reserved for the select few—it exists within all of us, waiting to be unleashed.

And that is where Lady JB Owen comes in.

If you know JB, you know she is unstoppable. She doesn't just talk about *impact*; she embodies it. She is a force of nature, a woman whose vision goes beyond simply publishing books. She is here to ignite others and change humanity.

Lady JB has impacted me in ways that are hard to put into words. She doesn't just suggest you can achieve great things; she instills in you a burning desire to reach your full potential, a feeling that resonates deep within your soul. She sees something in people before they see it in themselves. She pushes. She challenges. She elevates. Her passion for storytelling and empowerment is not just a mission but a movement.

Through Ignite Publishing, JB has created more than a platform for sharing stories—she has built a global stage for transformation. She gives people the space to tell their stories and own them. To turn their experiences into tools for impact. To share their Ignite Moments in a way that inspires, connects, and creates lasting change.

That is the *magic* of what she has built.

That is *why* this book is unlike anything else.

The stories in *Ignite Impact* are real. They are raw. These are stories of people who overcame challenges, conquered self-doubt, and found their true voice. These stories are not fairytales but testaments to resilience, courage, and transformation.

As you read them, you will find yourself reflected in these pages.

You may recognize your own struggles, discover the words you've been searching for, or experience an Ignite Moment of your own; that realization that you, too, have a story worth telling and an *impact* worth making.

Because here's the truth: your story is your greatest asset. It is your proof of perseverance, your testament to growth, and your gift to the world. Every challenge you have overcome, every lesson you have learned, and every break-through you have experienced holds value.

Someone, somewhere, needs to hear it.

That is why books like *Ignite Impact* matter.

It is more than just a book. It is a catalyst for connection. It reminds us that we are not alone. It has the power to turn our pain into purpose, our lessons into leadership, and our experiences into something greater than ourselves.

So, if you take one thing from this book, let it be this:

Your impact is already unfolding. Right now. At this very moment. Through the way you show up, the energy you bring, and the stories you choose to share.

The only question is…

Will you fully step into it?

As you turn these pages, let these stories do more than inspire you; let them challenge you. Let them push you to think about your legacy, the influence you are making, and how you choose to show up in the world.

When you reach the last page, don't just close the book and walk away.

Take action.

Start sharing your own story. Make choices that align with the *impact* you want to create. Live in a way that ensures your presence in this world leaves it better than how you found it.

Because *impact* is not just something we leave behind.

It is something we create every single day.

And the time to start is NOW!

Here's to your success.

Queen of Pitch,

Forbes Riley

Lady JB Owen

LADY JB OWEN

"The impact you seek may not always be the impact you make."

My intention is for you to feel the vast magnificence of who you are and bask in the glory of all you have to give the world. You were born with many gifts and so many treasures within you. Exactly as you are is perfect and divine. If we could all share our uniqueness, achieve what we aspire for, and support others in being themselves, our impact on humanity would be insurmountable. Life itself would flourish, and goodness would prevail. Being a magical piece in the infinite makings of the world and doing your part in uplifting others is the impact the world needs.

WE ALL MAKE IMPACT

It was Sunday evening, and I was just finishing my last *story polish* for the day. I had met with numerous authors over the last three days and completed nineteen story polishes, back-to-back, in a desire to get the book *Ignite Impact* to the finish line. I often stack my story polishes, using my weekend to immerse myself in the heartfelt stories that authors write to fill a book. I have been doing this practice for over seven years, having published over eight hundred authors and twenty-six compilation books, polishing every story personally.

I am used to this intense pace, and being with my authors this way is one of my favorite things. I feel so lucky that I get to sit with them, just the two of us, sharing a time in their lives that has fundamentally impacted them. I use my weekends to polish stories because that is when I am most relaxed and able to go *deep* with them, listening to their story as they read aloud every word to me. When I hear their voice, I begin to meld with them. I feel invited into their world, and in a way, I travel with them back in time to when their story occurred and when their *Ignite Moment* first took place.

It may sound odd, but I *feel* them in their rawest form, and I *see* them in those moments, making the decision and facing the consequences of the outcomes. I often say I am channeling them, interwoven in the mix of the story they lived and witnessing the meaning they assign to that occurrence afterward. It is as if I am there, like a trusted friend, a confidant, a spirit beside them as they invite me in. As they read their story, I sense a portal open, and I am at their side, going through the things they have endured. I am with them through and through.

During my polishes, I often feel as if I am sitting next to them as they read to me. It is as though I am in their world, watching their life, plugged into them. I experience what they experienced and see life through their eyes. It is a very intimate process, filled with the tremendous highs of success and happiness and crushing lows of anger and regret. It is deeply personal and vulnerable, and throughout the entire polish session, I am a part of them, feeling their deepest emotions and connecting directly with what I believe is the essence of their soul.

Often, in my polishes, I notice something they didn't. Like a visitor in the room, I have a unique perspective, an alternative vantage point that allows me to glimpse what happened to them from a different viewpoint. Gently and carefully, I offer a tiny idea or ask a simple question that opens their mind to an alternate perspective and enables them to find a different meaning than the one they originally formed. Sometimes, in my search for clarity, I ask a poignant question they have been wanting to hear, "Was it all about you?" "Was that the only choice you had?" "How could it have been different?" "What if you were not to blame?"

In those intimate moments of deep retrospection, I have them look at that situation in a more empowering way. At first, I see them struggle internally, almost wrestling with the question. But always, over time, with me as their support, I see them shift, make a new connection to what happened, and their eyes light up. They start to form a new thought, a new neuro pathway in their mind, outside of the one they have been holding onto. Through that simple invitation to ask themselves a thoughtful question, they begin to unfurl and unravel the decision they made, unpacking the actions and ultimately uncovering a deeper truth behind the truth they have been clinging to.

That moment of ignition toward a different thought is one of the most precious things I get to witness. It is a moment of compassionate self-awareness and true enlightenment. It is as if a flame has been struck inside them, and a light begins to shine. Using the passage of time, the sacred space of the story polish, and the retrospection of their maturity, they see what happened differently and begin to transform. I watch as unexplored connections are made and witness them softening, relaxing, and awakening to entirely new opinions than the ones they had before. Most importantly, I stand in awe as they forgive, embrace, and find themselves after being estranged for so long.

Few words can describe the feeling I have when I see this shift because it is so magical and precious. I get to be there as they let go of all the blame they carried, remove the burdens they had to bear, and no longer succumb to the shame they placed so dauntingly upon themself. I see the inner battle finally over, and the love they had tucked away blossom in its place.

These moments are often accompanied by tears from both myself and the authors. Tears that came with pain and sorrow, clenched fists, and a trembling voice soon subside, and before we know it, those tears have shifted to glistening rainbows and illuminating cheeks of joy. They find the laughter, begin to smile, and rejoice in the freedom they suddenly feel. They are eternally grateful for the chains they have uncuffed themselves from and the liberation they reclaim and decide to own.

I get to be with them in these moments, in the genesis of aroused new thought, and the revelation of what they once believed so emphatically is no longer the case. Somehow, in telling their story and reading it to me, they allow me to help them see what they are longing to reveal. They form new reflections like, "I did the very best I could," and "I know it wasn't my fault." They awaken to the decision that 'I am not to blame' and 'This is no longer my truth.' In these powerful moments of self-reflection and desired inner peace, they shed themselves of decades of harmful thinking and dissolve a lifetime of restricting beliefs.

We all assign meaning to events, and since we are the stars of our lives, we inject opinions and blame ourselves. We can't help but assume that when things unfold, it has to be because of us. Our minds, egos, and human needs compel us to formulate *why* it happened and *how* we were responsible. Most of the time, that blame comes when we are in a situation where we are unable to see the world is made up of other factors; some we have control over and others we do not. Too often, our meanings are subject to our limited knowledge, conditioned patterns, or imposed ideals. Nonetheless, we create unrelenting definitions and discouraging opinions of ourselves. We then carry them with us until one day, we decide, consciously or unconsciously, that we are ready to take on a new meaning and find a new path. We decided to *polish our story* and remove all the tarnishes we placed upon it.

I believe this desire for a better way of living is what guides an author to work with me. Add in the loving care of the Great One, who works in their favor, they find themselves sharing their most private moment with me in a polish, saying what has been hidden yet wanting to be released. Knowingly or not, they decide they deserve more, and even if it is trepidatiously, they want to embrace their greatness.

I didn't understand this deeply personal 'polish' process when I began the company Ignite Publishing™. Helping people *write* their stories was my first agenda. Being a systems person, serial entrepreneur, and one with an 'anything is possible' attitude, collecting stories, editing, manufacturing, and publishing them seemed straightforward and doable. I researched, mapped out the process, and took each step with the precision of building a business and formulating an influential publishing house.

Like most entrepreneurs, I accessed the problems, innovated a solution, and worked out the logistics along the way. I knew the steps that needed to happen to achieve results. Yet, when I began, I had no idea what investment had to be made in the authors themselves. I didn't realize Pandora's box would open and the Kraken would be unleashed when you ask someone to share the moment things vastly shifted in their life.

Our very first book of thirty-five women sharing their impactful stories threw me into the necessary steps of helping them manage and process their past. Knocking on the doors of old wounds and impactful moments meant performing emotional triage. I wanted them to dig deep, uncover challenges, and write about their hardship poignantly to help inspire someone else. Luckily, each author was willing and eager to move from how they were thinking to discover something better. I met with each of them to check in and lend support. Those meetings turned into them reading their stories to me so I could listen to their setbacks and offer my guidance. Intuitively, I had them read what was on the page, not talk it out. I had them recite what they wrote, what they crafted, and the words inside them waiting to be expressed.

To say that process made a difference is an understatement. Within days, each author felt better, old wounds were healed, and forgiveness for themselves and others was abundant. I watched each one of them come alive in remarkable ways. Their changes were profound, electric, and contagious. Each one was learning from the other; the entire group was elevating. Beautiful things were unfolding all because they assigned a new meaning to something they had labeled as a setback and their fault.

I stood back and watched them in joy and elation. Each one had begun writing their story with broken feelings and hurtful opinions about themselves, only to be transformed and enlivened by shifting their thinking around the 'story' they had made up about themselves. In writing their story, they began rewriting the beliefs they formed *because* of their story. Their story became *a story*, not a definitive in their life. They mourned for the person in the story and saw them with compassion and empathy. They detached themselves from the circumstances and walked away from the pages of that chapter completely renewed.

It was exhilarating to be the catalyst of such magnificent shifts. I was hooked, unable to look away as each shone like a blazing comet. Their worlds bloomed, their outlooks flourished, and the future before them was free and clear of the inner turmoil that had been holding them back. As they lit up like blazing candles, they lit up those around them. They became beacons of hope and possibilities, igniting others in their wake. I watched them in total admiration, knowing the impact they were making was also inspiring others. That solidified my knowing that helping them share those moments was the most significant impact I could make in my life.

That began an endless quest to tell more stories, write more books, and integrate a mandatory process where every author must attend an impactful story polish. I wanted to create a container of safety for the author to share openly, and like a bee to honey, I witnessed the moment when they recognized their divine greatness. Helping people write their Ignite Moment became an Ignite Moment for me. I was creating my own burning embers, an infinite supply of flaming fuel to transform myself. Each story was an enriching resource that ignited me. Every author was a spark toward my inner enlightenment. I realized each 'Ignite Moment' was like a cataclysmic birth of life itself, the very epicenter of the human and the soul coming together in divine convergence.

Imagine the impact that ensues when what you thought no longer exists, and in its place is a new thought, a more empowering one that forms into existence. Envision the energy, the expansiveness, the breaking and exploding of a construct so that a new paradigm of thinking can emerge. Consider all the molecules that move, the cells that change, the atoms and electrons that shift and form so that something else can materialize in its place. From there, a supernova of newness emerges, and not just one thought is created; a kaleidoscope of thoughts flows like an endless waterfall of possibilities into a pool of vast limitless. In that moment, you are forever changed from what *was* to what can *be*.

Many see what I do as just helping a writer write their story. They don't realize that during a story polish authors have the ability to create a seismic ripple in the fabric of all humanity. Some may see Ignite Moments as only sharing a fragment of one's life, but I see it as forging a gateway to a better life for *everyone*. One person can ignite lives and impact humanity on a global scale. Each one of us plays a part in the interconnectedness of us all. When one person decides the impact of a situation is no longer going to stop them from being who they were born to be, they shift the trajectory for everyone. They chart the path and pave the way for more revelations to occur. A single person in the aspiration of greatness creates a cosmic stream of possibility throughout humanity. Their energy can not be ignored, and their magnetism forms a neverending trail of what can be created universally.

How can we not be influenced by the igniting of a flame? How can my life not be affected when you ignite yours? These questions had simple answers. When I asked myself what I could do to perpetuate more of them unfolding, my mission was clear. A vision of humanity was shown to me in lights turning on all around the globe. It was as if I had a view from outer space as souls were lit up across all continents. Their lighting inspired the lighting of more souls awakening by their impactfulness. The world was a Christmas tree of light from people who had shared their stories, and one story sparked the flame in someone else. Their most difficult moments were a gift for them to be 'present' in the 'presence' of their magnificent greatness.

If eight billion people inhabit this earth, then eight billion Ignite Moments should be shared, expressed, and drawn from. This is the unlimited source of energy scientists have been searching for: the energy of *awakening* our true selves. There is no greater impact than the one we have when we see the glistening light of who we are and step into our existence, enveloping ourselves in our divinity.

Some people complete a story polish not knowing such an impact has transpired in themselves. They may only see a trickle of it, a fleeting glimmer, but it is a start. What they don't know is *I see it*. I see them. I see the pain and human suffering they have endured, and more importantly, *I see what is on the other side, ready to emerge.* I see what life has offered them through the darker human emotions, yet tethered to that is the greatest of all human gifts: their life force.

Others feel the impact of their Ignite Moment immediately, yet have to shield themselves from the karmic light until they're ready. Some take that moment in breathless sips and simmer in the change, allowing it to gradually build to its peak. Many go all in, basking in the light, singeing the old to oblivion, and never looking back. Yet, without realizing it, each one breathes life into themselves. I have seen this emerging beauty hundreds of times and humbly felt its undeniable force.

After all these powerful polishes, I have learned we all have Ignite Moments, those profound moments when life hands us an opportunity to become a better person, to rise above, and to do things differently for our highest evolution. We all have a choice and opportunity to embrace those moments and make the most of them. We may not know when or where an Ignite Moment will emerge, but what we do know is that it is genesis, it is life, and it is the beginning of something grand and exquisite. Within each Ignite Moment is the gift of greatness and pure inner magnificence.

I have had so many of my own Ignite Moments and have been blessed to experience energetically hundreds of others in this lifetime. Each one has left a lasting and life-changing impact on me and started a chain reaction of Ignite Moments globally.

The impact you seek may not always be the impact you make. Your work is to find the moments that once *defined* you and let them *refine* you into your greatest self. *Your Ignite Moment was given to you by something greater than you to bring forth the greatness in you.* Read that sentence a few times. Maybe even write it out. Let it be the first line in the new story you rewrite about yourself. Allow the knowing that within you lies your greatness, which will activate a new thought and create outstanding new beliefs that will forever impact your life, my life, and all of humanity.

IGNITE ACTION STEPS

Be willing to embrace the new you. Let go of everything that no longer serves and replace it with the best version of yourself. You have the ability to define who you are, so be intentional about who that person is.

See all moments as gifts and blessings. Nothing happens haphazardly or for no reason. Everything is part of the interconnectedness of the universe. If it has happened, it happens for a reason. If it is unfolding, then learn from it. If it has been placed in your life, then be excited to see the gift on the other side and the present and presence it will bring.

Lady JB Owen — Canada
Chief Humanity Officer™, Speaker, Author, Publisher,
CEO of Ignite Publishing, JBO Global Inc. & Ignite Moments Media
jbowen.website
igniteyou.life
ignitehumanity.life
Lady JB Owen
Lady JB Owen
Lady JB Owen

Ignite Your Impact

Impact is more than just what we do. It is the energy we bring into the world, the way we uplift others, and the ripple effect of our actions, whether big or small.

Throughout this book, you have read stories of people who turned challenges into purpose and ordinary moments into extraordinary transformations. Now, it is time to turn inward and reflect on your journey. How have your experiences, choices, and actions shaped the world around you? What impact have you already made without even realizing it?

Use the reflection pages throughout this book to dive deeper into the impact you are making in the world. Let the stories you read here mirror your journey, revealing new insights and a greater understanding of how far you have come. When we take the time to look back, we gain clarity on the challenges we have overcome, the lessons we have learned, and the ways we have already made a difference.

Let these reflection questions Ignite a desire within you to create more impact, not just in your own life but in the lives of those around you. When we live with intention and when we choose to uplift, support, and inspire our impact multiplies. We become the ignition point for something greater, setting off a chain reaction that extends far beyond what we can see.

Ask yourself...

- What does "impact" mean to you?

\
\
\
\
\

- Think of a time when your words or actions positively affected someone else. How did it make you feel?

\
\
\
\

Elaine Valerie Thompson

Elaine Valerie Thompson

*"When we look in the mirror and love what we see,
we can welcome another's love in."*

Deeply loving yourself is a journey that beckons you forward. The words others speak may cloud your reflection, but your true light will glow with patient self-discovery. As you embrace your authentic self and stand firmly in your deepest truth, you will naturally draw the one who recognizes your heart's essence. Lovingly know that you will awaken to divine love when you open your heart to see beyond the mirror. May this story be a guide and reminder that as you nurture self-love, you create space for the love you deserve to flow into your life.

Beyond The Mirror

The snow-capped mountain tops reminded me of icing on a cake, towering high, austere, and proud, a view I had never seen. Below them, the glass-like glistening lakes reflected nature twice. These were the Earl Mountains and Mirror Lakes of New Zealand. At that moment, reflecting on my opportunity for love to unfold, it felt just like the icing on the cake. My heart skipped a beat. *Had I finally been blessed with a chance to paint my life as a colorful landscape?*

It was my second campervan holiday, a time to live with this man, my soul mate, in awe and wonder. We were embracing the simplicity of nature and a life of just being: waking up with the ocean announcing the dawn, dancing with the untamed natural wilderness that had become my new haven, and the essence of wet, sweet, woody aromas like maple syrup slightly toasted in a pan. It was a stark contrast from life as it had started in New Zealand two decades prior! This new topography had been a slow crawl, but through learned mindset techniques and immersing myself in my newfound Faith, past narratives that did not serve me well had been relinquished. This new existence was one of steadfast wholeness, reinvigorated by God's presence, fresh eyes to see, and attuned ears to hear. *How was that even possible*? I thought. Once defined by dark depths of hurt and sadness, my current life had a brand new canvas that reflected the bright colors of limitless possibilities ahead.

Reflecting back on our first-ever campervan holiday three years earlier, my suitcase was bulging with summer dresses and shoes, way more than needed! My life's journey, up to that trip, had been filled with both physical and emotional trauma. I had forgotten how to celebrate myself; feeling feminine had morphed into a rigid keeping myself together. Yearning to adorn myself in bohemian abstract color and decorate my hair with colorful scarves, I dreamed of embracing a frequency of confidence and elegance tinged with fun. Every moment with this new man encouraged me to embrace my heart of wonder. I tingled with new sensations of quirkiness and joy, lifting my once-fractured self-esteem. On that holiday, the campervan had been blessed with a full-length mirror. Embarking on this second adventure on wheels, *was I being tested? Had the Lord presented me with an opportunity to live life without a mirror?* Filled with dread and despair, I turned to my soul mate, "We don't have a mirror! How will I manage to put myself together?"

My loving soul mate whispered the words, "Darling, you don't need a mirror. You're naturally beautiful as you are," and finished with a warm and reassuring smile. This holiday was in the midst of winter, a time to hide behind wooly hats and scarves. *What was my message? Did it have a deeper significance?* My innate faith whispered. *Could this be a sign God would help me rewrite my past mental narratives, along with erasing a kaleidoscope of memories and feelings I once had of my dysmorphic reflection in my mirror?*

Originally from London, growing up was filled with love. Maybe my pink candy outlook and magnetic aura shone brightly as a mirror for those who reflected the polar opposite. Wondering how people could be so scathing and destructive of my kindness and genuineness, my empathic love for the world and others had been quashed in the corporate jungle. I'd become unconsciously blind to the gradual paralysis of my self-love, so much so that I stopped listening to my intuition. My twenties and thirties were filled with constant noise in my head and a deep yearning to repair my self-esteem. Looking for external validation, I fell prey to a fatal attraction, a relationship that would deeply impact my calling and heart in a 'not-so-positive' way.

We were polar opposites; he was an accountant and all about numbers and control, and my vibrant frequency was of love and joy, a natural healer and nurturer. We met at my workplace. I was assigned as his recruitment manager, and he became my candidate. His energy was overly confident, a little too supercilious with an abstruse accent. His presence was unsettling, yet I remained his consultant for five years. He tried many times to ask me out, but mixing work and personal life was never an option. Then, one day, he tricked me into meeting him. I should have known right then to trust my intuition. He wanted to talk about leaving the work contract I had placed him in, and we were to meet at a wine bar. I remember the words he said, "The only way I could get you to meet me would be to talk about work!" Memories of how we became a couple still evade me, but six months later, we were engaged. Twelve months later, I suddenly found myself on the other side of the world.

Leaving England and saying goodbye to my mom was heart-wrenching. As we hugged and sobbed, I sensed her concerns, but I felt I was too deeply entwined to turn back, as a date at the altar was already set.

Surrendering everything to follow his desires and needs, my path descended into a pit of unfathomable hurt. A journey of sabotage began as the love I once had for myself plummeted. His actions and words led me to doubt myself. That began the *impact* of disconnecting me from my true essence and preventing me from living my desired purpose.

The frequency and energy leading up to the wedding reminded me of the inconsistency of New Zealand weather: four seasons in one day! Something felt off! The groomsman's computer housing all the speeches and photos had been stolen. My Mom's hat, the perfect accessory to a delicate, flowing, soft lilac dress, had gone missing on her flight. My future in-law's dog had consumed the corner of the wedding cake, a big deal to some; to me, it caused chuckles of amusement! Then, when exchanging the rings, the wind rose, and the celebrant wavered as she was gently nudged by the decorative pillar when it toppled onto her. It was too late to say no. Trusting things would change with this man, I still said, "I do," two tiny words of commitment that would have little *impact* on him.

The waters had been stormy long before we married, and almost immediately after the wedding, life's landscape was far from my dreams. Verbal abuse and physical and mental trauma became my new norm. I see now that when our connection with ourselves has too many cracks, our frequency reflects what we see in the mirror, we attract into our lives what and who do not serve us well. My dysmorphic vision of my reflection was fuelling what I had attracted.

The honeymoon, a sacred time to bond and create memories, became an *impactful* life story that cut deep. Recalling wine thrown in my face, my wedded heart was broken. Just days after saying, "I do," he left that night to party with a group of strangers. Our moments together were unimportant to him. My love language of quality time was broken and insignificant; he ruled the roost. As I went to bed that night, there in the hotel bathroom, his just-worn wedding ring sat shiny and gleaming at me in the soap dish. Feeling the *impact* of emotions dense and deep in my stomach, fear washed over me, and I struggled to breathe. *What will the morning bring?*

As a spiritual being, I know we have the power to create the life we desire, and my new marriage was not it! Yet, I still had more to learn.

Experiencing over two years of imprisonment and fear with my family on the other side of the world, he had forbidden me to phone them. "It's too expensive to call England," he would say. He stole my passport and locked it away. My heart spoke, "Start planning your escape." *But when? And how?*

Wasn't true love about being embraced in one another's arms? Going to bed and waking up with a golden glow, warming each other's souls, and pouring awe and wonder into every cell of our bodies? My soul was grieving as this man squandered my devoted heart's essence.

Months later, on a Friday evening, seeking solace and rejuvenation from a long working week, I retreated to the comfort of a warm, soothing bath. The bathroom door rattled, and I said, "I'm having a bath."

"Open the door," he shouted.

I replied, "I'm in the bath."

Next came the words, "I'll break the door down!"

It all happened so fast: the hole he punched in the door, fleeing naked and dripping wet, lying sopping and breathless, face down on the bed. My heart pounded with fear.

"Stop sobbing," he said reactively. He then switched gears and threatened, "I'll call the police and say you started it." As he followed through on his threat and dialed, it was already too late; the police were banging at the door.

They took me away! Broken yet needing to rise back up, this heartrending and tormenting encounter had *impactfully* propelled my plans into motion.

Easter seemed the perfect time to orchestrate the escape that had been one year in the making. He had announced he was going away yet again. Already aware of betrayal and deceit, I had made copies of the incriminating emails and texts. There was also underwear left in our wardrobe, far too big to fit me. This was not a work trip! I can recount the words I said so strongly, so profoundly. "If you go, I won't be here when you return!"

In retaliation, his ego spoke, "You will never survive without me." He picked up his bag and walked out.

Feeling at my safest sleeping in the spare room, most nights saw me creeping out from the sheets, away from his energy, and relinquishing the torment of the hairs standing up on my skin! Sleeping with the bedside lamp lit that night, my intuition was on high alert. Fearing his return, I woke before the alarm rang. The sun had not yet risen. My heart knew that seeing the sunrise on a new day would be the blessing that would shine on my purposeful path.

Easter Sunday, a time of resurrection, was a day already filled with the *impact* of history, a time to rise from anything not serving ourselves well. For me, it was to be the severing of my marriage, a day that would liberate me from any fear around my safety and my sanity. Shaking yet empowered, running on autopilot, two suitcases barely squeezed into my small car, my family of teddies with faces confused, I pulled out my keyring. Unwinding the key, it spiraled into freedom. *Was I unweaving myself?* I thought. With no shackles and taking none of our shared belongings, I felt my heart racing. My focus was ahead. Clothes, slippers, teddies and me. This was us now. With each step filled with fortitude, I stood at the front door. The impact of my decision was clouded with the unknown. The heavy air and burden of this marriage had stifled my soul and pulverized my self-worth. I took a breath and reconsidered my reflection in the mirror. *It was time to walk away.* The door closed with a hollow, final, *impactful* thud.

Finding myself alone, homeless, at the beach, the bright yellow and orange hues once again adorned my presence. Our minds can question the decisions we make. I thought *life wasn't meant to be one of torment and suffering.* My intuition was just reawakening.

As I sat embracing the early morning and watching the sunrise, I saw a colorful landscape that had long disappeared. *How would he react to my leaving?* I thought. He could and would cut me from the bank account. Now free from his painful torment, his outbursts were no longer stopping me from embracing my strength to paint my new existence positively.

That Easter Sunday evening, placing my cash card into the machine, it became a deep dark hole that swallowed the card. *So what now?* Sensing the *impact* and heaviness of my journey, I glanced to the sky, where the stars were twinkling. Closing my eyes that night, I trusted that my intuition would reveal the plan for my survival.

Life wasn't easy for many years, especially receiving a phone call from immigration and traversing another journey of proving the marriage was not one of convenience, even though it was over! He never stopped haunting me as I navigated the painful divorce.

Now, glancing out of the window as the wheels of the campervan spun joyfully along the road, my forever Soul Mate was carrying us toward new adventures. This campervan holiday had been an opportunity to reflect, review, and reinvent my reflection in the mirror. It may have taken two more decades to attract a relationship exuding love and one where I felt nurtured, but this time, I knew I was loved for my authentic self. I had found self-love by seeing beyond my once dysmorphic reflection and didn't need to see my reflection to love myself. Life was now defined by knowing that *we need to love the person we see in the mirror before we can truly allow another's love in.*

Deciding in my later life to walk with the Lord brought an unsurpassed feeling of peace and comfort. Life unfolded how He had planned it. Being introduced to a Neuroscience called FlowCode™ and qualifying as a Certified Coach enabled me to silence the voices and the inner critic in my head and recode past mental narratives that did not serve me well. When I became more conscious of 'being' versus 'doing,' intuitive messages came to me in numerology and nature signs. 10:10 became a number I regularly saw, and in Christianity, it relates to 'completeness and divine order.'

I am blessed and grateful that the Lord, in His divine plan, has brought a godly Soul Mate into my life who is now my fiancè. This time, when I say, "I do," I know that it will be a journey filled with awe and wonder, rich with mutual respect for one another and sealed with God's blessings. Our love isn't about the reflection in the mirror; it's about the frequency we generate together. The love I have gained for myself doesn't come from another. It is forged from within.

We shine our hearts' true essence when we embrace our authentic selves. Changing the thoughts on the inside changes the frequency on the outside. The Bible says,

"What is seen is temporary, but what is unseen is eternal." May you gaze beyond the mirror and realize the love you desire for yourself lies within.

IGNITE ACTION STEPS

Do you really need a mirror to validate who you are? Shine your heart's true essence for everyone's highest good.

- **Explore activities that calm your mind and negative inner chatter.** Meditation, Theta Waves, and Breathwork such as those found in the Neuroscience of FlowCode. Enjoy seven days of living life in Flow, which can be found in the resources section.

- **Morning Prayer Walking.** Take time to connect with nature, pray, or connect with a higher source to set the scene of what your day will attract.

- **Discovering your intuition.** Be aware of signs through numbers, nature, or messages you receive; be curious to explore more about them and let them lead your steps.

- **Learn to understand your partner's communication style.** Engage in personality assessments such as *Crack Your Code™* to begin speaking one another's language. (Link can be found in the resources page.).

- **Stop, take a breath, and reflect.** Take a moment to put a space between stimulus and response when your inner critic criticizes you. Using mindset rituals, such as being an observer, and finding gratitude and unity can ground you and help you see your truth. Remember you are exactly the way you are meant to be, a gift to many.

Elaine Valerie Thompson — New Zealand
Frequency Alchemist, Certified FlowCode Coach,
Intuitive Healer, Reiki Master Teacher,
Cellular Health Coach, Author, Speaker
thewellwishershaven.com
thewellwishershaven
the_wellwishers_haven

Ciara Caston Finley

Ciara Caston Finley

"True healing begins when we embrace our scars not as marks of pain but as symbols of resilience and transformative growth."

My intention is to shed light on the impact of sexual abuse and raise awareness about the long-term effects. This is not an easy story to tell, but it's one I feel compelled to share. For years, I've carried the weight of my childhood trauma, but now I understand my words have the power to inspire, heal, and transform. This is another step toward continued healing, both for me and anyone who might find themselves in similar pain. I hope my words bring you comfort and courage, reminding you that you are not alone. I see you, I hear you, I love you!

Peace in the Pieces

I was eight years old and living in our small, three-bedroom home with my baby sister, older brother, my mom, and her boyfriend. My older half-sister had moved away to live in another state with her dad. The house was a maroon brick color with a worn wrought iron post at the entry where the paint had started to chip. It sat closest to the corner of the street, right next to a firehouse. I was fascinated by the friendly firefighters, who always seemed larger than life, waving and smiling as they passed. Outside, the yard was alive with lush green shrubs and trees– peach, banana, and pecan –that felt like a world of possibility, vibrant and full of life. But inside, the walls seemed to close in, and the air was often heavy with tension, which was a stark contrast to the beauty and vitality just beyond the door. It was a place that should have felt safe, but safety was a luxury I never knew. My mom's boyfriend cast a shadow over every corner of our lives. His presence was suffocating, a storm of chaos that we couldn't escape. Brokenness seeped into everything, becoming part of who I was, a reflection of the world around me.

He wasn't just an alcoholic or a man filled with rage; he was something much darker. His abuse made me feel like the foundation of my world was crumbling beneath me with each passing day. My mom bore the brunt of his rage, but none of us were spared. He would beat my baby sister with belt buckles for anything he deemed necessary.

My older brother tried to protect us in his quiet way, but even he was just a pre-teen navigating a nightmare. I'll never forget the day my mom's boyfriend pressed a gun to my brother's head, his voice cold and steady as he threatened to kill him if he ever interfered with their arguments. After calling the police, I was frozen and helpless, watching my brother's life dangle on the edge of a psychopath's fury. His anger was dismissed when the police arrived; no charges were pressed. The relief of his departure proved to be only temporary.

His wrath towards me came in the form of sexual abuse. From the time I was eight until I was thirteen, he used me in ways I never had the words to describe. At that age, I didn't fully understand what was happening to me; I only knew that it hurt and felt wrong. He would threaten me, using my love for my sister as a weapon. I believed he would try to do the same to her if I didn't lay still. I was too scared not to. At a young age, I took on the role of my sister's keeper, hoping to shield her from the pain I had endured. Wherever I went, she came with me. My friends became her friends, as I wanted to protect her from the world I knew.

The pain was unbearable, searing in a way that felt like my body was betraying me. He didn't just touch me inappropriately; he silenced me by covering my mouth with his hand and raped me over a five-year period when I was most vulnerable. Afterward, I would run to the bathroom, lock the door, and cry silently, almost suffocatingly, trying to stifle my sobs so no one would hear. My privates burned with pain, and my heart ached with confusion and shame. Each tear that fell was a reminder of how broken I was and how trapped I had become. I was living in a world that wasn't safe, and I felt that no one could help me.

No one could save me. No one!

My fury towards him intensified as I entered my pre-teen years. I wanted him dead! I even tried poisoning him…but nothing happened. Whenever he was intoxicated and arguing with my mom, I'd strike him on the head with the hardest objects I could find. Still nothing. The deepest part of me knew his path of self-destruction would eventually do the job for me.

I try not to remember everything about him. Sometimes, it's the small details that haunt me most: the smell of alcohol on his breath, the way his eyes seemed empty yet burning with anger, and the sound of the front door slamming that signaled he was home and everything was about to get worse. Those moments etched themselves into my memory, reminders of a childhood that was anything but innocent.

For years, I convinced myself this was what life was supposed to be like. I thought that maybe every child carried these same hidden burdens, that this was just part of growing up. The sexual abuse finally stopped when I started my menstrual cycle. But mental abuse followed, with his brutal words cutting deep, calling me horrible names and insisting that no one would ever want me. Even while it was happening, I tried to bury it all so deep within me that eventually, it disappeared from my conscious memory altogether. Numbness became my shield, protecting me from the weight of the abuse. It was as if my mind had locked it away in some unreachable corner to protect me.

The trauma infiltrated every part of my life. On the outside, I thought I was going about life as if nothing had happened, but internally, it bled into my whole being. I didn't realize then that any relationship I entered, whether casual or personal, became a mirror of what I felt I deserved. I found myself unknowingly welcoming betrayal, exploitation, and abuse of my time and energy. I struggled with self-esteem issues and often felt I wasn't good enough, feeling unclean, unworthy, and unexpecting of unconditional love.

Fear, anxiety, and depression easily identified who I was. Blame consumed me as I took responsibility for everything that went wrong in my life. At times, the weight felt unbearable, and the thought of escape seemed like the only relief. I wanted to die and end the anguish, but even then, I was too much of a coward to harm myself, just as I was too afraid to speak up for myself during the abuse.

It wasn't until my adult years, when I became a parent, that the walls I'd built around those moments began to crumble. Seeing my children's innocence and vulnerability, I was able to unearth memories I didn't even know I had buried.

At first, it came as flashes: quick, disjointed images that I tried to push away. But the more I tried to ignore them, the stronger they became. One night, while rocking my baby girl to sleep, I was overwhelmed by a wave of intense emotion that left me breathless. The impact of it all hit me at once, and I couldn't stop crying. I didn't understand why. Looking down at her peaceful face, I saw myself. I saw the little girl who needed to be protected, held, loved, and shielded from the evils of this world. The memories came flooding back: the threats, the pain, the violation, the helplessness, the name-calling. It was as if my body had been waiting all those years for the right moment to tell me the truth.

Confronting the past wasn't easy and certainly didn't happen overnight. I am still on the journey to wholeness, and just recently, in my forties, I shared this with those closest to me. For a long time, I felt ashamed that I hadn't stopped him, ashamed that I'd let it happen. I've had countless days where I couldn't even get out of bed, experiencing the familiar feeling of an immobilized body. I couldn't look at myself in the mirror for many days because I never liked the girl staring back at me. That lack of love for myself carried me through many relationships where I settled for the bare minimum because I didn't think I deserved better. I toggled through long-term abusive relationships. It took me years to understand the shame I carried was never mine to bear.

The more I reflected, the more I realized that it wasn't my fault. I was a child! I was powerless against a grown man who preyed on my innocence. I began to recognize brokenness not as an end but as a thread connecting me to the possibility of something stronger, something whole. That understanding was the first step toward healing, and every step, no matter how small, moved me closer to loving myself.

Letting go of the torment was a slow, painstaking process. There were moments when I doubted I'd ever break free from the suffocating grip of pain and violation. But over time, I came to understand a profound truth: I am nothing like him. That realization was freeing. It allowed me to reconnect with my own tenderness, compassion, and grace, qualities that had always been a part of me. Unlike him, I had never felt the need to harm others because I understood far too intimately the weight of that kind of suffering.

Through self-reflection, the guidance of self-help books, and the Word of God, I began to uproot the lies he had planted in my mind and replace them with the truth of who I am—who God says I am. Seeing the innocence and softness in my children reminded me of my own gentleness, reigniting a part of me I thought was lost. Slowly, I started to believe I was deserving of my own forgiveness. I wasn't defined by his actions or the pain he caused. I was worthy of healing, love, dignity, and peace.

The trauma didn't just mute the negative parts of me; it suppressed my positive expression as well. Yoga, meditation, and eventually cooking were a big part of quieting my mind and opening up creativity that had been locked within for so long. Choosing to speak in public, join the praise and worship team, start my own business, and write this story have been meaningful steps toward reclaiming my voice and finding the courage to express myself again.

God has been my constant source of healing. I have journeyed from trauma to triumph. My value remains intact because God continues to breathe life into me. Through my challenges, I've learned that God does His greatest work through broken people. His grace has carried me through it all, and *"it is sufficient for me as His strength is made perfect in our weakness"* (2 Corinthians 12:9). His unwavering love carried me through, guiding me one breath at a time, one day at a time. My faith has allowed me to share this story with strength and peace instead of despair.

Today, I am stronger than my affliction. The scars are part of me; they provide a testimony for me, but they don't define me. Together, we can break the silence and show that survival is not just possible but courageous and something to be proud of.

Some people may not understand how deep these scars go, especially if they've never experienced anything like this. It's easy to think someone should just 'get over it' or 'move on.' But trauma doesn't work that way. It changes how you see the world and interact with people for years, if not a lifetime. Before I could muster the courage to talk about it, I picked up my pen and wrote the words that seared my heart. Speaking my truth out loud for the first time was still one of the hardest things I've ever done. It felt like ripping open a wound I'd tried so hard to forget existed. Whenever I tried to speak up, it was as if I was muzzled. It took five years before I could even dribble out pieces of what I went through to my husband. His love and care have allowed me to feel safe and know that I am no longer fragmented, even if I only shared my story in fragments.

If you're reading this and find yourself in these words, please know you are not alone. Healing is possible, and while it takes time, every step forward counts, no matter how small. Don't hesitate to speak up even if it has nothing to do with your trauma, even if you're doing it afraid. You can get through it. Part of the 'trauma bond,' the attachment that embeds itself in every aspect of who you become, silences us in general. The more you open your mouth, the more empowered you become to tell your story.

True healing begins when we embrace our scars not as marks of pain but as symbols of resilience, allowing the light of our growth to illuminate even the darkest corners of our souls. This sentiment resonates deeply with the Japanese art of *Kintsugi,* where broken pieces of pottery are mended with gold, highlighting the cracks rather than concealing them. Kintsugi teaches us to embrace imperfections and view them as part of a richer, more intricate whole.

Similarly, in our personal journeys, acknowledging and integrating our past experiences, including the painful ones, contributes to our unique strength and beauty. By illuminating our 'cracks' with the wisdom gained from overcoming adversity, we transform our wounds into sources of light and inspiration and find peace in the pieces of our past.

Opening up about past trauma can be intimidating, but it has a huge impact on freedom and healing. It's never too late to begin reclaiming your power. Take it from me: I was stifled at a very early age, and now, at forty-four years old, I've finally shared my story without feeling suppressed.

You are not alone, and taking even one small step forward is a tremendous act of courage that will bring you peace, love, and dignity.

Ignite Action Steps

Below are several ways that can work together to help you discover renewed peace.

1. **Lean into Faith and Spirituality**
   - Reading scripture, prayer, meditation, or spiritual guidance can aid in finding peace and strength.
   - Forgive yourself for any misplaced guilt or shame; healing is about giving yourself permission to grow and become the person you were always meant to be: strong, resilient, and deserving of love and peace.
   - Forgive the offender, as this frees you from their control over your thoughts and life. However, forgiveness is deeply personal and should be pursued *if* and *when* it feels right for you.
   - Seek counsel from compassionate faith leaders who understand and support survivors of abuse or trauma.
2. **Write It Down**
   - If speaking feels too difficult, writing a single thought or journaling can help release emotions and bring clarity.
3. **Practice Self-Care**
   - Set boundaries by limiting contact with individuals or environments that feel unsafe or triggering.
   - Engage in mindful practices like yoga, meditation, or breathing exercises to help you find balance when feeling anxious or overwhelmed.
   - Utilizing creative outlets, such as art, music, writing, cooking, etc., can serve as powerful tools to express and process emotions.

4. **Educate Yourself on Healing**
   - Read books and articles or watch talks about healing from sexual abuse to understand that you're not alone and healing is possible.
   - Examples include *The Body Keeps the Score* by Bessel van der Kolk and *Healing the Wounded Heart* by Dan Allender.

5. **Be Patient with Yourself**
   - Healing is a journey, not a destination. Allow yourself the time and grace to process emotions, setbacks, and breakthroughs.
   - Celebrate your courage for addressing the trauma and taking steps toward recovery.

6. **Seek a Safe Space to Share**
   - Start with trusted individuals such as a close friend, family member, or mentor who you feel will respond with empathy and support.
   - You don't have to share everything all at once. Start by sharing small fragments of your story; it allows you to practice and builds your strength with each retelling.

7. **Engage in Therapy**
   - Find a faith-based, trauma-informed therapist specializing in childhood sexual abuse.
   - Explore modalities like EMDR (Eye Movement Desensitization and Reprocessing) or CBT (Cognitive Behavioral Therapy) to process unresolved emotions and manage negative thought patterns.

8. **Build a Support System**
   - Join a support group specifically for survivors of sexual abuse.
   - Sharing experiences with others who've endured similar pain can foster connection and healing.

Ciara Caston Finley — United States of America
International Best Selling Author, CEO, Chef Extraordinaire
Healed, Whole, Fearless Leader
desideratakitchen.com
Ciara Caston Finley
desideratakitchen

Andonia Reynolds

ANDONIA REYNOLDS

*"Through the wisdom of the horse, I found the strength to lead,
the courage to heal, and the truth of who I am."*

**May this story remind you that the answers you seek are often found in
the quiet presence of those who truly see you, whether horse or human.
Trust in the journey, embrace the lessons, and allow yourself to be guided
back to wholeness.**

BLACKHEART'S GIFT

Often, when I am in a place of disconnect, I realize I haven't seen my horses for
a while. It's a connection that, for some, might be lost, but for me, manifests as
aching in my bones, like I misplaced my soul. When I see them, a great weight
is lifted, and I feel clear in my thoughts as the wisdom of the horse moves
through my veins. With the horses' calming presence, I began my journey of
helping others understand the message they were meant to hear. And I began
to listen to my own.

My life purpose began before I was born; when my mother was six months
pregnant with me, she met Shilo. She followed an impulse to purchase her.
With no fence to hold her, Mom came home with a filly. It was the beginning
steps of transformation that would lay the path I would follow in helping

horses while helping people. An imprint on my heart and mind led me to hear the guidance of these mystical animals and the gift of sharing their teachings.

When I came into the world, I was screaming at the top of my lungs, the fourth child who was full of life and wild. I gravitated to the outdoors and was often found playing with the dogs, cats, or, more often than not, the herd. Dirt was always smeared on my face as I ran barefoot around the farm, and my hair a mess and everywhere. There, I developed a sense of the horse's adaptive and observant ways: always teaching and always learning.

I often joke that English is not my first language, as confirmed by my mother; I mostly spoke gibberish in my early developmental years. The horses taught me, through their body language and synchronicity, how to speak my truth. If I was upset, put me in a pen with horses, and I would connect with them for hours. Sometimes, I would just lay on the back of a horse while it grazed, looking up at the sky and watching the clouds shift from one shape to another. I could feel the barrel of the horse expanding under me with each breath while I listened to the sound of it eating grass, *crunch, crunch, crunch*, as it slowly moved forward. In those moments, a feeling of complete peace through the connection of the horse enveloped me.

Through school, I was labeled 'different,' and often, I was the one bullying the bully. I was to bring justice to this herd of children; no bully could take me. My energy was big and intimidating, but I could get along with the majority. Even though I was liked, I wasn't always wanted and had one friend who accepted me as I was, but that was enough. I continued to shine bright, always on a mission. My competitive nature and my love of sports and art often put me in leadership roles. I expressed my opinion, wanted or not. Often, I was sent to the principal's office because I didn't agree with teachers' feedback or would advocate for fellow students if I deemed they were being mistreated. I wasn't afraid of conflict or resolution. I had built a sense of confidence through the behavior of the horse and was becoming the leader I was meant to be.

When I would arrive home after school and get off the bus, I would run to the fence. I whistled for my four-legged companions. The sound of their hooves was like thunder running toward me, a deep, powerful rumble vibrating through the ground, into my feet, and out through the top of my head. Excited to see me, they would kick out playfully as they galloped across the field to greet me. One by one, as they circled me, I experienced an undeniable joy, knowing I was part of the herd. As we silently shared a moment, the horses would carry on grazing except for one, my heart horse, my Blackheart.

Blackheart was a liver chestnut; his coat would shine in the sun. His eyes were a deep brown with a Roman-shaped head, strong and well-defined. Our first meeting was at the Rock Lake staging area, where we were packing horses up with gear and preparing to enter Willmore Wilderness Park along the eastern slopes of the Rocky Mountains. Blackheart came off the stock trailer with a few other horses that had recently been purchased from the auction and potentially saved from being sold for meat. My godfather, Dave, pulled me to the side and directed me to toss a saddle on Blackheart's back because I was going to ride him in.

Being only fourteen at the time, I asked Dave what he knew about this horse. Dave's response was simple and to the point, "I don't know, that's what you're gonna find out."

I shrugged and walked over to saddle him up. As I introduced myself, I noticed on his rear right hip he had a black spot shaped like a heart, hence his name, Blackheart. His eyes made me think he might be a survivor, observant and prepared for anything to happen. As he stood quietly taking me in, I grabbed my saddle, slung it on his back, and moved around him cautiously while seeing if he had any 'triggers' I needed to be aware of. He seemed alright, but I still didn't know how he would be once I got on his back. It wouldn't have been my first rodeo, and I was fully prepared to ride any buck he was willing to give.

I untied him, walked him to a safe place to mount up, and grabbed my left rein to pull his nose into my toe. In case he wanted to take off, he would just turn into a circle. I slid my boot into the stirrup and lifted myself onto his back. I let a long breath out as I checked his mind to see if he was ready and willing to work by turning him around to the right, then the left, and backing him up. No problem. He was well trained, and Dave might have scored a good horse for cheap.

It was time to hit the trail, and Blackheart and I were leading out with a few other wranglers, guiding twenty-seven loose horses carrying our gear. I was feeling pretty good about my new ride. One hundred meters ahead was a trail that I needed to block so that the rest of the horses wouldn't go that way. Before I knew it, I was about to have the ride of my life, and Blackheart would see what kind of rider I was.

As I went to block the pathway, suddenly, I was riding a bull. He was kicking, pulling, tossing his head, backing up, and trying to run forward. We were crashing into the pack string of horses passing by. Blackheart dropped his head between his knees and started backing up into the green park gate. I looked over my shoulder to the right, where it dropped off, and I knew what was coming next was going to test my faith.

He let out a big grunt, and his front feet lifted off the ground as he carried us both straight up, standing only on his hind legs. I clutched my legs around his barrel, grabbed a handful of mane, and pulled myself up and over the saddle horn onto his neck. We were balancing on the edge of the drop-off, but I was also concerned that we would smash on top of the park gate. I did everything I could to not fly off his back and lose my horse to the herd that was now fifty yards ahead.

I yelled with every force of my power, "Enough!" and pushed him forward with all I had. As he landed hard on his front, I dug into my seat as though my tailbone was a brake, shutting the power off to his hind end. I felt a source of energy flowing out, grounding both of us as I took over as the leader. Vibrating with adrenaline, I controlled my breath and touched the side of his neck, reassuring him everything would be okay. It was then a connection was made, a silent agreement that he could trust me, and I could trust him.

Over time, I had gotten closer to Blackheart, and we were inseparable during the summer. Often, when he was napping in the meadow, I would go and lay near him, watching his muzzle twitch and hearing him make small huff sounds like he was calling out to something as he dreamt. Curious about where he was, I often felt a sense that he was running and free.

When summer came to an end, I would not see him again until the following season. It was like this until I was eighteen years old. Every year, I would ask Dave if I could buy him, and he would say no, even when I tried to trade my summer wages and tips. My sales pitch stated none of the wranglers liked him and he was too stubborn to be a guest horse, but his answer was still the same. Until one year, my godfather was diagnosed with prostate cancer and was selling everything.

Given the circumstances, my mother went to see Dave and negotiated his purchase, bringing him home to me. Blackheart held my core memories of the mountains and spending my summers with my godfather, even long after Dave passed. He was more than just a horse; he was the gift that kept giving. He was my strength when I was weak, my voice when I couldn't speak, and most importantly, my friend.

After Dave's passing, I went through a breakup and left for college to major in Western horsemanship. I wanted to bring Blackheart with me, but I was on student loans and couldn't afford the boarding fees, so I took him back to Mom's. It was hard to leave him behind because of our connection, knowing I wouldn't be seeing him for a while. When it was time to go, he stood at the fence, watching me as I drove away. I felt anxious, as though I was leaving a part of myself behind in him, and my guilt ran wild.

When I arrived at school, it was spent mostly in the classroom, 80% theory and 20% hands-on. As someone who struggled academically, this was not what I expected when I enrolled for my Equine Science Diploma. During the first three months I spent adjusting to the school environment, I found myself amongst second-year students. It was easy to meet people, but I still felt out of place.

An old friend had found out I was living forty-five minutes away and took me out for my birthday. I didn't want him to know how much I had missed him, so I was on guard. My protective shield was up, observing him just as the horses had taught me. At one point, he went for my hand in public, and I pulled away, rejecting him. Confused by my sudden change in body language, he asked if I was embarrassed. I looked him in the eye and said, "I don't know what this is if we are friends, dating, or just a hookup. I know that if you want that part of me, that's a relationship, and I love hard."

Taken back, he paused. "Can I think about it?" implying I wanted to be his girlfriend.

With a straight face and a shrug of my body, I said, "I don't care what you do, but don't take my hand if this is nothing."

Later that night, he cutely asked me to be his girl, and I agreed. We carried on back and forth between my school and his place for the remainder of the year. He would come and watch me ride. Scared of horses, he would push through his fear and walk around them at the barns to reach me, knowing that if he wanted this gal, he would have to love horses. As he continued to court me, I was grateful that, like the horses, I could speak my truth and set boundaries that instilled trust and understanding.

College didn't get easier; in fact, it was disappointing. I had made friends and even been the mistress of ceremonies for the Christmas formal. I had made a good name for myself but did not desire to be there. The more conversations I had with the instructors, the more I felt resentment. A feeling of not being understood was present, and at one point, I was told I would never achieve the highest riding levels for coaching. It was then I decided to quit. I carried that anger for a long time, giving those words more weight than I should have.

History repeated itself as I struggled to find my worth in a world that I didn't seem to fit into. I longed to feel like me again, the part that I left behind but couldn't remember where I left it. It had been almost a year since the last time I had felt whole, the last time I had felt that treasured connection with something deeper.

I carried on into the city with my partner. Worried I had quit because of him, but I just needed to leave. My internal struggle continued, battling all my demons from my past choices. I stood there in the mirror like an empty vessel, as I had in my previous relationship with two accidental pregnancies that resulted in miscarriages. I struggled with the memory of holding Dave's hand and saying our final goodbyes, wishing I had spent more time with him. Tears running down my face, I felt all the shame resurfacing. I knew it was time to go home, time to see my horses and find that missing piece.

At first, Blackheart didn't want to be caught, running away from me in the field. Frustrated, I chased after him with no result. I decided to grab some treats to coax him in. I put the rope over Blackheart's neck and yanked his nose over to put the halter on him. I brushed him quickly and abruptly tossed the saddle on his back. He wouldn't stay still. "STAND!" I yelled over and over again and gave him a little tap on the shoulder. "Stop moving," I said, but he kept pacing back and forth, pushing me with his head and then his shoulder.

When I finally got him into the arena, I jumped on his back and pushed him forward. He stood stiff, bracing himself on the ground. I kicked and kicked, then used my lead shank to smack his hind end forward. Nothing but stubborn, he dug in, going nowhere. *No good horse.*

Instantly, all my rage and anger flooded out of me, and I screamed at the top of my lungs. "That stupid school ruined everything, even this." I fell apart on Blackheart's back. Bawling uncontrollably, I was broken. All the bitterness, hurt, and pain from losing Dave, quitting school, failing, and losing the pregnancies erupted, and I blew up. All the anguish I had been holding onto poured out, and I took it out on him, my heart horse.

While I was losing myself, Blackheart just stood there, giving me the space I needed to feel all I had been avoiding. He did his job and stood strong, holding space for my emotional breakdown. He knew I needed him. Yet, he also knew I needed to check myself and rein my attitude. His stubbornness was forcing me to see myself and have some self-reflection. He wasn't willing to give in to my demands until I dealt with what I was internalizing. He was being true to himself and his boundaries. He was the mirror I needed to reflect on my behavior and how I was truly feeling deep inside.

I caught my breath and touched his neck. "I'm sorry," I replied.

I felt him relax under me, and the tension in my body was gone. I picked up the reins gently and softly and asked him to walk forward. He agreed. We both took a deep breath, moving forward with renewed trust and understanding. I had let go, and together, we both moved on.

We had one of the most amazing rides as though an invisible thread attached our hearts and minds. As we flowed like the wind in unified rhythm and cadence, I felt my soul returning to my body, more complete. In his beautiful Mustang wisdom, he guided me back to feeling whole once again.

Though Blackheart has passed, I carry his lessons and wisdom everywhere I go. He impacted my life so profoundly, and I am grateful I listened to the message I needed to hear. His wisdom was a reflection of my wisdom, something I let go of and needed to reclaim. He helped me find my calling and my meaning amidst his Mustang teachings.

Now, I am back with the herd, supporting others through their transformation and guiding them through the Mustang ways. Horses can teach us so much if we take the time to listen and observe their subtle gestures. They speak the unspoken but obvious truth. I hear and see the things we often try to hide through the language of the horses as they can look through us and mirror our inner thoughts. I have made the Wisdom of Mustang the foundation of all that I do.

The gift of the horse's knowledge can bring you back to connection with yourself and guide you toward a brighter future. When you are willing to look within yourself and journey there, you'll discover the truth you seek. Your purpose, your mission, the reason you are here, the reflection you are supposed to see, and the clarity you need will be revealed authentically.

IGNITE ACTION STEPS

- **Listen to the Quiet:** Take time to sit in stillness with nature, animals, or yourself. *What emotions arise? What messages do you hear?*

- **Revisit a Moment of Connection:** Think back to a time when you felt truly seen and understood. *How can you invite more of that into your life?*

- **Lead with Trust:** Just as horses respond to confident, kind leadership, practice stepping into your own strength while allowing space for trust and connection.

- **Honor the Lessons:** Reflect on the mentors, human or animal, who have guided you. *What wisdom have they left with you? How can you apply it now?*

- **Return to Your Herd:** When life feels unbalanced, reconnect with what grounds you, whether that's time with horses, loved ones, or a place that feels like home.

Andonia Reynolds — Canada
Founder of The Many Hats We Wear, Western Horse Academy, Mustang Wisdom, Lil' Bee Daycare, Equine Specialist, International Best Selling Author, Cognitive Behavioural Life Coach, Social Work Diploma
andonia@manyhatswewear.com, manyhatswewear.com,
westernhorseacademy.com, mustang-wisdom.life
🄵 *The Many Hats We Wear*

Peter Giesin

Peter Giesin

"Ignite Moments forge the strength to rise into our most authentic, extraordinary lives."

Every 'almost' moment holds the power to transform and reimagine your story. My journey from shame to impact has shown me that scars are not endings but beginnings. You can uncover the strength to turn pain into purpose through the courage of vulnerability. Embrace your authentic power. You are enough, and your most extraordinary chapter is ready to be written. The pen is yours; the page is blank. Dare to rise and begin again. Your story starts now.

The Power of Almost

The stench of stale sweat and cheap floor wax clung to the gymnasium air, thick and suffocating. I stepped up to the free-throw line, the basketball in my hands feeling alien. My palms were clammy; my pulse thundered in my ears. My coach's voice echoed somewhere in the background, but it was swallowed by the storm churning inside me.

I dribbled once. Twice. The sound of the ball hitting the floor seemed deafening; each bounce was a pulse of tension that reverberated through my chest.

My breath was shallow, a desperate attempt to steady myself, but the nausea surged relentlessly. Cold and unforgiving.

Then it happened... my knees buckled, and I doubled over as the sour burn of vomit clawed its way up and spilled onto the polished hardwood floor.

A stunned silence fell, heavy and suffocating. The noise of the crowd, the whispers, and the muffled laughter came rushing back as if the gym itself had taken a sharp breath. A hundred pairs of eyes locked on me, each a dagger of disbelief and judgment. My cheeks burned hot, shame spreading through me like wildfire. *You're a failure,* the voice in my head hissed, sharp and cruel. *You'll never be enough.*

Something inside me cracked that afternoon. It wasn't the kind of crack you can fix with a bandage or time. It was deep, a jagged fault line that I didn't know how to mend. That moment imprinted itself on me like a scar. The echoes of humiliation rippled through me, a constant reminder of the person who had knelt on the gym floor, drowning in shame and unable to rise. In the solitude of my bedroom, I searched for refuge. The world outside felt unbearable, its weight pressing down on me with every sideways glance and quiet laugh that lingered long after that day.

Yet, within the pages of well-worn books, I found a lifeline. Night after night, I lost myself in tales of heroism and transformation, their characters braving storms far greater than mine. On those pages, I wasn't the boy who choked under pressure. I wasn't the kid who couldn't measure up. I became the hero of a thousand stories: brave, resilient, and whole. Each turn of the page became a quiet rebellion against the voice that told me I wasn't enough. As I lost myself in these stories, there was a tender voice, softer than the one that mocked me. It was tentative, barely more than a whisper, but it carried with it a message that I didn't yet know how to receive: *Maybe, just maybe, you have your own story to tell.*

The echo felt like light breaking through the edges of a storm. It wasn't hope, not yet, but it was something close. And yet, the other voice that clung to the memory of that gymnasium floor was louder and more insistent: *What could you possibly have to say that matters?* For years, the two voices would battle within me. One fed on doubt and failure, while the other dared to imagine something more. The seeds of transformation quietly took root in that small, fragile tension.

Those stories didn't just show me what was possible; they gave me language for the ache I carried. I began to see that heroes weren't perfect. They stumbled, they doubted, and they failed. And yet, they continued. Their flaws weren't weaknesses; they were what made them real and their triumphs meaningful. For the first time, I began to wonder if the jagged fault line inside me wasn't just a scar. Maybe it was a map, a record of where I had been, but also a guide to where I might go.

Books became my sanctuary, a place where I could imagine a version of myself I hadn't yet met. They didn't fix the voice that murmured, *You're not enough,* but they gave me something to stand on when that voice felt overwhelming. And in those humbling moments, a fragile hope began to form. I didn't know it then, but the stories I read were planting seeds of transformation. They were forging the truth that our wounds don't diminish our potential for growth. They prepare us for it.

In college, I dared to believe that maybe my story mattered. It was a fragile belief, like a spark in a storm, but it was enough to push me forward. I enrolled in a creative writing course, each assignment a tentative offering of the 'self' I had kept hidden for so long.

Writing wasn't just an academic exercise. It was an act of hope, a quiet rebellion against the voice that lingered: *You're not enough.*

For the first time, I allowed myself to imagine a future where my words could matter. Something inside me shifted when my professor scribbled encouraging notes in the margins of my essays. It wasn't just validation; it was a crack of light breaking through the walls I had built around myself. Then came the essay I wrote, an expression of myself that I never imagined before. I poured myself into it for days on end, doting on every word and unleashing a newfound vision of my literary brilliance finally coming alive.

"This raises questions about its originality," my professor said, her voice clipped and her eyes avoiding mine. "I need to submit it for review." Her words didn't just land... they detonated. My chest tightened as shame surged, sharp and immediate. *Not originality. Anything but that. Was she implying plagiarism?* My mind raced, a hundred tangled thoughts fighting for attention, but one rose above the rest: *What if they're right?*

The academic board hearing felt like stepping into a courtroom where my identity was on trial. I sat at the table, gripping its edge so tightly that my knuckles turned white. My pulse thundered in my ears, and the air in the room felt heavy and stifling.

"I wrote every word," I said, my voice cracking under the moment's weight. "This essay isn't perfect, but it's mine. All of it."

They nodded, their faces impassive, as if they hadn't just shattered my fragile belief in myself. The scratch of their pens against paper felt like judgment rendered in real-time. When they finally cleared me of the charges, the relief I'd imagined didn't come. Instead, shame lingered like a bruise, deep and unrelenting. *I must be a fraud.*

That doubt burrowed into me deeper than I cared to admit. I'd always known that writing was vulnerable, like opening a door into the most private corners of myself. But after the accusation, vulnerability no longer felt brave. It felt dangerous. Every time I sat down to write, the voice in my head grew louder. *Why bother? You're not good enough.* Slowly, that voice chipped away at the spark I had found. The part of me that longed to create and pour my soul into words grew quieter until it was barely audible. I wasn't just burying my stories; I was burying a part of myself.

Adulthood came quietly, not with fanfare, but with a series of roles I slipped into like a well-worn coat. I became a devoted husband, diligent employee, and caring father. On the surface, everything looked whole. I wore competence like armor, each task and responsibility a shield against the parts of myself I didn't want to confront. But beneath the surface, I was a man divided. The shadow of my untold story followed me, silent but ever-present. It lingered in the moments, avoided risk, let opportunities pass, and smothered my creative spark for safety. I told myself that I was doing what needed to be done. The discontent didn't go away. It grew.

Late at night, I would find my wife in the kitchen, her back turned and her shoulders trembling. She cried quietly, her face streaked with tears and her wedding band discarded on the counter like a relic of some forgotten dream. I wanted to reach for her and close the aching gulf between us, but the words I needed were locked inside my chest. Instead, I retreated, hiding behind the comfortable numbness of routine. At work, I drifted through endless meetings and told myself I was being productive and that I was providing for my family, but deep down, I knew I was hiding, hiding from the possibility of failure. Even with my daughter, the light of my life, I felt the weight of my absence. She would chatter excitedly about her day, her laughter weaving through the drab fabric of my world like a bright thread. But hours later, I realized I couldn't recall a single detail of what she had said. I was there but not present, my mind locked in a fog. She deserved more than the shadow of a father, but I didn't know how to give her what she needed. My life was slipping through my fingers like sand; each moment was another grain in an hourglass I couldn't flip.

The silence in my marriage stretched until it finally snapped. The distance between us had grown over the years, a chasm neither of us knew how to cross.

There was no shouting, no accusations, just the quiet unraveling of a thread that had been fraying for far too long. Becoming a single father of two young children was a role I took on with determination but little grace. I convinced myself that if I could just do enough, I could compensate for all the ways I had fallen short. But the truth was harder to admit: I felt like an imposter. Every time I looked at my children, I felt the weight of their unspoken questions: *Are you really here? Do you see us?* I felt like the fraud I was being.

Amidst the wreckage, something stirred. It was faint, a call against the roar of doubt, but it was there. *You don't have to stay here. You don't have to live this story.* In a desire to radically change my life, I flew to Barcelona to attend a world-schooling event. I was looking for transformation, not a relationship. But then it happened in a whirlwind when JB and her kids swept into our shared apartment. Her energy and laughter seemed to fill every corner of the room. She moved with purpose, her presence magnetic, as though she carried her own light. I watched her navigate with a calm intensity, and for the first time in years, something inside me stirred... a faint flicker of possibility.

JB was unlike anyone I had ever met. She approached life as if it were a story waiting to be written, and she was determined to be its author. Her questions weren't casual; they dug beneath the surface, peeling back layers I hadn't even realized I was hiding. There was the quiet rhythm of co-parenting, shared laughter, and long walks through Barcelona's streets. JB radiated a vibrant presence that didn't demand attention but invited it, inviting me to imagine something larger, something more between us.

It took a few months, but romance began to stir. We decided to join our families. Just one problem: she lived in Canada, and I lived in the United States. My courage was questionable, and I didn't see how it could work. I didn't know how to rewrite the story of my failure, worries, and irreparable belief that love, joy, and a happy ending were impervious to me. Trepidatiously, I flew to Canada to see her. For days, we talked, laughed, and imagined what a life together might look like. It was everything I wanted, and it terrified me. When I returned home, fear got the better of me. I called JB and told her, "We should just be friends," succumbing to my old habits and limiting beliefs.

Her response was devastatingly direct: "Why would you settle for being my friend when we could be so much more?" Sucking the air out of my chest, her words haunted me. For days, I wrestled with the safety of the familiar and the pull of the unknown. Finally, during another phone call, I found the courage to speak my truth.

"I don't want to be just friends," I said, my voice trembling. "I want us to be legendary in love." The words hung in the air, vulnerable and electric. Saying them felt like crossing a threshold, I couldn't return from. Choosing JB wasn't just about choosing love; it was about choosing to rewrite the story I had been telling myself for years. It was daring to believe that I could create a life filled with connection, growth, and profound meaning.

"I've spent most of my life feeling like I'm not enough," I said. "Every failure, every 'almost moment' feels like proof that I'll never measure up. I carry this shame, this fear, that if people really knew me, they'd see I'm not good enough."

The words came tumbling out, raw and unfiltered, and each one left me more exposed than the last. I spoke about all of my failures and feelings of not being seen. I admitted to the parts of myself I'd been afraid to confront and ashamed to name. When I finally stopped, my chest heaved with the weight of what I'd just released.

JB listened, her expression soft but steady. "You're not your failures," she said, her voice full of tenderness. "You're the man who keeps rising in spite of them. That's the man I want to spend my life with. We get to write our story. Let's make it legendary."

Her words impacted me like a key opening a locked door. For so long, I had seen my scars as evidence of my inadequacy. At that moment, I found proof of something else. *I am the author and the hero of my own becoming.* The revelation stopped me cold. For years, I had buried the part of myself that felt capable. Yet now, I felt able to reclaim my voice and use it to shape our destiny. I realize that I am the storyteller; I have the sacred alchemy of turning the raw material of my experiences into something golden. It's not about erasing the scars I carried. It's about seeing them as evidence of growth, as markers of the journey that has brought me here.

Our stories are an invitation. They are an offering to anyone who has ever felt invisible or doubted their worth. They are a reminder that transformation is possible, even in the face of doubt. Your 'almost' moments are not failures. They are powerful catalysts for growth, impact, and transformation. They are the stepping stones that shape us into the people we are meant to become. Transformation isn't about erasing your past or pretending the scars don't exist. It's about learning to nurture those scars with grace and seeing them as growth and positive impact. Every one of our experiences is part of the process and the moments that define our extraordinary lives.

IGNITE ACTION STEPS

- **Reframe a Past Failure Through Self-reflection:** Think back to a moment when you felt like you fell short. Look at it again, not as an ending, but as a lesson. *What strength did you uncover in that experience? How can that hard-earned wisdom propel you forward today?*

- **Identify Where You're Playing Small:** Be honest with yourself: *Where in your life are you holding back? What dream, goal, or version of yourself have you been afraid to step into? What's one bold, courageous step you can take today to start living more authentically and unapologetically?*

- **Share a Vulnerability:** Open up to someone you trust. Share a fear, a struggle, or a long-held dream you've kept hidden. Pay attention to how vulnerability shifts the relationship, and notice the courage it ignites in you when you allow yourself to be seen.

The world doesn't need more perfection. It needs courage. It needs people like you who are willing to embrace the messy, imperfect, extraordinary work of becoming. So, take a deep breath, square your shoulders, and step forward. Your story is waiting to be lived, your greatness waiting to be unleashed.

This isn't just my story—it's yours, also.

Peter Giesin — Canada
CoFounder & CTO at Ignite Publishing, Software Evangelist,
Author & Adventurer
✉ *peter@igniteyou.life*

Melody J Carberry

MELODY J CARBERRY

"How we are within the world mirrors how we are within ourselves."

My intention for this story is that you see how powerful you are and the impact you alone can imprint on your family, community, and globally. When you realize your value and potential, you are limitless about what message or meaning you can leave. It does not matter if you are subtle, like the ripple effect of a stone skipping across the water in a pond, or powerful, like a meteorite melting into the Earth. Your impact can be the difference that someone needs or perhaps everyone needs. I invite you into my story, and you can decide for yourself what your impact will be and where you see the potential for you to shine through.

GOOD GRACES

In my early years as a server at the Riverboat Restaurant, I had some of the best customers. It was a family-owned establishment and one of the busiest in the heart of the downtown area. One particular group of insurance men who came for coffee a couple of times a day used to call me the "Thank you Lady." They appreciated my happy demeanor, quick wit, and attentive service. I was cheery and ready to jump in and lend a hand wherever needed. Making sure everyone's cups and bellies were full, removing plates as necessary, and never leaving a table without a genuine smile and an uplifting "Thank you." These simple acts of kindness earned me the badge of this memorable nickname.

While in the company of other acquaintances, I knew outside the restaurant that it was an automatic reflex to help out if someone needed something. At times, they would tease me for such acts of kindness. They didn't seem to appreciate my eagerness to support them. It wasn't long before I realized some of these people were not my people, nor was I in the right place being around them. Kindness was a character trait worth keeping, and I refused to change this fundamental part of who I was and still am. Being in service has always been a gift I cherished and wanted to be known for.

For forty-five-plus years, I delighted in the customer service industry moving from hospitality to aesthetics to client support in the health industry. I was in my fifties, working at a great job with kindred spirits, when the world came to a *pause*. We had all been informed that the clinic we so completely loved coming to each day would close. I was stunned! I had never been let go from a job before; we were all handed our "walking papers" together. Although I knew it was not my own doing, it shook me with an impact I was unaccustomed to.

I took some online classes as I have always found value in being a student. This would fill my time until the weather turned warm enough to get into the yard and garden, where I could redirect some energy outside. I also spent some time with a friend, having lunch and visiting her in her clothing boutique. It was divine in her quaint little space. We were both on the same nutrition program, and it was great sharing lunch with someone who was also doing her inner self-work. Fashion, a friend, food, and fun…. *What could be more fabulous than that?*

Naturally, I started to spend more time in the boutique. What began organically became a part-time position. The fashion industry has always been my passion, but this was my first time working in a clothing store. I always prided myself on being able to put a great outfit together. I loved adding pearls to everything, matching the perfect pair of shoes, and designing a unique style for myself and my customers. Customer service was like breathing to me. Starting all those years ago as a server, my life has always been devoted to customer satisfaction, and I was good at this. I knew several of the clients already and loved getting to know many of the others. I have always believed in *Women lifting up Women*, which was a good fit. Helping someone feel fabulous about how they look and feel in an outfit can be a game changer. I adored being there.

It was a beautiful way to build back some of the confidence lost over the events of the *pause.*

I was becoming proficient at work and feeling great about the business's direction. My friend and boss was a very driven entrepreneur. We first met many years ago when she had another boutique in the same building where I taught a theory program for hairstyling. We developed a lovely friendship.

Things were busy, and the boutique needed more space. The Christmas season was a telltale sign, as we were bursting with inventory and an abundant clientele. Her aspirations for expansion were imminent. I was thrilled to attend buying shows with my friend and happy to participate in the day-to-day operations and responsibilities. It was an incredible insight into an industry I held in high regard.

Over the weeks, the transition from friend to employee became tested. There were a couple of instances where I found myself at the short end of remarks that felt uncomfortable and perhaps inappropriate in front of clients. She was my boss and my friend, and the lines were becoming tangled. Brushing things off as pressure from the time of year and growing pains from the expanding enterprise, I wanted to support her bold, big venture. I felt the impact I was making and enjoyed what I was doing and the clients I was working with. It was easy to overlook those pinchy moments… until it wasn't.

It was a few weeks before Christmas, and I was accused of not filling an order for a client she had texted me about that morning. Unhappy, she was sticking to her story as though I was being untruthful. Upset, it wasn't until I showed her the text that she realized it was her mistake. She then blamed it on the client even though it was her shortcoming. I was not used to communicating this way. She was stretching my core belief that it is more important to be kind than right. I felt shaken at the implication. I realized not many people in her life challenged her, especially in her most intimate inner circle. For me, this was a sacred circle of friendship and trust that mirrored who we inherently were.

Nothing could have prepared me for how she spoke to me in a very public display the week leading up to Christmas. I had barely recovered from the past accusation. As discomfort set in between us, her communication style became less supportive.

One very busy morning, the husband of one of my best girlfriends came in to find a Christmas gift for his wife. He patiently waited towards the front of the store until I was free. While he waited, my boss took a moment to dress me down in front of the entire clientele. I was mortified and hoped perhaps he had not heard it all. In the flurry, I walked over to him and asked if he could come back in an hour when I could devote my time to shopping with him. He headed out, asking if I was okay, and I said, "Yes," thanking him for his willingness to come back to finish his purchase, which turned out to be no 'small purchase.' He put together a beautiful gift for his wife, for which I was very grateful. It was the most perfect basket with purple ribbon and tissue lovingly arranged, ready to take home and eagerly be placed under their tree. The details and pride taken in assembling that gift felt amazing. It was a pleasure to go the extra mile for both of them. Many friends supported me by shopping at that store and purchasing from a 'local' boutique. Girlfriends, their husbands, and daughters, including my own, all spent handsome sums of well-earned money in helping both myself and the business.

It wasn't until the holidays that we got together that my girlfriend shared with me that her husband was appalled about the way I had been spoken to that day. He asked me if she talked to me like that often and said he would not return to spend another dime in her store. I felt embarrassed yet, in some way, relieved. It was freeing to have someone else say the words I was thinking, a witness to what was becoming more common than I cared to admit. Finding diplomacy in something I had no control over was also becoming more difficult. At times, my boss was incredibly generous, but a lack of courtesy and absence of respect shadowed it. It felt like an apology that would never be spoken.

I was looking forward to a little break, knowing that the store would be closed between Christmas and the first week in January. The boutique was moving to a much larger space. After a few days of Christmas celebrations, it was time to launch operation 'New Location,' an inspired time. I manned the exit strategy for the current location while the Boss managed all things business on the receiving end. The mission went tremendously with a great support crew and several hands on deck.

Eureka!! New Year, new location, grand reopening, and the sense of gratitude for being part of this big, bold adventure. Through the view of my rose-colored glasses, this felt great. With a new hire in place, talk of moving me into a management position would free up some time for the Boss to work on new business avenues. Everything was happening so quickly, and we needed to stay focused. I felt invested in the purpose and contributed a few pieces of decor to the new space, which felt good. Making sure to ease any scheduling conflicts and being poised for any tasks that came up each day gave me the comfort of being of service. It could be, at times, a very fickle place to be part of someone else's dream. Giving everything I had, hoping that the ripple effect I was creating wasn't swallowed up in the wake of a larger stone. I could feel a shift between us, as if she needed the help but wasn't ready to allow it. There were so many mixed messages to decipher while navigating all the changes.

One Saturday morning late in January, I began the day anticipating it being wonderful. When the Boss arrived, there was a mood that entered with her. Bringing an uncomfortable feeling, one I had become familiar with. There was a visitor in the store on Friday, a friend of the boss's. He was such a divine presence that it was easy to connect with him. Truly heavenly, I felt that in all sincerity. Perhaps I expressed my gratitude to meet him, or I spoke to him for too long. Naively, I was unaware of what I had done.

Before the meeting on Saturday morning started, a derogatory comment came flying out of her. She never directed it to any specific person. It was not meant for the new hire but was said in front of her. I was so surprised and in disbelief that I needed to think for a moment if that actually happened. Trying to process, I took a brief moment to collect myself and invited her to see if there was a conversation she and I needed to have in private. She negated my offer and continued dressing me down in front of the other staff member. It had become common, but THIS was on a whole new level. In all my years as a Director of Operations, an Instructor, and a Business Owner, I have never spoken to anyone in this manner. She meant to put me in my place, and she did!

My mouth became devoid of moisture, and my breath instantly soured as if I had been delivered a blow to my stomach. An emotional blow, the kind delivered with great precision, knowing the level of hurt it wielded. I am a lover, not a fighter. People who are fighters know how to deliver with damaging accuracy. It was a 'win at all costs,' and I was unprepared for the battle. I needed time to process. I couldn't speak. I also couldn't walk out at that moment. I am no quitter. I stayed that day. There was a full backroom of stock that needed to be processed, so it was easy for me to retreat into the back to lick my wounds in recovery. Spending the next few days with a migraine from the stress, I knew I was left with only one choice. *Do I stay, or do I go?*

The next day, I was struggling. I kept repeating in my head that *we are made to do hard things, and you've got this*. Well, I most certainly did not have this. The minute I walked into the boutique, my legs crumbled under me. I needed to find a chair, feeling that I would be physically sick. I sat with my head in my hands. I couldn't believe that I wasn't strong enough to get through this; my skin was not nearly thick enough. I tried talking myself out of the physical things happening, but it was not working. I decided to leave, clearly still rattled from the impact she left from our last conversation. Using the migraine headache as my way out, I excused myself and went home.

Over the next couple of days, I began writing her a letter. After about fifteen rewrites, my outpouring went from seven pages to just less than three. I wanted to tell her my feelings without the anger and judgment behind it. With my heart involved, I chose kindness. I am a 'kind' fighter, not a *right* fighter. The goal was to let her know how her words and actions impacted me and that, as a result, I would not be continuing my employment.

This is a portion of what I shared...

My Dear Friend,

I am sharing this letter with you as I feel a deep sense that there will be no closure unless I honor myself and find the courage to bear both my gratitude and my soul.

Women lifting up Women can mean so many things. To me, at the core, it means everyone leaves with their dignity intact, even in the face of conflict, no matter what the outcome is. When there is no allowance for this process, someone is always left feeling less than they are. I will always choose to be kind over being right, so this will more often be me. I am okay with that, but please do not mistake my kindness for weakness. It is a choice, not a misguided behavior.

Knowing this, it is hard for me to see a way forward. Having had some time to process and work through the physical responses around the experiences and, ultimately, the choice, I knew I had to make. In your words, my friend, I need to honor myself and not compromise who I am. With all this said, I honor the same for you...

Clear of what I wanted to say, I knew for sure that *words matter*. I could express my hurt in a way where I showed up for myself. Only with the urging of a wise and beautiful friend who insisted it was a gift of kindness for both of us, not just for me, did I find the courage to speak my truth. It became easier to think I would enter the boutique one last time to give my notice and hand in my key. I was able to make peace with my ripple and allow time to heal this impact. Within a few months, I received a text that my boss had found some clarity about why she had treated me that way. Finding my worth and my words, I became able to stand in my own power. I had a voice that would leave both of us with our dignity intact. After all, this wasn't about who she was but about *who I was.* Of course, if you know me at all by now, I didn't leave before saying, "Thank you!"

How we are within the world mirrors how we are within ourselves. You are magnificently powerful. Standing up for your values allows your greatness and potential to shine. Being honest *is* kind. Being right isn't always kind. Find your balance, take a deep breath, and courageously discover what impact you will create in your life and the lives of others.

IGNITE ACTION STEPS

- **Spend time with yourself in quiet reflection.** Having a sense of connection with who you are inside can help you navigate the terrain when things are difficult. Know who you are and the value you bring to the table. Always know your worth.

- **Breathe deep, long breaths in and out.** Doing breathwork can help you be calm and focused when going into an anxious situation. Repeat until you feel the calm come in.

- **Engage in conversations from your heart.** Invite the possibility of resolution with dignity for all sides. The most courageous conversations come from your heart. Speak your truth lovingly.

- **Kindness benefits everyone.** Being kind over being right is a powerful goal. Find ways to inject kindness into difficult conversations. Showing kindness maintains a higher frequency, which, my friend, is a gift for you.

- **Engage in *heartful* practices.** Meditation, breathwork, or yoga to help cultivate deeper connections with yourself. Align your heart and mind to experience a life with less conflict and judgment, leaving the door open to more love and joy.

- **Tap into your inner wisdom.** This is where courage, vulnerability, truth, and self-love reside. Sometimes, life will hand you the lessons you need to learn, so learn them well. Let your impact reflect your beliefs and what you wish to imprint. With practice, you can navigate life with greater ease and purpose.

- **Speak to yourself kindly.** Ensure your self-talk mirrors what you put into the world. Say the things that will uplift you! Raise your vibration, which will influence how the world sees and experiences you.

Melody J Carberry — Canada
Author, Speaker, Reiki Healer, Hairstylist, Director of Op, VP Dirt Werx Ltd,
Essential Feng Shui Practitioner
msha.ke/melodycarberry
Melody Carberry
melodycarberry

Your Ignite Moment

Every person has a moment when something shifts, a realization occurs, or a challenge sparks a transformation. It could be a difficult experience that forced you to grow or an unexpected opportunity that changed your path.

That moment, whether big or small, had the power to shape you. Recognizing these moments allows us to see how our experiences prepare us for something greater.

- What is one moment in your life that shifted your perspective or inspired change?

- How has that moment influenced the way you live today?

Christine Lang

Christine Lang
BA(Econ), CPA, CGA, CCS

"Courageous steps forward always start with the decision to change."

What I have learned is many of my belief systems were not created by me. My money story, my worthiness, and how I approached life were given to me by my mother. The lack of success in my life was a direct result of what I learned from my family. My biggest wish is that we all choose the direction of our lives and not allow our past to dictate our future. You can decide to do, be, and think differently. Once you decide you want to change, asking for help is crucial. You don't know what you don't know, and by seeking support, you can move forward, shifting past old beliefs and unhealthy behaviors. By taking courageous steps, you move into unexpected treasures.

The Journey of a Resilient High School Dropout

I'd just turned sixteen, and it was the second week of grade eleven. The principal called me into the office. I was used to being there, but that day, I was confused with the request, given the year had just barely started.

He sat me down and earnestly said, "Christy, you have two options. You can leave voluntarily, or we can ask you to leave."

I was shocked! I couldn't believe my luck! "I can leave? Where do I sign?!" I rejoiced.

I was so happy, I thought to myself as I headed home. *What did I need in high school? I have street smarts, I'm cool, and I have no use for it.*

When Mom arrived home that evening, I smugly told her I'd quit school. She was furious. "If you aren't going to go to school, you have to work and pay rent," she yelled.

I looked her square in the eyes and said, "If I'm working, I won't be paying *you* rent." Yep, I was a total rebel without a clue. No job and now, nowhere to live.

The next few years were spent angry and resentful, working many lousy part-time jobs and making minimum wage. I was a bartender and a waitress, worked at a tanning salon, pumped gas, and spent a season as a receptionist at a motorcycle insurance company. I even sold roses in the bar! Partying almost every night to numb myself from the life I was living, I moved from one cold, damp apartment to another. I barely had enough money to feed myself. The one time I went home and asked my mom for help, she said, "No." That's when I knew I was completely on my own. Sink or swim. No plan B.

Life had always been hard. The rage in me didn't start at sixteen.

My dad died accidentally when I was six and my sister was three.

As a child, I didn't feel like I was the 'victim' of my mother's anger, but I was definitely the recipient of it. While my sister was quiet and stayed in her room to read, I battled with Mom on a daily basis.

Starting at around age thirteen, I began stealing her car when she was at work or in bed. I got away with this for a long time until one night when I was around fourteen. Coming home in the wee morning hours from being out all night, I saw the light on in the kitchen window. Knowing a blowout fight was coming; I carefully parked the car exactly how she had left it. After replacing the odometer I had removed from the dash, tilting the steering wheel the way she left it, and perfectly aligning the tires, I closed the driver's door as quietly as possible. I had learned all these tricks over time to avoid her accusations.

When everything was back in place, I looked up and the kitchen lights were off. I knew she knew, and my heart was racing. While I would still lie to her and say I was home the whole time (I was a great liar and could often convince her she was wrong), she wasn't buying it that night.

Sneaking successfully into my room, I sighed with relief as I took off my favorite leather jacket, just as she burst in screaming at me. I have no memory of what she was saying, but I do remember her furiously lunging at me. As a young and nimble teenager weighing only one hundred and ten pounds, I could outmaneuver her heft of three hundred pounds. Grabbing my jacket and purse, I ran down two flights of stairs to the back door. For a heavy woman, she was fast on her feet that night and caught me just as I was trying to unlock the door (that lock was so friggin' hard to turn)! She spun me around and slapped me across the face hard. I slapped her back. She was stunned into silence. I told her that was the last time she would hit me. Turning around, I unlocked the door and slammed it as I left. That was the last time she ever put her hands on me.

Within days of our physical altercation, I left home for the first time. When I went to Social Services, I was devastated to find out they wouldn't help me. Because I was still a minor, my mother was responsible for me. It didn't matter if our relationship was volatile or that she hit me. I left and burst into tears, knowing that I had no choice but to relent and go home.

I boldly walked in the front door and told her I was staying and she was obligated to take care of me. I went up to my room, locked my door, took the screen out of my window, and sat on the overhang with tears streaming down my face. I was fuming that everyone else had control over my life except me.

Control has always been a part of my relationship with my mother. It started when she became pregnant with me. My parents were married at the end of January, and I was born at the beginning of September. The math doesn't quite work. My dad was a very good man and wasn't about to leave his pregnant girlfriend unmarried. Years after my dad had died, she told me I was a 'weapon,' *that was the word she used*, and that she had become pregnant so my dad would marry her. She used having a baby as a way to control him. Control became our family theme.

Her plan, in many ways, backfired because my dad fell in love with me the moment he held me. Our relationship was always amazing. I was Daddy's little girl. My mother grew to resent the fact that my father loved me more than her. Her jealousy festered, and she treated me terribly, creating in me a deep sense of shame of not being worthy of love and 'not enough' just as I was.

My mother's plan B was to have another child, my sister, and she decided that child would love only her. She intentionally drove a wedge between my sister and me. My mother would often say my sister was the smart one and I was the pretty one. The implication was that I was the stupid one, and my sister was the ugly one. From an early age, I developed a deep sense of unworthiness that began to define how I valued myself and set in motion destructive behavior that got worse with time.

It wasn't until I was an adult and spent years working on my trauma that I realized where all my rage came from. My dad was the one person who loved me unconditionally and made me feel safe. When he died, I was only six, which created a vacant hole that I tried to fill with partying, boys, and bad behavior. I didn't realize it at the time just how alone and abandoned I felt.

The man my mom married when I was eight was a raging alcoholic and abused us emotionally and verbally. When I was about ten, I started playing with makeup and loved making my face up! The late 1970s fashion was all about blue eyeshadow, and I had a bright, beautiful palette. The internet and TikTok™ didn't exist yet, and my only style reference was my beloved *Tiger Beat* magazine. Blue eyeshadow for days! I didn't care; I loved wearing it and paid a severe price for my brazenness. My step-father called me gutter trash, a slut (I hadn't even kissed a boy!), and told me I was going to be a loser for the rest of my life. His cruelty went on for a few years, but the day he called my sister a slut, I was done! My sister spent all of her time riding horses and reading in her room. *Slut? Are you kidding me!?*

At fourteen, I confronted my mother and demanded it was him or us! I was determined that my sister and I were leaving. I had no idea where we were going, but we were absolutely leaving. She chose us. For the first time, she chose us. And it was the first time I felt the power dynamic shift; I felt like I was in control. This control was fueled by white-hot anger. There is something dangerous about a fourteen-year-old feeling power from rage.

Being a high school dropout wasn't surprising and set me on a path of self-sabotaging behavior. I was exposed to dangerous people and regularly put myself in jeopardy. One day, a threatening man came after me, looking for money that was owed to him. He spent the next three days parked outside my apartment, intermittently banging on my door and threatening me while I hid in my closet. I was petrified. I couldn't call the police because it meant I might also be arrested.

Once he left, I decided I couldn't live in a constant state of fear, working miserable part-time jobs and putting myself in situations that could very easily have taken my life. The first step to making a change was to go back and get my high school diploma. I was incredibly nervous about becoming a student because I believed what I had been told about being stupid. Returning to school, I took on student loans and multiple minimum-wage jobs to just pay the bills. It was worth it. Surprisingly, I liked being there, and I was good at it! My confidence was growing. My B grade average was a far cry from the Ds and Fs I was used to getting. Because my confidence was growing, I finished with an advanced diploma that would help me get into college, where I earned a business diploma in accounting and landed an amazing corporate job!

To the outside world, I was a success story and looked like I had my life together. That corporate job helped me buy a cool car ('81 Corvette™), rent a nice apartment, and amass a smoking shoe collection. What people didn't know was I had created crushing debt. I was using 'stuff' to pretend to be more successful than I was. Any meager savings I did have inevitably went to pay a credit card bill. I was dodging credit collectors and using money from my line of credit to pay bills. I was terrified of losing my job. All I could think was *I had a great job and was drowning! Why was I so messed up with my money?*

The shame I felt about my financial situation was palpable because I was a smart, educated woman who should have known better and been able to get ahead. I was working in a corporate treasury department and definitely should have been doing better! I was completely out of control.

A few years into my new job and 'successful' life, I stood in front of my kitchen drawer filled with unopened bills. I opened it and tried to shove one more unpaid credit card statement into that overflowing drawer. It wouldn't fit. The crushing shame I felt was so heavy, like I was wearing a concrete vest. I was frozen and couldn't breathe. All I could do was cry. Cry over the decisions I had made that had me still trying to fill the hole of unworthiness. That's when I realized that something HAD to change; *I can't live like this anymore.* That was my impact moment.

The madness had to stop!

I decided to make a change. My debt was the first thing I thought about when I woke up and the last thing I thought about before I fell asleep. I did everything to keep my shame a secret. There wasn't anyone to turn to for help. Even if there was, I don't think I could have borne the humiliation of telling anyone what my life had become. I bought books and tapes on money management, investing, confidence, and worthiness. Anything to help me find the path forward. *My "success" was smoke & mirrors, and I wanted real success like other people seemed to have.*

I became so motivated to change. I wanted real wealth, not just stuff. Even more, I wanted relief from the pain I had created, to feel safe and secure. The first step was to read every day, listen to investment conversations at work, and eventually join a women's business group. Slowly, I began to understand money could serve me and provide me with the freedom I desperately wanted.

Even though I did so much research and found tools to test, something was still missing. I needed a mentor, and I found one in a woman at the bank. She spent more time teaching me about investments and how to think about them rather than trying to sell me a mutual fund like many others had.

That's how I got started. I put my credit cards away and set up a plan for both paying off my debt and putting money into investments. In those days, I only had a very small amount every payday; half to my credit card and half into savings. I started to feel hopeful and in control, like maybe I would be okay after all.

Years later, when I was in my late thirties, I found a true mentor. This woman was a financial advisor unlike any other I had ever met. She helped me figure out why I had a dysfunctional relationship with money and how I could change it. It started with my belief systems. Her unconventional philosophy enabled me to understand wealth is about how I *think* about money and what it lets me do. She encouraged me to talk about my shame and reframe my feelings of unworthiness. It's because of her I decided to become a financial advisor and guide others the way she helped me.

While I was taking courageous steps forward and feeling successful, I was still giving the world the middle finger. Using my attitude of '*F***you, watch me*' was exhausting and soul-crushing, constantly having to prove myself. (And I did prove myself). I was successful in real estate, created a million dollars in assets before I turned forty, and had a successful corporate career where I regularly worked my way up the ladder.

There was so much I faced from a young age, and becoming a victim would have been an easy road to take due to all the things I could not control. Yet, through it all, what I know for sure is I am a survivor. I have been surviving since my life began because no one thought I could or would make anything of myself. That '*F*** You watch me*' attitude worked for a very long time until it didn't. I finally decided to stop being angry and prove myself to the world. I made a crystal clear decision. I was done with that, and I was determined to see what I could truly accomplish if I set my mind to a goal!

A couple of years after meeting my second mentor, my newfound curiosity and drive to discover what I could accomplish allowed me to start my own business. I started part-time, and four years later, I was full-time. I had six months of expenses saved and gave myself permission to go back to a finance job if I fell on my face. This year, I will celebrate eleven years in business for myself full-time!

What I know for sure is my past does not have to dictate my future. I have proven myself to myself over these last eleven years. Even though I still get scared, I love to show myself what I can accomplish. Having this story published is yet more proof I can do anything I set my heart and mind to.

Working from a place of love and wanting to be of service is far more fulfilling for your soul than being powered by rage. Whenever you feel stuck in fear or frustration, helping someone else can make you feel better. And more often than not, your problems will seem to find workable solutions. Courageous steps forward always start with the decision to change. You always have a choice so choose yourself. Choose joy, fun, and happiness. Make yourself your biggest asset.

Ignite Action Steps

Below is a framework I have used for my life. I hope it helps you find the same control and freedom.

- **Decide you want to make a change.** Deciding is key. Even if you don't know what the answer is, just deciding you want things to change can start to open your heart to ideas that you can try. Sometimes you will need to decide again every day! Not only is this okay, but it is completely normal and expected. Remember why you want to change, pick yourself up, dust yourself off, and keep going!

- **Ask for help from someone who has what you want.** No matter how big or small your idea is, there is someone out there who is a few steps ahead and can show you a path.

- **Take small, consistent steps.** This can be the hard part because fear and your self-worth can get in the way. That little voice in your head might tell you that you can't. Decide again. Take one small step forward; it feels great! It isn't until you look back that you realize how far you have come!

- **Rinse & repeat.** You are going to fall down, doubt yourself, and want to hide under the covers. Remember the reason you want what you want. Stand up, dust yourself off, and start from the top.

Ready? You got this!

Christine Lang — Canada
Coach, Advisor, Speaker, Author
liveabiglife.ca
christine.lang.3597
christine-lang-financial-advisor
live_a_big_life

Dee Taggart

Dee Taggart

"The smallest decisions add up to make the biggest changes."

My wish and intention for you reading this is to bring awareness and find motivation to embark on a journey to elevate your personal frequency. Through the small actionable steps you take, you can expand your life in all categories. My hope is that you gain insight, relatability, and connectivity to your own lived experiences. Discover opportunities to reflect and bring awareness to the course of your thoughts that may be preventing you from moving forward. Hurts and heartaches can mend and won't last forever. You can experience heaven here on earth as there are better things in store for you if you design your life with thoughts, words, and stories that positively impact you.

The Impact of One Decision

At twenty years old, I never could have imagined having four children under two. Most people my age were getting sent off to college and moving out to have fun and explore life as an adult for the first time. I chose a different path. I fell deeply in love and found myself getting married young, at just nineteen. I always thought I would marry later in life, like twenty-seven or older, by which time I would have had more life experience and be able to figure out 'adulting.' I had barely had a chance to learn who I was as an adult before I had to become a responsible mother.

Only a year into being married, I had the biggest, most joyous 'surprise.' I found out that I was pregnant. Nine months later, I gave birth to my first child, a little boy. He was only four months old when life threw me another curveball. Family circumstances required me to take care of my nieces and nephew; a twin boy and girl born five days before my little guy and an additional two-year-old girl. Becoming a mom for the first time was a lot to juggle mentally, emotionally, and physically, but then adding three more infants to the mix definitely amplified the struggle. I always see myself as very optimistic with a positive 'can-do attitude.' However, a reality set in that I could never have been prepared for. Many thoughts started swirling in my head: *Oh wow, can I do this?* Then I thought, *My family needs me. I am already home.* Followed by, *How much harder can it be? Can I juggle these new babies? How will I cope alone?* Then, I wondered, *Would I have to suppress my dreams and ambitions for these kids?*

I found myself working the best I could to learn the ins and outs as a young mother with basically triplets. As if that wasn't enough, I also had a rambunctious two-year-old toddler girl with a curious mind and an unstoppable energy. Thankfully, I wasn't totally alone. My parents lived in the same neighborhood. I was counting on them to help me out, but they both had full-time day jobs and were only available in the evening. They covered me while I worked part-time in a warehouse from 5 to 9 PM, four nights a week. Multitasking to the max, I felt defeated most days as I studied for my bachelor's degree in Exercise Science online while the kids napped. My mind felt weighed down as the constant inner chatter started to chip away at my confidence and discouraged me.

I remained strong and positive the first week, soaking up every moment with those pure new souls. There is something special and heaven-like about having babies and being their source of love and care. By week two, life started to settle in. It was manageable at first. Then it became hard and something needed to be done. The repetitive routine slowly started stacking up and became more overwhelming to manage. The same cycle of feeding, changing, and feeding again was draining. These little humans relied on me for everything. I was depleted, craving help but convincing myself I could handle it alone, all while dealing with shame around the thought of failing them.

I was having a moment of comfort and reprieve on the large sectional couch we had in the living room of our home, the one that sucked you in like you were sitting on a cloud, almost feeling hugged. I was exhausted from these new motherhood responsibilities, a whirlwind of daily negative thoughts and emotions that flooded my mind, body, and soul. These precious babies who were reaching for me with desperate cries, diapers, bottles, and endless demands that came at me from every direction began to break the optimism and positivity I was trying so hard to maintain. I couldn't remember what it felt like to be alone in my thoughts, let alone feel like I was 'good enough.' I felt like I was losing myself, having four little ones in my care while still trying to pursue a degree, maintain a job, and be a wife. *I don't know who I am anymore. I don't know what I enjoy or how to move past these feelings. I am beyond exhaustion. My hobbies have disappeared. I am just giving all I got.* My hopes, desires, and dreams had been swept away.

One morning, I was up early with the four littles. It was around 7 AM, still dawn with light gray skies. I was sitting on the couch, drained and tired, with bags under my eyes. Having already been up twice in the night feeding and tending to crying babies, it was time for another round of feeding for each of them. Pulling myself together to try and feed three babies at once, I was empty, a shell of myself. Two of the babies were propped up on pillows on my right and left nursing, and the third one was on the ottoman in front of me, sucking on a bottle with my one free hand. My arms and back ached from being hunched over. I was holding off putting on a TV show to distract the two-year-old until I had finished feeding the babies. Just as I was set up, feeling like a dairy farm cow, the sweetest voice cried out, "I'm hungry." Trapped in my position, I felt inadequate. I could not move; I was stuck! A storm of thoughts started brewing inside my mind. *I can't do this. I'm not enough. There are too many of them. I'm failing at this. I can't meet all their needs. Heck, I can't even meet my own needs. I'm breaking.* I was surrounded by babies who couldn't talk to me, thank me, or appreciate me. The weight of everything felt too heavy to bear. At that moment, the core belief I created was *I am not enough.* That became my new belief and the story that I told myself, shattering my self-worth.

The softness of the cushions pressed into me as if they were trying to hold me together when I was falling apart. It was at that moment that I became aware that *I wasn't capable.* Everything became still. I was aware of what was happening, this negative belief that was forming, but I didn't seem to care. That usually small voice in my head suddenly became very loud. The one that came up many times throughout my life now screamed at me even louder: *I'm Not Enough!*

Once that negative belief settled in, I spiraled out of control. I stopped caring about myself and started reaching for comfort food to numb the stress. Before I knew it, I was too drained to make healthier choices. My lack of energy had me creating unhealthy habits. *I can't be healthy and take care of these kids,* I told myself. Often overindulging, I ate scraps from leftover meals or had a double portion to prevent my hard work from going to waste when my husband wasn't home for meals. When I was working late nights, I would get the double-wide greasy pizza slices to hold me over. I allowed no prioritization or time in my schedule and daily routine for personal exercise and no space in my day for self-care. My schedule was always about everyone else, and when I did think about getting my mind and body right, the thought would be so fleeting. I would say to myself, *It's too late. It's too hard. What's the point*? I was attacking myself, sabotaging anything that could give me hope, and denying myself permission to take the time I needed to heal or recharge. The idea of a healthy body became something I didn't deserve, something for people who had time, energy, and discipline, things I didn't have anymore. My only goal was to survive and keep the kids alive.

I constructed my own prison, boxing myself into a mentality that had no hope for a better future. The more I repeated those negative thoughts, the more it became a victim mentality. *I can't do it. I'm too tired. I'm not enough. It's too hard for you. I have too much to handle. It's the kids' fault that I don't have time. I can't help it.* I was convinced that my struggles were too big and overwhelming. I started to believe that I was stuck in this place of poor habits forever, with thoughts of negativity preoccupying my mind. It wasn't just the exhaustion of caring for the little ones. It was the exhaustion of fighting against myself. Clouded in my doubts, I accepted this sad reality as truth. I did not see a future where I could be my optimistic, positive, vibrant self anymore.

A year of that mental turmoil rolled by. One late winter morning, I was sitting in the driver's seat of my white Dodge Durango™, heading down a back road and feeling the weight of the world pressing down on me. Not even the hum of the engine could drown out the noise in my head and the feelings of my body, the way it moved with just an all-over heaviness. It felt suffocating to be inside my own body. My mind screamed. I could feel my body tense. As if the extra physical weight of my body wasn't enough, the mental and emotional cries from within woke me like a jolt. *I have had enough!* I was not okay with how

I was feeling and felt crushed internally. It was like my spirit was speaking up: *You can't go on like this anymore, you're hurting yourself.* This wasn't a new voice; it had been with me for years, whispering, sometimes faintly, sometimes louder, but on that day, it wasn't whispering anymore. My spirit was shouting. The truth had hit; *I can't keep going like this*. I was unhappy. Feeling unworthy and unlovable, *I had had enough!*

For the first time in a long time, the full weight of that realization hit home, and in that moment of clarity, the pain of the voice in my head became something different; an Ignite Moment. I could see things for what they were. If I was being honest with myself, I had been ignoring my body and my spirit, avoiding it, pretending I could push through, but there it was, undeniably waking me up. My body and spirit were crying out for change, and I was no longer okay with complacency. I wasn't just carrying the pressure of my responsibilities. I had the emotional weight of the stories I had been telling myself: I was not enough, nothing I did mattered, and I wasn't worthy of feeling good or of taking care of myself. That debilitating narrative was created from all the times when I felt unseen, unappreciated, and unloved. I had internalized those words and allowed them to shape my world; things had to change!

At that moment, a spark was struck, a realization that I needed to change. I needed to take care of myself and be a leader for not just me but everyone who depended on me for their care, guidance, and motivation. I needed to begin, to change, to make the effort. Something shifted internally, and I realized that if I wanted to feel better, I had to align my choices with the desire for better health. I didn't have a plan, the answers, or even a clear path forward. But in that moment, I decided: I would stop waiting for the 'right time,' I would no longer wait for a miracle to happen, and I would make an *impact* in my own life.

The miracle was in the decision. The first step was the decision to do one small thing each day that stretched me, made me uncomfortable, and, hopefully, would create a snowball effect to improve my overall well-being. *What if I drive myself to a gym and just park outside?* It was a small step. The next day, I pulled up outside the gym. Once in the parking lot, the thought came to me: *Maybe I could check to see if the daycare would accept four kids, and I could see how much it would cost.* I told myself at least if I walked inside, just one small step through the doors, I would be moving forward. When my feet hit the reception floor, I discovered that I could add child care to the membership for only an extra ten dollars a month. I signed up to commit and ensure I returned. This small step was enough for one day. I left feeling uplifted. It was the first time I had invested in myself in years. A big part of me still wasn't sure that I was going to follow through and do the work it took, but I was moving forward.

Three days later, I went back to the gym. My conflicted mind told me tomorrow was a better day, but I knew I needed to take action today! Embarrassed in my leggings and oversized t-shirt, I sat in the car, battling internally, pausing, and hesitating. Finally, I went inside and put the kids in the daycare for ninety minutes. I went straight to the cardio cinema, where they dim the lights and play movies. I thought *I could hide away from all the athletic, toned people. I won't feel so uncomfortable. I don't fit in.* I sat on a cardio bike and peddled for the whole time while watching a movie. I felt so proud and accomplished that I had finally taken action on my goals.

I didn't have any illusions that everything would change in an instant. But I did understand; *I am choosing to change one thing. I am making one small decision.* I chose myself for the first time since motherhood had swept me away. I was choosing not to be bound by the lies in my head or confined by the 'story' I had been living. I was choosing to take a step toward something better, even if it felt small or impossible. That was the moment of impact, the moment I gained momentum for everything to start changing, the moment I realized that the smallest decisions add up to make the biggest changes.

Over the next few weeks, after breakfast, I continually showed up at the gym, hiding and cycling away. After two months, I noticed the weight dropping off my figure. I lost twenty pounds, gained more momentum, and saw that I was capable. My internal story was beginning to shift because my mind now had evidence that I was doing the work and results were taking place.

Despite all the heavy, blocking, negative thoughts and emotions that had clouded my reality, one truth began to stand out: *Feelings aren't facts, and thoughts aren't permanent.* Just because I experienced the feeling and thought of not being enough didn't mean they were true about who I was or who I am today. Through understanding how to shift my internal dialogue and that small actions can lead to results, I noticed that my thoughts created my feelings, and those feelings drove my actions. It sounds simple, but it impacted how I viewed myself and the world around me. One thing I've learned is that emotion is energy in motion. It's like the law of physics we all learned in seventh grade: *energy can't be destroyed or created; it can only be transformed.* That Ignite Moment, the thought that I have had enough, showed me where I was stuck and sparked the desire for total transformation, re-creating myself from the inside out.

That is where my true healing began. I desperately wanted to feel better physically and to break free from the patterns that kept me locked in depression and negativity, and it had to start from within. I had to learn how to move that energy, transform it, and use it for fuel to set myself free from the control those thoughts and feelings had over me. During this time, I discovered that true wellness wasn't just about the physical body. It's about tending to every aspect of my well-being: physical, mental, emotional, and spiritual.

Unhappy with how I felt in my body, I started with the physical because that's where I felt the most disconnected. Once I began to master the change in my health and fitness, I knew I had to heal on a deeper level and continue to rewrite other negative beliefs and thought patterns. I focused on my spiritual body, beginning to shine a light on the darkness and bringing awareness to those false stories I'd been telling myself. Awareness became key to it all as I heard that inner voice and decided a change was needed.

You can't change what you're not aware of. Caring for my mind, body, and spirit became the foundation for raising my vibration. Every small step, every positive action, led me to a better, higher version of myself. Now, I see that true wellness isn't just about looking a certain way; it's about how you feel, how you treat yourself, and how you show up for your own life despite your external circumstances.

The journey is ongoing; every small step and decision leads to a better overall feeling and sense of worthiness. If you are willing to bring awareness to the thoughts that need changing and take small, actionable steps, you have the power to transform. Know that the hurts and heartaches internally can mend and won't last forever. There are better things in store for you. You, too, can design and create heaven here on earth with your thoughts, words, and stories.

Ignite Action Steps

- **Small Decisions Lead to Big Change** - Start by taking small, uncomfortable steps toward self-care and health to create a snowball effect that leads to lasting change. It's not about waiting for the perfect moment, making one decision can positively impact your overall well-being, helping you to build worth, power, and confidence in yourself.

- **Awareness** - You have the capability to change the stories you tell yourself, and that shift in awareness is the key to your overall well-being. When you stop accepting the negative narrative that says you can't or aren't enough and start rewriting your story based on that awareness, you transform your life for the better in all areas and categories of wellness.

- **Holistic Healing** - See your healing from a multi-dimensional perspective and understand that your mental, emotional, physical, and spiritual well-being are all interconnected. Taking care of your mind, body, and spirit is the foundation for raising your vibration and aligning with your true essence.

- **Self-Worth and Transformation** - You can transform energy and the belief that you aren't enough into a more empowering belief of strength, resilience, confidence, and value.

Dee Taggart — United States of America
Speaker, Author, Transformational Coach, Mentor, Impact-Driven Leader
herXpansion.com
thedeetaggart

Aligning Your Life with Your Purpose

The most impactful lives are built on purpose. When your values and actions are in sync, everything feels more meaningful, and the path forward becomes clearer. Living aligned with what truly matters to you creates a sense of fulfillment that no external achievement can replace.

The stories in this book show how people have aligned their lives with their true calling, often through moments of challenge, growth, and self-discovery. Now, it is your turn to explore how your values guide you and how you can create a life that reflects your deepest purpose.

- What are three values that guide your decisions?

- How do your daily actions reflect those values?

Jessica Sinclair

Jessica Sinclair

"Learn to roll with the tides of life and truly experience what it is to live."

I hope that reading this story will bring you hope. While things may not seem okay right now, they *will* get better. You always have a choice in how you respond. Your circumstances don't have to hold you hostage. You can overcome them and create something beautiful.

The Rainbows After the Storms

If there's one thing I have learned about life so far, it is that it comes in waves, ebbs, and flows. There are the highest highs, the lowest lows, and a lot in between. I've also come to know that every time I've thought *I'll never survive this,* I do. Or when I've thought *it can't possibly get better than this*, it does. It's in learning to roll with the tides of life that we truly experience what it is to live. I have not always had this perspective. I used to think that life was happening *to* me until I learned life was happening *for* me.

It all began... when I was just fifteen and saw Logan for the first time. I immediately felt an electric charge course through my body. His captivating blue-green eyes, longer blonde hair, and athletic build had me swooning instantly. He kissed me that night, taking my breath away, and I remember thinking, *I'm going to marry this boy one day.*

Unfortunately, the universe had other plans, and our relationship was a short-lived whirlwind that lasted a couple of spring months. We parted ways suddenly, and both continued on our own paths.

Six years later, we unexpectedly reconnected on a drunken summer night and quickly became inseparable. If I wasn't crashing at his place, he was at mine. We spent as many waking moments as we could together. I felt that same certainty from when I was fifteen rushing through me all over again. He was who I was supposed to end up with. The next three months together flew by and felt like a dreamy fairytale. My heart was at home, safe and held.

The hard reality was that a previous relationship tore his heart. Giving him the space he needed to sort out his feelings, I chose to walk away. My heart shattered. I was devastated like I had drowned in that choice to put things on hold. And yet, this was just the beginning of life happening *for* me.

The next day, I found out I was pregnant.

I was terrified! Newly single, I was unsure whether my now ex-boyfriend was going to be around for us or not. *What am I going to do? This was never my plan.* One thing I knew for certain, however, was that I loved the baby so much already and that with or without Logan in the picture, I would be the best mama to this precious angel.

Over the next few weeks, we shared minimal contact. He was caught up in a storm of emotion while I was trying to navigate how my life would change with this beautiful little soul soon coming to me. I was heartbroken thinking of raising my baby without their daddy at my side, nervous because I didn't have many answers, but also excited because I knew my greatest adventure was only about to begin.

The swelling excitement was, unfortunately, short-lived. Just a few weeks later, I went to the emergency room, experiencing unusual pain and heavy bleeding. After receiving an ultrasound, the doctor came in and told me that I had miscarried my sweet baby.

The grief of the heartbreak and my loss crashed into me like a tsunami. Still reeling from the loss of the relationship I thought was fated, this news swept me to depths I didn't know existed. I felt everything and nothing at all. I wanted to scream, but no noise would come out. My mom held me as I cried and cried until I faded into sleep.

The days became a blur as I cried until I had no tears left. I felt emptiness like I had never before and willed darkness to encompass me entirely. I packed up the little outfit and the tiny baby blanket I had bought into a box, along with the thoughtful package the hospital gifted me to provide some support during this monumental loss. I knew I needed to try to find some kind of 'normal' in the nightmare I was living. Twelve days later, I returned to work on Christmas Eve.

Two hours into my shift, I felt sharp pain unlike anything I'd ever experienced before. It was radiating from my abdomen so intensely it made me physically sick and on the verge of losing consciousness. I rushed to the emergency room, and finally, after nine and a half hours of excruciating pain, I was given an ultrasound. This was when they discovered that I had a second *ectopic* pregnancy (a pregnancy that occurs outside the uterus). Now, not only was I grieving my recent miscarriage, but I was also suffering the earth-shattering loss of another baby. Before I had time to wrap my mind around this rare circumstance, I was taken into emergency surgery to address this life-threatening situation.

The surgery was successful, but I needed help through recovery. I spent the holidays on the couch at my parents' house feeling entirely void of life, utterly empty, and like I had failed at everything: failed at my relationship, failed at pregnancy, and failed at keeping my babies safe. I was amid so much anguish; the weight of all the sorrow felt like I was drowning in the sea of tears that wouldn't stop coming.

Logan eventually visited me, and while I resented him for not being there through the whirlwind of loss and heartache, I still loved him. He held me close as the salty tears stung my face, and my nose burned red from all the tissue I'd been using. Being in his arms again made me feel a small shard of hope for something positive in the chaos that was raging within me.

Feeling fragile, I kept Logan at a distance to try to protect my aching heart from another blow. A few weeks later, we slowly started building our life back together. As our relationship blossomed, we moved in together. After a few months and some therapy, I started to feel like myself again. I missed my babies every day, but it became easier to exist in a world where they were watching over me rather than here with me.

We decided we wanted to try for a baby again, and not long after, we found out we were expecting! I was elated yet terrified of the thought of losing another baby. Due to my previous ectopic pregnancy, I had an early ultrasound. With Logan at my side, we saw this little one's heart beating and were immediately overwhelmed with tears of gratitude. Finally, I could breathe! I was so relieved and overjoyed to know that this precious babe was growing on track and so wonderfully, amazingly alive within me. We started planning for the baby's arrival and anxiously awaited the next ultrasound. We were back at the clinic five weeks later to have our twelve-week scan.

My perfect, beautiful baby had stopped developing at nine weeks.

The world stopped entirely as a hurricane of devastating grief encompassed me. My body had not yet recognized that my baby didn't make it, and the doctor said that it could be weeks before it did. I opted to induce the miscarriage that evening and was connected with resources to support me through this tremendous loss. I spent countless hours in therapy, working through the layers of grief, shame, and guilt. My home felt empty and lonely, so I moved things around, trying to fill the space I had arranged for my baby, whom I would never meet.

As the weeks passed, my mom suggested to Logan and me that we should get married if we wanted to bring a baby into the world, as we clearly wanted to build a life together. We began planning within a week. I bought my dress the next month, and we started nailing down details shortly thereafter. Logan proposed during our family photo session, surprising me! He got down on one knee, whispering the question with deep sentiment. It was such a pure and perfect moment, surrounded by our families. Once more, I felt on top of the world! We picked our wedding date that night, setting it for just shy of a year later.

We spent the next twelve months planning, expanding our lives together, and falling more in love. We focused on what made us happy and forged our friendship in meaningful ways. Twenty-four hours before our wedding, I was out grabbing a few last-minute touches for our big day when I felt a huge urge to take a pregnancy test.

As it turned out, we had a baby on the way! We cautiously shared the news of this beautiful blessing with our closest friends and family at the rehearsal dinner that night. I was getting the wedding of my dreams with the man of my dreams, and I just found out about this glorious child we had prayed for. We were over the moon!

Our wedding was perfect, our honeymoon was magical, and this pregnancy was going to plan. Although I bled off and on through the first trimester, this baby was safely in my belly, developing as expected. Throughout the pregnancy, I often felt caught in a storm of anxiety yet anchored in Divine protection. I knew this baby, and I were being watched over and protected by my other three angel babies.

I went into labor at almost forty-one weeks pregnant, and the next thing I knew, I was holding the most beautiful baby I had ever laid eyes on. It felt surreal, and for a moment, I almost panicked, but then a wave of peace and love poured into me. As I heard her first cry, my heart healed so purely and wholly, and I embraced her warmth as she was placed on my chest. Her presence in my life had a tremendous impact, showing me that all I had been through was *for* me, to awaken me, to gift me this precious moment: the 'coming together' of my new family.

A rainbow baby is a baby born after loss, the beauty after the storm, signifying joy and hope after a period of grief, guilt, and loss. Adalynn was the greatest blessing and healing I had ever received. Being her mama came effortlessly to me. It felt like she was meant for me all along. We watched her grow in awe of this precious life gifted to us every day. She was perfect. Before I knew it, a year had passed, and our delightful little girl had grown into a curious toddler. Our home was filled with laughter, love, and sleepless nights. We relished every moment, feeling like life couldn't get any better.

We started dreaming of growing our family once more, and within just a few short months, our wish was granted! Even though there was some fear due to our previous experiences, we were comforted to hear this sweet babe was growing on track. I was as prepared as possible, feeling ready for this baby. Delighted to welcome another daughter, I was feeling confident in the mother I had become and loved the life we were creating. We moved into our first home in the dead of winter, and I started nesting right away, preparing for our newest addition to arrive soon. Life was perfect.

In the wee hours of a cool Spring day, we welcomed Emersynn into our lives in the comfort of our home. Peace washed over me as she arrived earthside, safely in my arms. The first few days felt natural. However, I noticed pretty quickly that something started to feel off. Before too long, I was experiencing intense postpartum depression. This was such a contrast to the early days with Adalynn. It felt like the joy I had experienced before had been turned to dread. I cried a lot, was quick to anger, and had thoughts of self-harm. I was exhausted; surviving, yet in no way thriving.

My doctor prescribed an antidepressant and referred me to a therapist and a group therapy program for postpartum moms experiencing similar heart-wrenching pain as I was. It was such an agonizing time for me. My package was complete — the house, the marriage, and two incredible daughters - yet I was struggling with it. I should've felt like I was on cloud nine, yet I was floundering to stay afloat most days. *Was there something inherently wrong with me?* I knew my family deserved a stable and present mama, so despite the pit in my stomach around all the support I needed, I dove in head first.

I started seeing a therapist individually every two weeks while attending group therapy sessions weekly. After months of feeling more like a shell of myself than a person, I started to feel seen and understood. It was so healing to speak with other moms experiencing things similar to mine. This transformative time provided stability, tools, and support that helped me feel like the mom I knew I was at my core.

Towards the end of the ten-week therapy program, I yearned to continue my healing, at first for my family and then for myself. Despite my progress, fear crept into the back of my mind. *What support would I have when this was over?* Within days of this thought, I was scrolling through Instagram™ when I noticed a coach I previously connected with had recently shifted her niche to conscious parenting. Her energy reminded me of how alive I felt when Adalynn was born, and I longed to regain that feeling. I immediately booked a call with her that evening. She ignited something within me as she described intuitively healing, returning to myself and my purpose.

Exhausted from fighting the currents of chaos within myself, I was ready to feel inspired, peaceful, and happy. I knew this was the person who would guide me toward the wholeness I was seeking. Thirty minutes later, I sheepishly walked out of our spare room to inform my husband that I had invested $12,000 into the healing I'd so longed for. His jaw hit the floor. I understood this was a considerable investment, especially since maternity leave meant a decrease in our income, and I was relieved when Logan was incredibly supportive. I didn't have the funds, but I knew I needed to prioritize my healing and invest in myself *for* my family.

The impact of choosing to invest in myself rippled into every area of my life. This coach was teaching me a new way of being, giving me a perspective I would never have seen. I was deep-diving into my wounds, creating healing on a raw, introspective level. She had a profound and intuitive way of bringing forward what I needed and what would best support me while lovingly nurturing me through each step. She gave me a safe space to bare the depths of my soul and offered a hand to raise me higher than I had ever been. The freedom and lightness that washed through me was revitalizing, like I had taken a deep breath after being submerged underwater for too long. I felt as though I had been *reborn*.

I gained a new perspective that if any of my previous pregnancies had come earthside, I wouldn't have the incredible girls I do now. Nor would I have the self-compassion and trust in the Universe that I do now. Even on the hardest days with my girls, I still have immense gratitude, as I remember a time that I would have given anything to have hard days with babies I never got to meet. I learned that I could either become my circumstance and be held hostage to it or heal beyond it and create something impactful *through* it. While I may not always have a say in what happens to me, I discovered that I always have a choice in how I respond. I get to choose the blessings and cherish how they have happened *for* me and my greatest good.

Now, I connect with my intuition and heart, finding safety within myself to discover and explore life with curiosity, openness, and patience. I've connected to who I am at my core - not who my experiences had shaped into me. Recognizing the divine timing, the spiritual knowingness, and the frequency of desire and love, I discovered myself, my truth, and my purpose. Investing in myself was the catalyst for building the foundation for completely stepping into who I am. Now, I use my experience to support women in finding peace, purpose, and joy no matter where they are on the waves of life. I show them how to embrace authenticity, balance, and flow so that they can impact their lives profoundly and meaningfully. Life's gifts are often wrapped in unforeseen ways, but they are always filled with blessings designed to richly impact our existence.

You get to experience your highs as deeply as you are willing to experience your depths in life. The lows can feel breathtaking, heartbreaking, and insurmountable, yet they pass. The highs can have you on top of the world, feeling invincible and empowered, and they, too, will pass. When you learn to roll with the tides of life, you experience the impact they offer: the love, the peace, the pause, and the clarity. Treasure these moments. Honor their presence, for they are a present wrapped divinely just for you.

Ignite Action Steps

You are your greatest investment! Invest in yourself. Get help to heal your trauma and explore your pain. Be open to trying multiple things to find what works best for you. Stay curious and keep opening yourself to new possibilities. Embrace each moment. Immerse yourself in the present while also taking action towards what you desire in the future. Do things today that your future self will graciously thank you for.

Jessica Sinclair — Canada
Transformational Life Coach, Reiki Master, Soul Guide, Energy Healer
msha.ke/SacredRebel
 Sacred Rebel
 sacred.rebel.soul

Yun Rhee

Yun Rhee

"We are magical beings on a magical planet where thoughts become things."

My wish for you is to feel the profound truth that your power comes from within. Life's greatest journey is discovering who you are, the infinite potential within you, and the joy of falling in love with yourself. As the creators of our own reality, investing your time, energy, and resources into understanding your potential will unlock your soul's unique blueprint, allowing you to live as your highest expression. In a rapidly changing world, this self-awareness will ground you and unleash the limitless possibilities of what you can create.

Keys To The Kingdom

I remember the day so vividly. I was in my big corner office on the top floor, speaking with my coach at the time and feeling confident and overwhelmed. On the surface, I had everything: a thriving career as a team leader at Keller Williams™, the largest real estate company in the United States. I was overseeing the growth and performance of their market center. I also worked with my husband, managing our real estate sales team, a fix-and-flip company, buy-and-hold investments, and a commercial real estate portfolio. At home, we were raising two beautiful girls. Life was full, busy, and precisely what I thought it should be. At that time, my coach asked me a question I wasn't prepared for. "Yun... who gets the best version of you?"

My mind instantly jumped to the people I love most: my husband, my daughters, my parents, and my closest friends. *Of course,* they *got the best of me. I mean, that's what I was working so hard for: to provide for them, create a legacy, and honor all the sacrifices my parents had made for me. That's what it was all about, right?* But as I opened my mouth to respond, something inside me froze. I couldn't say it. Because deep down, I knew it wasn't true.

In full integrity, I had to admit it; the people I loved most were actually getting the worst of me. They got whatever scraps of energy I had left after juggling all the roles and responsibilities I had piled onto my plate. And the worst part? *I had no idea how or what I wanted to change it into.* That realization brought me to my knees. At that moment, it felt like my entire world cracked open.

I was operating in survival mode, utterly unaware of the programs running my life. *Guilt. Shame. Pressure. Hustle.* These invisible forces were driving everything I did, and they had been with me for as long as I could remember. They created the programs I was operating from, programs such as 'needing to work harder and harder' to create 'more and more success,' 'money was hard to achieve,' and 'doing things' to make others proud of me. I had so many limiting belief systems that I wasn't even aware existed.

I grew up as a very sick child with many health complications. My parents had immigrated to the United States from South Korea in search of the American Dream, and they worked an average of twenty hours a day just to make ends meet. They sacrificed everything for my brother and me, and at some deep, subconscious level, I believed I was a burden. That belief became a deep-rooted program. An inner silent voice in my head telling me I had to work *really, really hard* to prove I was worth it. I had to ensure their sacrifices meant something. That pressure shaped me into who I was sitting in that room. Someone who was successful on the outside but completely disconnected on the inside. Someone who had no idea who she really was or what she truly wanted.

Of course, I wanted to be a great daughter, wife, and mother. But the truth was, I wasn't showing up as any of those things. I was exhausted. I was drained. And I was giving the worst of myself to the people who deserved the best. And even more than that... *I had nothing left to give to myself.* That realization was like staring into a mirror and seeing someone I didn't recognize. *Who was I, really? What did I want? How had I let things get to this point?* These questions impacted me deeply and pushed me to want to discover my truth.

As my coach's question settled in, my body reacted before my mind could catch up. A rush of heat spread through me, and it felt like I'd been punched in the gut. My thoughts spun in all directions, a whirlwind of anger, frustration, sadness, and utter disbelief. Tears welled up and streamed down my face. I sat there, blindsided by one piercing realization: *What am I even doing this for?*

At that moment, the carefully constructed life I'd built began to unravel. Titles, achievements, and responsibilities – all the things I thought defined me– suddenly felt hollow. I had been living on autopilot, chasing success without ever stopping to ask myself what success truly meant. That one question opened my life, sparking a series of serendipitous events that felt too perfectly aligned to be coincidence. I was so curious to learn and understand myself that I started to ask many questions, and like magic… I was led to answers that I wasn't even aware of.

I was introduced to *Thinking Into Results* by the Proctor Gallagher Institute, where I encountered a simple yet profound explanation of the relationship between the conscious and subconscious mind, helping me to understand *why* I had been operating the way I was. The guilt, shame, and relentless pressure weren't *me*—they were deeply ingrained programs I'd absorbed throughout my childhood. Beliefs like, '*You have to work hard for money,*' or '*life is so hard,*' had unconsciously dictated my actions. Seeing these patterns with such clarity set me on a path to rewrite them.

Something inside me clicked: *I need to learn more.* That realization ignited a hunger I hadn't felt in years. Despite all my outward success, I had no idea who I truly was or what I genuinely wanted. I dove into personal development with a newfound curiosity, and for the first time, I began to explore the limitless potential within me.

As I leaned into this journey, I felt a deep sense of recognition, and it was like my soul had found something it had been searching for all along. Life wasn't just about building skill sets to get ahead; it was about discovering my infinite possibilities. This awakening stirred a connection to something greater, and the desire to make an impact awakened in me.

As I allowed myself to dream again, ideas and desires I'd buried for years began to surface. It wasn't easy at first. I had spent so long focused on what I *had* to do that I had never permitted myself to even consider my own desires. I started small, grabbing a notebook and writing down anything that came to mind. It did not matter how irrelevant or silly it seemed. The act of writing broke the dam, and the floodgates opened.

I realized that to dream bigger, I had to clear out the mental and emotional junk cluttering my mind. Guilt, shame, and survival programming no longer existed in my life. Letting them go made space for something new: *the freedom to embrace my truest self.* I was excited to start discovering more of myself and find the magic inside of me.

Letting go of old stories inspired a profound shift in my life. Opportunities, people, and experiences I never imagined began flowing to me, completely outside my usual reality. Instead of questioning or overanalyzing, I consciously decided to *say yes.* Each 'yes' opened a new door, offering lessons and perspectives that expanded my world in ways I couldn't have planned. My family went from traveling once a year for three days to exploring new destinations one to two times a month. In less than a year and a half, our business multiplied, and our rental portfolio grew from twelve doors to over four hundred units. Life was transforming rapidly, but it wasn't without its challenges. Growth never is.

I came to understand that obstacles aren't punishments; they're opportunities for our souls to expand and evolve. By tending to the three planes of existence – spirit, intellect, and body– I began to see challenges not as roadblocks but as invitations for growth. Every obstacle brought new clarity, deeper self-awareness, and a stronger understanding of my potential.

As I embraced this new chapter, prioritizing who gets the best version of *me,* I committed to saying yes to the things that stretched me. One of the first was hiring a coach, an investment in myself I had never considered before. I also began attending mastermind groups with people equally dedicated to their growth. It was like stepping into a completely new world where the possibilities were limitless, kindness and collaboration were the norm, and success wasn't a competition but a shared celebration.

This shift was a breath of fresh air, breaking down paradigms that had unconsciously ruled my life for years. Stories like '*Money is the root of all evil*' or '*Rich people are greedy*' no longer held power over me. In this new environment, I discovered people who were wildly successful yet deeply generous. They shared their knowledge, supported others, and genuinely wanted to see everyone around them thrive. These new belief systems shattered every misconception I had about success and wealth, showing me that abundance doesn't just change lives; it elevates everyone it touches.

I knew I was on the right path because, for the first time, I was beginning to uncover the truth of who I was and what my soul came here to do. The more I said yes, the more I committed to my growth. Daily study, meditation, and journaling became non-negotiable habits. Through those practices, I began uncovering parts of myself I hadn't known existed. I became more aware of what I truly wanted: the experiences I wanted to create, the people I wanted to surround myself with, and doing the things that mattered most to me. And through the process of self-discovery, I tapped into one of the most profound truths I've ever known: *the truth of Oneness.*

I understood that everything in this universe is energy and that I am energy, the center of all that exists, intricately connected to everything around me. The limits I once believed in were illusions shaped by the paradigms and programs I inherited to protect me from emotions I feared to face. But as I learned to work with energy, to uncover these paradigms and create habits that expand my awareness, I discovered the wonder of infinite possibilities: I can BE, DO, and HAVE anything I desire because I am infinite.

That realization was like finding the *keys to the kingdom*. It wasn't about chasing external success anymore; it was about creating from a place of *alignment* and a deep knowing of who I am and what I'm capable of. My impact was now unfolding.

Through the journey of studying and personal growth, everything in my life began to shift. Our real estate business grew significantly and with it, our wealth. Opportunities seemed to flow to us effortlessly from all directions as if the universe itself was conspiring in our favor. And while the material success was rewarding, what mattered most to me were the changes happening within my family. My marriage began to thrive in ways I never thought possible. My husband and I were more connected, aligned, and supportive of each other's growth than ever before. My relationships with our daughters deepened as I learned to show up for them with more presence, love, and patience. These were the things that truly filled my heart, the things that made every step of my journey worthwhile.

As I continued on that path, something extraordinary began to happen: I started to tap into my spiritual gifts. I felt alive. Amazed. Powerful. Elevated. I realized how we are born with supernatural gifts far beyond what we've been taught to believe. The superpowers we've been told that are fictional or only for superheroes are what we've been conditioned to believe. The truth is that those powers and extraordinary abilities exist in *all of us.*

As I started to unlock my soul's blueprint, I began to see the truth of who we are as humans. *We are spiritual beings who are having a physical experience and are the creators of our reality.* The outer world we see is not separate from us; *it is a mirror reflecting the frequencies we emit into the universe.* When we understand this, we gain the ability to shift our reality by creating from within. This is what it means when people say, *"The truth will set you free."* The journey to freedom is the journey of discovering your truth, finding your purpose in your existence, truly learning to see your experiences as reflections of your inner world, and reclaiming your power to create intentionally.

That one question, "Who gets the best version of you?," became the catalyst for what has impacted me to continuously discover the infinite version of myself while helping others to do the same. I now ask that question to all my clients and help them unlock their greatest potential and have them fall in love with being curious about who they are. *Who gets the best version of you?* has given them clarity to create a life of impact for themself and those they love. It's a question we should all ask ourselves.

If there's one thing I want you to take away from my story, it's this: *you are the creator of your world.* Every person, place, and circumstance in your life exists because, at some level, you created it. Whether consciously or unconsciously, your soul brought these experiences into your life for one purpose: *to grow, expand, and uncover the truth of who you are.* But here's the challenge: most of us go through life giving our power away. We let our circumstances define us, we let old paradigms control us, and we let fear keep us small. It's time to change that.

True power comes from taking full accountability for your life. It comes from understanding that you can shape your reality not by changing the outer world but by transforming the inner world. When you take your power back, you begin to see the magic that's been inside you all along. You start to understand the three planes of living – spirit, intellect, and body – and how they interact to create your experiences. You begin to see how your energy shapes everything around you. You realize how *magical* you truly are.

The journey is not about perfection; it's about *curiosity.* It's about falling in love with the process of discovering who you are and what you are. When you approach life with this kind of inquisitiveness, everything changes. You'll start to see yourself and others with more clarity and compassion. You'll live in harmony with the laws of the universe, creating a life filled with magic and miracles. And most importantly, you'll experience the freedom and joy that come from knowing yourself deeply and authentically.

My invitation to you: *get started.* Dive into personal development. Do whatever it takes to uncover the truth of who you are. Because when you truly understand yourself, you'll understand others. And when we all begin to understand one another, we'll create a world of harmony, love, and infinite possibility. *We are magical beings on a magical planet where thoughts become things.*

The power is already within you. It always has been. Empower it, and step into the life you were born to create.

Ignite Action Steps

1. **Reflect Honestly:** Ask yourself, *Who gets the best of me?* Awareness is the first step to reclaiming your power.

2. **Seek Growth:** Surround yourself with mentors, coaches, and communities that challenge and inspire you.

3. **Commit to Daily Practices:** Use meditation to calm your mind and journaling to explore your desires, patterns, and dreams.

4. **Embrace Opportunities:** Say yes to experiences that stretch you and reveal more of your potential.

5. **Trust the Process:** View challenges as opportunities for growth and trust that your outer world reflects your inner journey.

6. **Take Ownership:** Recognize that you create your reality. Design a life that reflects your highest self.

Yun Rhee — United States of America
Chief Empowering Officer and Energy Expert of EHE, Speaker, Trainer,
Practitioner
yunrhee.co
elevatedhumanexperience.com
yun.rhee.3
yun.rhee
yun-rhee

Kimberly E. Beaudoin

KIMBERLY E. BEAUDOIN

*"Forgive yourself, and you can finally see the beauty
of life through all the pollution."*

My wish for the reader is to know that there is light at the end of any darkness. No matter how low your life may seem polluted with abuse, addiction, or loss, there is always a way to emerge into a peaceful existence. Others can have a devastating impact on you, but I want you to know that it is possible to heal yourself. You can become drunk on self-love and high on life.

RISING UP

It was 'date night' with my young son Jesse every Monday. We would make time together hanging out on the couch in the basement with blankets and popcorn. The buttery fragrance would linger throughout the house. We had a special bond after I left his father. One night, Jesse told me, "Mom, I know what you do for us. You buy food, put gas in the car, put a roof over our head, get the oil changed, and do so much. Thank you for looking after us like that, Mom. I just love you." Jesse was a kind-hearted, gentle soul who always cared for me and his younger sister. I made sure I would lie down with each of the kids every night to ensure they felt safe and knew I was there for them.

A few months prior, I made arrangements to leave their father. I had secretly taken counseling for two years and finally mustered the courage to move out and away from my husband, who was a very abusive man. I felt a sense of freedom and purchased a little two-story, four-bedroom home. Jesse had the bedroom downstairs on the main level, and Alyshia and I occupied the two bedrooms upstairs. The house was very choppy, with small rooms everywhere, and we wanted to do some renovation work. A family member found a handyman who was the son of a local businessman. We hired him. He seemed polite and eager to get started fixing a humble home.

We rebuilt a deck and had the kitchen opened up. I was happy to see the changes. It filled our hearts with joy as the new space allowed us to have friends over. The handyman would be at our house when the kids went to school, and he would still be there at night wrapping up projects when the kids went to bed. Some nights, he joined us for dinner at the kitchen table. We connected more as a family in our new life and home.

Months passed, and our handyman found extra jobs to keep himself around our home. I worked in a hair salon and started to hear rumors that this particular person was a pedophile. Initially, I thought it was gossip, but the stories grew. One day, while cutting someone's hair, I was listening to one such story. I could feel every cell in my body begin to burst into rage, and heat came out of my ears. My whole body tensed, and my teeth clenched. I had spit coming from my mouth in disbelief. My eyes felt like they were on fire. My hands flailed around in the air, asking if anyone knew if he was actually convicted. There was silence.

Back home, I thought about how kind he had been to us as a family and how good a job he had done. *Maybe it was all gossip. Perhaps it was all just people spreading lies.* I am a trusting person and want to believe the best in people. I decided to dismiss the allegations. I needed proof.

The jobs around the house were coming to an end. One Saturday late afternoon, a beautiful summer day, my phone rang. When I picked it up, the Handyman told me he had gotten tickets to a rock concert and that I was going with him. I said "no" immediately. I had a friend over for supper but didn't even have a babysitter. I said I was not going out with him and hung up the phone.

A half-hour later, he showed up with his two younger sisters at my front door. He said, "I'm not taking 'no' for an answer; you are coming with me. I brought my sisters to babysit as well." He was smiling and charming, mixed with a little aggression, and I felt ambushed with little choice. We went to the concert.

After the concert, he began acting strange. In the name of fun and foolishness, he went into the stairwell of the parking lot and turned on the fire hose, pouring water out of the spout like a tsunami. He left it running. I was in shock and scared. We then came across a pub and went in. I had to go to the bathroom. He ordered beers while I was gone, and as I sipped mine, I noticed little bubbles coming from the bottom. Something didn't feel right. Everything went numb and cold from the top of my head to the tips of my toes. My eyes were going fuzzy, and my legs felt like a thousand pounds.

I have no recollection of how I got into my car. He drove. We were on the highway just coming off the overpass, and I struggled to get words out of my mouth. Everything moved in slow motion as I tried yelling STOP. He was driving my car like a madman. I have no memory of how I made it out of the car, onto the sidewalk, and up the thirteen stairs to my bedroom. I couldn't even hold my head up or lift my feet. I was paralyzed — a deadweight. For the next two and a half days, I was in and out of consciousness with little flashes when I could move my eyes from side to side. Helpless, he took advantage of me many times over. I was trapped in hell.

One thing I do remember is him pinning my hands over my head. He was naked and leaning in close to my right side. I could feel his warm breath on my face and his voice whispering to me, "Kim, the rumor is true. I do like little boys." I couldn't move. Having his way with me over and over again until he was satisfied shattered my life into pieces. All I could think of in my haze was, *How could this have happened?*

After nearly three days of unimaginable trauma, he left me angry, in shock, and in disbelief. I told someone, but they didn't believe me. There was no proof. The Handyman seemed so nice. Wondering if anyone would believe me, I stayed silent, feeling alone and broken, like darkness had overcome me. I didn't tell the children, I wanted to spare them from the entire ordeal. I dimmed my light and buried my feelings inside.

My perpetrator continued to drive very slowly around my neighborhood at all hours of the night. A couple of weeks later, he parked in front of my house, trying to get my kids to come and have a peek and pet his duck. I chased him out of my yard, yelling and screaming at him to never come back. Fear and terror ripped through me, shouting, "You are not welcome here!"

As the months went on, I noticed a change in Jesse's behavior. He stopped coming home after school and would turn up around 9 PM. He was only eleven years old. I was worried. He got caught in possession of dope in his locker and then started getting into fights. He was suspended from school for three days and then suspended again. Finally, after three months, he was expelled. Even though he was beside me, I couldn't grab him. He was slipping away. *What did I do wrong?* I felt I had failed as a mom and buried my emotions even deeper.

Jesse became very self-destructive. He got caught stealing. He was so engulfed in his own shame he would hit himself so hard on the face that he had lumps, bumps, and bruises. I felt helpless watching *his* light diminish; once so bright, he was slipping away, deeply burrowing his emotions.

The school had placed him in a facility for troubled youth. Jesse was seeking love but came up empty, distraught, and defeated. He made more bad choices as I exceeded and exhausted every possible avenue available to help him. A few times, I had to call the police and ask them to come and remove him from our home. I also needed to keep my daughter safe. Torn between protecting my daughter and helping my son, I was at a loss.

One particular time, Jesse started smashing the four big mirrors on my closet doors. Then, he grabbed his hair and tried pulling it out. A policeman came and calmed Jesse down, telling me about P-Chad Orders regarding minors, where the parent would have to go in front of a judge and convince the authorities to apprehend a child who was a threat to himself and others. Such an order would allow police officers to pick Jesse up and take him to a safe house for five days, where he would have the opportunity to become clean and sober and get the help he needed.

I took their advice. Unfortunately, it didn't work, but I was hopeful and tried multiple times as Jesse worsened. The fifth time I called the police needing a P-Chad Order, two cop cars drove up onto my lawn in a blazing pursuit, one racing up the left side and another tearing up the grass on the right side. It was like a scene from the movie. At that moment, I watched, devastated, as they removed my son from my home. The choice played hugely on my morals and values as a mother. I was dying inside, defeated, knowing this was the *only* choice I had. With a pit in my gut and feeling like my heart was being ripped out of my skin. They took custody of Jesse.

Things did not get better. When Jesse turned sixteen, he was at an age when he could be on his own. From then on, he lived between family members here and there. He became a functioning addict at the age of eighteen, but I still remembered the gentle soul he was and hoped he could make a fresh start, always believing his sliver of light would shine through.

One evening, while watching the television program Canada Intervention™, a number came up at the end of the episode. The next day, I called the number to the treatment center. I talked to my parents, and we made arrangements for an addiction worker to fly out. We were going to do an intervention with Jesse. *Maybe this could be our solution.*

We set ourselves up in a local hotel in the city. Tricking Jesse into thinking he had a job interview, he walked into the hotel room and faced all the people who loved him. Although it was tough love, my hope hung in the air. His first reaction was refusal to go to any treatment center. Feeling ambushed, he asked to get some air and went for a walk outside. Upon his return, he agreed to commit. Always the optimist, I had a bag of clothes packed for him in the car, and the very next moment, Jesse and the addiction worker were on a flight to the recovery program. It was such a relief. My body, mind, and soul finally felt peace, as if I was waking up for the first time in years. I saw a light at the end of the tunnel.

For four months, Jesse was on the road to recovery. My load was lightening. Not long after he came home, he fell into his addiction again, even deeper and darker this time. My pain and frustration reached new lows. I was losing all hope.

At 3 AM one night, I got a phone call from the city police. Apparently, masked men were breaking into Jesse's house where he was babysitting his roommate's little brother. Jesse had put the boy in the closet and laid over him to protect him while calling 911. Jesse was in a drug-induced psychosis, and there was no one breaking in. He was so high that the invasion was all in his mind.

I was in shock. A forty-minute drive to his place took me only seventeen minutes. I turned the corner and drove into a SWAT swat team, swarming like ants, crawling over the entire neighborhood, lit up with red and blue. It was another movie scene. I couldn't believe my eyes.

An officer informed me that Jesse was shackled in the back of the SUV SWAT swat vehicle. They had taken him to a nearby hospital. As a mother, I was screaming within. The treatment from the cops was entirely inhumane. He was placed in a rubber room where they held him for five days to assess him. Upon his release, it felt like they just threw him to the curb like a piece of garbage. They never even notified anyone to pick him up. I cannot express how painful it was to witness all those heart-wrenching events and feel so helpless. For years, since my assault, I had been facing the volition of one thing after another. I was incoherent of my own existence. My light had been snuffed out completely.

Many hard years passed, and then, at twenty-eight, Jesse came to me and said, "I need help." It felt so uplifting that he was finally choosing himself. Jesse called the intervention treatment center where he had first gone. He organized it all. I drove him around, and he sorted the payments, the doctors', and the plane ticket to get there. He also asked if he could stay with me and if I could drive him to the airport. I was delighted. Before boarding the plane, he looked at me and said, "Mom, I just want you to know it's not your fault; I want you to know that I love you."

"I love you, too. You are so worth it. Never give up, my boy; I love you," I responded. My heart expanded with the same glow I used to feel during our date nights in his younger years.

Jesse was gone for almost three months. It would be another Christmas without him, but he was in the best place; he was getting clean and sober. He was making a life for himself, and I was very proud. When he called me from the center, I had never heard joy that clearly in his voice. He had so much love for life, and his enthusiasm deeply moved me. He said to me, "I finally got it, Mom. All I need is God in my life." I truly felt whole from his conviction to God and experienced heavenly light reigniting my soul.

As a new year arrived, an ad on social media kept showing up in my feed to *start the year fresh. Want to live a stress-free life? Come join a free four-day experience!* I signed up for their workshop on New Year's Eve. We had to pick one word that we wanted to bring into our lives for the coming year. Mine was *peace*. That's all I had envisioned. Peace.

During those four days, Jesse's face played over and over in my mind. There was a giant puzzle of my life that formed in my mind's eye with three pieces that were missing. While in meditation, the three missing pieces came together: the assaulter, Jesse, and me. *Oh my gosh, it became clear.* The Handyman had sexually assaulted Jesse. He had not just assaulted me but also my son. I knew I had discovered the root of Jesse's deep turmoil and inner anguish. That was the reason my kind-hearted, caring son had transformed into a lost soul. He had turned his pain inward, just as I had. He kept his dark secret all to himself the same way I did. We both protected one another by hiding the truth and closing off ourselves.

Four days into the new year, I got the worst knock on the door a mother could ever get. My beautiful son had passed away. I was beyond the ability to process it. I couldn't absorb the news. My body and soul were broken. The impact was beyond words.

The next morning, I came down to the kitchen to face the reality that my son was no longer with us. I sat, staring into oblivion, trying to comprehend reality. My watch fell off my wrist, landing on the counter. I looked at the time on my watch and noticed it had stopped working at 8 PM, the same time the police told the news the night before. I stopped in my tracks, looked up to the Lord above, and said, "Thank you, I get it; time doesn't matter." My time with Jesse was a blessing, and my time with him is infinite.

As the years passed, I thought I would never come to the surface. Slowly drowning, I was trapped in a dark place for over three years and developed Post Traumatic Stress Disorder. I was barely surviving, not living, and needed a beacon of light to hang on to. On New Year's Day, three years later, I promised myself to get better, a promise I severely needed to keep. I knew that from the deepest pocket of my heart, and I had to rebuild trust within myself. I signed up for a retreat in Guatemala. It was life-changing. As I broke through barricades and hurdles of fear, I overcame enormous mountains of emotions. I removed impenetrable barriers and accepted life's past challenges. I was healing and went on to explore deeper connections within. I reclaimed my life and ignited the light I had forsaken. I forgave myself, embraced my emotions, and began to live again.

You can love yourself so genuinely that you are high on life with no substance required and be drunk on self-love. You can forgive yourself to the point of seeing all the beauty in life and emerge from the pollution. You are free; you are the beacon of light in *your* life. You can have peace knowing that whatever darkness you are facing does not need to last forever. It *is* possible to impact your future and emerge into a peaceful and loving existence. *Shine your light and be free for all to see.*

IGNITE ACTION STEPS

- **Find a community** - whether online or local, having people around you who are taking the same steps as you can be very powerful.

- **Sign up for a retreat** - there is something very impactful about spending time with new people in a new environment, carefully designed to surround you in healing practices that provide such a safe container. Treat yourself.

- **Forgive yourself** - hire a love coach or someone who can guide you on a path to learning how to lighten the load of shame, guilt, and anger. Learning how to forgive yourself and loving yourself deep within is essential to a life of peace. Never give up. You are worth it.

Kimberly E. Beaudoin — Canada
Business Owner, Operator, Author
Kimberly Beaudoin
scissors_edge.hair Spruce Grove
Kim Beaudoin

Angela H. Robinette

Angela H. Robinette

"Words are not helpful unless action supports them."

There will be times in our lives when we may face an uncomfortable or fearful situation that could inhibit us from helping others. Humanity cannot move forward if we allow our apprehensions to control our actions. If we embrace a call to action and appreciate the moments that stretch us, we will broaden our worldviews, welcome new opportunities, and develop lifelong relationships. I hope that my story will inspire you to act and give the universal gifts of time and compassion.

A Gift

Icy pellets of rain pecked at my windshield. I clenched my teeth as the rain tapped and the wipers chattered back and forth. I hated the chaotic sound and the view outside my window. Everything was gray; a streaky-gray windshield, a gray sky, gray trees, a gravelly gray road, and a gray single-wide trailer looming in the distance.

I glanced over at my student, Shakerah. Unlike the grayness that enveloped us, she wore a purple sweatshirt and had cherry-red fingernails. A few of them were chipped.

I gestured with my hand at the window. "In America, this is a popular color for inside homes. If I had to look at gray walls, I think I'd be depressed all the time," I said dryly. "What color were the walls in your home in Jamaica?"

"We have color, like a green room. It's the color of new grass. And a pink room," she responded directly.

"Your bedroom?" I asked, trying to develop a rapport with her. "Do you miss it?"

Shakerah shrugged. "A room is a room. I miss my mom."

"I know." I placed my hand on top of hers and squeezed. "Hopefully, your dad will get established quickly in Boston."

I hit a pothole, and my body jerked up and forward before my seatbelt caught me.

"What the hell was that?" I blurted. "Are you okay?"

"Ms. Robinette!" Shakerah guffawed. "You cursed!"

"I'll curse even more if I pop a tire, but I'll do it under my breath."

She continued to laugh. "You write up students for cursing, but you do it."

"Well, in my defense, I don't hit bone-shattering potholes in class."

"You are funny." Shakerah's smile widened, and her voluptuous lips tightened, exposing her brilliant white teeth. She shook her head. "You are a cool teacher."

"My idea of 'cool' is that you are learning," I quipped.

"Yes, Miss, I am. I like Scout in the book we are reading. She is like my sister, opinionated and hot-headed."

I had to smile and hold back a chuckle. *To Kill a Mockingbird* is one of my favorite novels, also. If I could meet a man like Scout's father, Atticus, courageous, intelligent, and thoughtful, I wouldn't be single," I admitted.

Shakerah laughed so hard I half expected her to snort. "He's too old for you. You need a younger man."

Even though I was concerned the pothole may have caused damage to my tire, I was grateful for the distraction. The burning chunk of apprehension bubbling in my stomach slightly subsided as we bantered with one another.

"Thank you for driving me home," Shakerah giggled. "That's our place." She pointed at the single-wide, which looked even grayer than the clouds and the road. I had no idea the gloomy trailer was her home.

I almost said, "No problem," but that was far from the truth: Bringing her home *was a problem*. There are a plethora of things teachers cannot do. This was one of them. Another was going into a student's home when a parent or guardian wasn't there. That was a big no-no that could get me fired, but I had to know the living situation for her and her siblings. There was a third concern

I had, which would not only lead to the end of my career but also send me to prison. Hence my burning stomach.

I hadn't been teaching Shakerah for very long, not even two months since the second semester started in January, but I had learned so much about her through the journaling I required my students to do. She and her siblings, a younger sister aged ten and an older brother aged seventeen, had moved from Jamaica to South Carolina at the beginning of the school year. They were living with their father's sister, and according to Shakerah, her aunt did not like having them in her home. I could understand that. Her aunt was a single woman in her thirties who had become the custodial guardian for three children she barely knew. What I couldn't comprehend, however, was that their aunt had left them home alone for a long weekend getaway with her boyfriend. That seemed neglectful.

When Shakerah had asked me for a ride home from school, I told her I couldn't have students in my car; then she said she would have to walk because her aunt was out of town. I thought about the busy road in front of the school and the closest neighborhood, which was over a mile away. I looked outside. The needle-like rain tapping on my classroom window changed my mind.

The harsh reality of where Shakerah lived brought me back to the present. I pulled up to the trailer. It looked even more dismal up close.

"May I use your restroom? The pothole jarred my bladder," I fibbed.

"What? Your bladder? Did you damage your kidneys, too?" she teased. "Yes, come in. I think it is good in there. In the bathroom."

I didn't really have to use the bathroom, but it was a legitimate excuse to get inside the trailer. I needed to make sure the home was in a livable condition and that there weren't any drugs being used. This was my third concern: As a teacher, I am a mandated reporter, which means if I suspect a student is neglected or abused, I am required by law to report it to the Department of Social Services (DSS). I felt prickly all over: down my arms and on the nape of my neck and scalp. Adrenaline soared through me. *It's not like I'm breaking into her house,* I thought, *so calm down!*

In front of me, Shakerah dashed up the three steps, pulled a single key from her back jeans pocket, and unlocked the door. I followed her in, but without a covered porch, we were both wet from the deluge of icy rain.

The door opened into the kitchen. There was more grayness – the floor, the cabinets, the refrigerator – but at least the trailer was warm, and the kitchen was tidy. A blender was on the counter, and a small pot was on the stove. Nothing unusual.

"The bathroom is there. On the left." Shakerah gestured.

The carpet that led to the bathroom butted up to the kitchen's linoleum tile. "Should I take off my shoes?"

"*Irie*," she responded, using a Jamaican word I did not understand. It sounded like eye-ree.

"*Eye* . . . what?"

Shakerah laughed. She had a deep, resonating laugh, like someone humming into a hollowed-out coconut. "'*Irie*' is a way to say 'it's all right.' No worries, Ms. Robinette. Keep your shoes on. My sweatshirt is wet. I'm going to change."

Good, I thought. *I'm going to snoop.* I turned on the bathroom light, but there was no fan. Too bad. I knew I needed to mask the sound of opening the cabinets. In all my life, I had never opened a bathroom cabinet door that wasn't creaky.

I turned on the hot water faucet to cover the sound and quickly opened the medicine cabinet, the cabinet under the sink, and the one above the toilet. I wasn't sure what to look for ... unlabeled pills? Needles? Bags of drug paraphernalia? A hand pipe?

I found a makeup bag, toothpaste, ibuprofen, several bottles of Victoria's Secret™ body spray, toilet paper, and a metal pick comb. I unzipped the makeup bag. Just tampons.

Her aunt was irresponsible but not a druggie. And she's neat. The cabinets were more organized than mine. I touched the running water with my index finger. It was hot. Good.

Flushing the toilet, I sighed. "Thank God," I murmured, feeling relieved.

As I entered the kitchen, Shakerah was opening the refrigerator door.

"Do you have enough food for the weekend?" I asked.

"No." She had her back to me, but I could sense her frustration.

I looked over the top of her head and saw a small container of orange juice, ketchup packets, a bottle of mustard, and a half-eaten hamburger in its wrapper.

"It's okay, Ms. Robinette. My brother works at McDonald's™. He'll bring home food after his shift tonight."

"You can't eat fast food for every meal," I sympathized. "Come on. Let's go to the store."

I decided I would not call DSS. Leaving them home alone for three nights in a drug-free trailer with heat and hot water was inappropriate, but not neglectful. Her brother was seventeen, and at fifteen, Shakera was old enough to babysit her sister, and I was taking her shopping for food. Calling DSS might make their situation worse if they were here illegally. I could not live with my shattered emotions if my phone call led to their deportation after all the sacrifices her parents had gone through to get them here. Ultimately, I wanted this sweet girl to have the American dream, to someday move to Boston, where her father was establishing himself, and have opportunities she would never have in Jamaica.

Three years prior to this impactful afternoon, my boyfriend, our daughters, and I had vacationed in Jamaica. As tourists, we were the country's primary income source. On the way to the all-inclusive resort, our bus drove through a rural area, and I saw homes made with concrete blocks. They weren't painted; they were just gray cinder blocks. The homes were small, smaller than my townhouse's living room. Sheets of metal were used for their roofs, and I distinctly recall one home having a bright blue shower curtain for the front door. It was attached to a shower rod with plastic rings. We had a great vacation, staying in a luxurious villa and eating scrumptious Jamaican dishes, but the poverty they lived in gnawed at me as I sipped a fruity cocktail on the beach. I wondered what the children in the rural mountainous areas endured: *Were they hungry? Did they have to travel far to go to school? Did they even have school buses?*

With our heads covered by reusable shopping bags, Shakerah and I ran into the grocery store. I shook off the rain and threw the bags into a cart.

"Lead the way, Shakerah. Get enough food for tonight and this weekend."

I expected she would head to the freezer section for frozen pizza and waffles and the snack aisle for chips and cookies like most American teenagers would do. I was wrong. In the produce section, she inspected three or four cabbage heads before choosing the one she liked best. She then grabbed a bundle of unpeeled carrots, a bag of potatoes, and two yellow onions. Watching her, I was in awe. I had made an assumption about her as a teenager without considering her Jamaican lifestyle and culture.

"On weekends, my mother would make ackee and saltfish for breakfast. I haven't had that since I moved here," Shakerah explained. As she told me about her mother's cooking, I felt as if I was unwrapping a beautiful gift, the gift of a world I did not know.

"Fish for breakfast?" I was surprised.

"Oh, yes, Miss. It is good," Shakerah said, smiling brightly. She steered the shopping cart toward the meat refrigerators. "May I get two chickens? My brother is skinny, but he eats so much."

I nodded yes but did not speak. I was not prepared for the overwhelming emotions that seared my heart. As she placed the chickens in the cart, I looked away. I batted my eyes to ward off the tears. This fifteen-year-old girl had taken on the role of her mother, buying fresh produce and meat to make home-cooked meals for the three of them. Her courage, dedication, and resilience were stunning. I realized how Shakerah was showing me the values and traditions that I had lost with my family. Her actions and thoughtfulness were incredibly impactful. I was moved and forever changed.

"This would be extra," Shakerah said, interrupting my thoughts. We were in the frozen entree aisle, heading to check out after adding milk and butter to the cart. "But could I get this?" She pointed at TGI Fridays™ Buffalo-Style Chicken Wings.

"Of course, Shakerah. You deserve a special treat." Like one of the puddles outside, it felt like my heart flooded with compassion and empathy. I knew I was helping her, but she was helping me, too. My entire perspective shifted when I saw what this courageous girl was doing, how devoted she was to her family, and the fortitude she had to endure in her situation: *we have to care for one another, and we have to act.*

After that rainy day in March, I spent more time with Shakerah, inviting her to help my cross-country team cut down trees to create running trails. I learned about Jamaican traditions, her mother, and her wish to become a nurse. I was thrilled to spend time with her. I met Novelet, her sister, and her brother Everton, whom I took to work several times. They were lovely children.

In late May, just two weeks before the end of the school year, Shakerah missed class three days in a row. I knew something was wrong, but the attendance administrator did not know where she was. She had not withdrawn, and she never returned.

I searched for her on social media but could not find her. Frustrated, I gave up trying. Years later, I received an early Christmas gift, a text message from her:

Goodnight, Ms. Robinette. I hope u remember me. It's Shakerah, the Jamaican girl from South Carolina High School. You used to be so nice to me and my siblings. I hope all is well. I always talk about how nice you've been to me…Hope to hear from you.

Since then, we have communicated through phone calls and texting. She is now a nurse, and her siblings have careers helping others.

Reflecting on this experience, I'm grateful for the impact Shakerah had on me. Because of her, I have become involved in many types of service, using my God-given skills to positively impact others. I owe my transformation to a girl who gave me a gift when she asked for a ride on a cold, dreary day and ignited a spark in me.

When you have the opportunity to help someone, do it. Take chances, trust your instincts, do what's right, and see how the gift you *give* is an unexpected gift you *receive*.

Ignite Action Steps: *ACT*

- **<u>A</u>ccept Challenges:** Respond by *doing* rather than *dwelling* on the adverse outcomes of helping others. It is integral that you replace excuses and fears with commitment, compassion, and generosity. Seeing challenges as gifts, not problems, can change your mindset.

- **<u>C</u>are More:** You should never underestimate the importance of caring for people on a personal level, even in situations that may create discomfort. Stepping outside of your comfort zone to help others will not only add value to your life but also to the people you connect with.

- **<u>T</u>ake Action:** Volunteer in your community. There are ubiquitous opportunities to help others, whether it's in schools, community parks, libraries, senior centers, churches, soup kitchens, men's or women's organizations, and homeless shelters. There is always a need.

Angela H. Robinette — United States of America
English Language Arts Teacher
angelainfinitepossibilities.com
robinetteangela, msrobinette_echs

Matthew A. Swierk

MATTHEW A. SWIERK

"Lead with the heart, and everything else will follow."

I hope this story reveals the strength of reclaiming your identity and step-ping into the truth of who you are. May you find the courage to question old beliefs, embrace vulnerability, and rewrite the patterns that no longer serve you. My journey reminds us that our greatest power comes not from perfection but from alignment with ourselves, our purpose, and the Divine. May these words spark a desire to live boldly, love authentically, and rise confidently. Know that you have everything within you to create a life of meaning and connection. The past does not define you; you are the creator of your future. Step forward with trust, and may your journey inspire others to do the same.

THE JOURNEY BACK TO ME

The room buzzed with a palpable excitement, a mixture of anticipation and curiosity. Bright lights reflected the energy that radiated from my wife, Yun. She has the kind of aura that makes you feel both seen and inspired before she even speaks. Cool air brushed against my skin, grounding me in the moment as I tried to manage the nervous excitement coursing through me. My hands felt clammy, betraying the calm exterior I was attempting to project. Around me, I heard murmurs as the attendees captivated and whispered their thoughts. Yun had been selected as a presenter at a high-level mastermind of entrepreneurs, and I was so proud. Yet, amidst the pride, something unexpected began to stir within me.

The room was intimate with fifteen seats arranged neatly on either side of Yun, creating a focused, almost sacred space for her presentation. She stood in her power at the front, poised and radiant, exuding confidence as she prepared to deliver her talk. I couldn't help but feel a surge of pride seeing her address this group; among them were high-level CEOs, people of influence and success, who had chosen to hear her speak.

Yun began to share her message about choosing *happiness*, her voice calm yet commanding. Then, an attendee interrupted with a sharp question: "What if I don't want to be happy?" His tone was snarky and aggressive, slicing through the room's energy like a knife. The room fell silent as his words hung in the air. I noticed side glances exchanged between audience members, their discomfort detectable.

My chest tightened, and I felt my hands clench involuntarily. A little bit of rage bubbled up inside me. *How could someone challenge such a simple, powerful truth?* I felt a surge of judgment toward the man, and an immediate thought crossed my mind: *If I had been given that question, I would have used my dominance to put him in his place.* But Yun, ever graceful, responded calmly, "Why would you not want to be happy?" Her poise, unshaken, diffused the tension in the room while I sat stewing, grappling with the contrast between her approach and my own masculine instincts.

I had always been Yun's biggest supporter. From the beginning of our marriage, we did everything together. We had built a life most would envy; a strong marriage, two incredible daughters, multiple businesses, and even several rental properties. It was a life I had dreamed of growing up in a broken home as a boy. Back then, I promised myself I would be the husband and father my family could count on. And, I had succeeded — or so I thought.

As I watched Yun take the stage that day, my excitement for her was suddenly overshadowed by a creeping sense of inadequacy. Her energy filled the room, connecting instantly and deeply with everyone present. She was magnetic, and the admiration in the room was undeniable. However, instead of basking in her glow, I felt a knot of discomfort forming in my chest. My intense desire to be seen and heard diminished the way it had throughout my childhood.

A thought surfaced: *What about me?* It was a whisper at first, but it grew louder as the day continued. I realized I had been in a 'lack mindset,' and she was fully in growth mode. Again, I questioned who I really was. I began to tune her out, detaching myself from her words and presence. It was easier to retreat into my thoughts than to face the growing gap I felt between us. I reflected on a conversation when Yun had asked me if I was happy. Without hesitation, I'd said, "Of course!" *Why wouldn't I be?* I had achieved everything I had set out to do: marriage, house, businesses, and stability. Her response was a statement that pierced through my carefully constructed facade; "You're not the man I fell in love with. I think you have settled in life."

Her words rattled me. I felt exposed and confused. I had given her everything I thought a good husband should. I subscribed to the mantra, 'Happy wife, happy life,' putting her on a pedestal and following her lead. In doing so, I had lost myself. My childhood dreams had been simple, and once achieved, I had stopped dreaming. I had settled, and it was clear that Yun had not. Her suggestion that we start pursuing our unique strengths felt like a betrayal, given that our direction had always been the same. I wondered who the man she fell in love with was and if I truly possessed any of those characteristics.

I had always been a high performer, driven to succeed in every venture I took on. The first business Yun and I ran was a dry cleaner. One of the primary roles that she assumed was working with the customers. I always admired how effortlessly she connected with people, as this was not something I naturally gravitated toward. She made each interaction personal, learning their names, asking about their families, and making them feel like they belonged. It wasn't long before the business felt like an extension of our home, and our customers became like family. We both knew 95 percent of them by name.

When times got busy, I would step up front to help with the workflow. At first, I thought of it as just lending a hand, but those moments turned into something much bigger. Interacting with customers allowed me to see how Yun worked her magic. People gravitated toward her, and soon, they started joking about me being 'allowed up front.'

Comments like, "Oh, Yun finally let you out of the back!" would come my way. I laughed along, not thinking much of it, and joined in with playful responses like, "Yep, she allowed me up front today," or, "I'm just her indentured servant." Sometimes, I'd even say, "Oh, I'm just a pants presser." Everyone would chuckle, and the moment would pass.

What I didn't realize at the time was how those small, seemingly harmless jokes were slowly chipping away at me. The more I fed into the narrative of being 'just' something or needing her permission, the more I started to embody it. My words, even spoken in jest, were shaping my reality. Without knowing it, I reinforced the idea that I was less than and that I wasn't the equal partner I believed myself to be.

Looking back, it wasn't about the jokes or the laughter but the stories I was telling myself. Each comment I made fed into a growing belief that my worth was tied to the roles I played, not the person I was. I was the behind-the-scenes man at the back of the house. That realization that I had settled was a subtle but powerful awareness that took years to recognize. What started as harmless banter became a reflection of how I saw myself; not as a high-performing partner but as someone who had withered into the shadows. My confidence was shattered.

I overcame my self-doubt by diving deep into one of the core programs we facilitate named *Thinking Into Results™*. I used a lesson on self-image to understand that I had deep-seated beliefs that were not true. What I had become was *not* my destination; it was a stop along the way toward living in alignment. I went deep into understanding that my beliefs had been created from emotional impacts as a child. The fear of failing was causing me to fail, and I simply would not let that happen. I started to ask the following questions daily: *Who am I? What am I?* If I wanted to change my belief systems, I needed to stop looking backward at what had transpired and instead have a constant focus on who I wanted to be.

One of the tools I used from the program was *Life Script*. The tool led me to mentally create the best possible life I could imagine and envision what my relationships could feel like. I created a movie in my mind that I played with clarity and confidence to influence my subconscious programming. It was not an overnight process and required constant attention and focus. Initially, stepping into my power and passion helped me become a better mentor with more confidence. I wanted to feel liberated by being vulnerable and sharing with others. Yet, my paradigm of divorce, shaped by the trauma of my parents' separation, surfaced with full force. I was terrified that I couldn't support my wife mentally, emotionally, and spiritually and that she no longer wanted me by her side.

For the first time, I confronted the fact that I had become codependent, which is a pattern of relying on others for self-worth and identity, often neglecting one's own needs and boundaries in favor of prioritizing another's happiness or approval. That realization filled me with shame. I feared that others would see the cracks in my carefully constructed image. My initial reaction was to swing in the opposite direction, to reclaim my power with a defiant, "I don't need anyone!" That only brought out the anger and aggression of a past self I had worked hard to leave behind. I felt like I was losing everything, including myself. My mind was racing and defaulting to survival mode, filled with lack, fear, worry, and doubt.

As I dug deeper, I began to question who I really was. *How many layers had I been hiding under?* I wasn't being honest with Yun, and more importantly, I wasn't being honest with myself. I felt like an imposter, saying one thing and feeling the opposite as I would agree to follow every path she had put us on. I told myself I wanted to support Yun, but deep down, I resented her growth because it highlighted my stagnation. I slid back into the belief, ingrained since childhood that my feelings and opinions didn't matter. That was a program I had carried for years, one born from a desperate need to be seen and heard but never feeling worthy inside.

Confusion consumed me. I didn't know who I was or what I was supposed to do next. Yun, in her characteristic way, approached me with love and compassion. She told me something that changed everything: "You can rewrite your story. You don't have to live by the beliefs that brought you here. If you want to change, you can start now."

Her words lit a spark within me that created a major impact. For the first time, I realized that I had the power to redefine myself. I didn't have to settle for being a passive participant in our relationship or my life. I began to reflect deeply on how I had been showing up. I asked, *Am I being the best version of myself?* The answer was *no*. I understood that I needed to honor and empower ME for our relationship to thrive.

The more I reflected, the more I realized I *had* a choice. I could stay in the current cycle, burying myself deeper in fear and insecurity, or I could break free. The fear of my life breaking down loomed large, but the alternative – aligning my body, mind, and spirit— felt like the only path forward. *The best way I could support Yun was to support myself first.* I realized that when I functioned at a high level and poured into myself, it allowed her the space to do the same. We could elevate each other by being the best versions of ourselves. My Ignite Moment arrived when I realized that my ego had brought me to this point, and it was time to rewrite false beliefs and programs that were holding me in a lower vibration. I paid close attention to my thoughts, feelings, and actions and diligently used the universal law of polarity to stay focused on the version I wanted to become rather than the version I was.

The transformation wasn't instantaneous. I had to face the uncomfortable truth that my identity had been wrapped up in roles I *thought* I should play. Growing up, I was torn between conflicting role models: my father's aggressive dominance and my mother's nurturing love. This left me confused about what it truly meant to be a man. *Was I supposed to take control at all costs? I wasn't sure.* Relationships then became a mirror for my self-doubt, reflecting the parts of me I didn't want to confront. In doing so, they also became the most significant source of growth. By focusing on the inner work of nurturing my needs and pursuing alignment, I found the strength to show up authentically—not just for Yun but for everyone in my life.

I turned to meditation to quiet my mind and seek guidance. Each day, I carved out time to connect with my higher self, asking for clarity and direction. Slowly but surely, I began to hear the answers I needed. The process was exhausting at times, but it was transformative. I learned to let go of the anger and fear that had been holding me back and started taking inspired action.

One of the most profound lessons I learned was the importance of acceptance. Yun and I had different talents and gifts, but that didn't make mine any less valuable. I stopped comparing myself to her and began to see the unique contributions I brought to our partnership. Instead of trying to measure up to her, I embraced the idea that we could empower each other by pursuing our individual passions. We all go through the same emotions, just at different levels. I learned that using my existing environment and beliefs to understand these patterns of the past was critical. Staying focused on feeling good in the present moment became a guiding principle. After all, we have a choice: to say, 'one day,' or make it, 'day one.'

The journey wasn't just about rebuilding my sense of self; it was about recognizing that each of us has an important message to broadcast to the world. Stepping into my power has been a profound example for my children. My desire is for my two daughters to step into their authentic selves and understand that a healthy relationship is about being the best they can be, not conforming to what they think someone else wants them to be. By living this example, I hope to inspire them to embrace their authenticity and find strength in their individuality. They now see that their parents can work together in different roles and create a life by design, not by default.

Following my passion and stepping into my calling has enabled me to establish a path of my own by creating a luxury travel company that facilitates transformation through travel, which opens the hearts and minds of others by using nature as a classroom. I have also created an environment of unconditional love and acceptance within myself and those I work with. Saying yes to God's assignment takes my ego out of the equation. It allows me to let go and trust that I have everything I need inside of me and that I am divinely guided. Being on *my* mission has been one of the greatest gifts I could give myself, my wife, and my family. We all carry limiting beliefs, but we also have the power to rewrite them. By stepping into my truth and embracing my gifts, I found a renewed sense of purpose and fulfillment and surpassed the man I was before.

My relationship with Yun is stronger than ever, not because we rely on each other to feel whole but because we empower each other to be our best selves. By choosing to lead from the heart, I've discovered that true strength lies in alignment *with ourselves, our purpose, and the Divine.* Through this process, I have learned to honor my individual journey while creating a shared life rooted in love, trust, and respect.

Life, relationships, and love do not come without their challenges, but each component flourishes when we embrace vulnerability and release old patterns. We open the door to deeper connection and growth. Leading from the heart has taught me that everything else truly does fall into place. It's a reminder that we all have the power to rewrite our story and create a life of meaning, courage, and *impact* — not just for ourselves but as an inspiration to those around us.

Ignite Action Steps

- **Self-Reflect:** Regularly ask yourself, "How am I showing up?" Success in any relationship requires both partners to be their best selves and support each other's individual journeys. Empowering each other is key.

- **Seek Guidance:** Connect with your higher self to improve your feelings. This could be through prayer, journaling, or meditation.

- **Take Inspired Action:** When clarity comes, act on it. Trust the guidance you receive and take steps that align with your purpose.

- **Meditate:** Take time daily to calm your mind, ask for answers, and create space for insights to come through. The practice of listening is just as important as asking.

- **Accept:** Understand that everyone has different talents and gifts. Recognize the value in your contributions and honor your unique path.

Matthew A. Swierk — United States of America
Leader, Guide, Adventurer, Warrior, Husband, Dad
MattSwierk.com
matthewswierk
mattswierk

Mickey Forsyth

Mickey Forsyth

"Self-care is not selfish but a necessary, loving gift for yourself."

If you, the reader, are a caregiver, I want you to make sure you don't lose your identity in taking care of someone else. Remember to support yourself at the same time as being supportive. Take time for breaks and give yourself grace so it's not such a hard road to heal and recover when things change. Hang onto hope and take things one day, sometimes even one moment at a time.

Lessons Of Care

My wife Dani and I lived in an endless cycle of constant money worries and physical setbacks for both of us. I stressed about money incessantly. I had no idea how we would survive financially. Love is fantastic, but it would not pay our bills. Out of sheer desperation, I took a customer support job while still attempting to run our technical virtual assistant business. Dani was in the depths of a crippling depression and struggling to cope, unable to provide our services anymore. After about six months of struggling, she took a customer support job at the same company as me. *Big mistake!*

As a transgender woman living with physical concerns and severe, chronic depression, Dani was not prepared emotionally or mentally for the toll of this seemingly straightforward job. The harassment, verbal abuse, and discrimination, under the guise of support from the employer, sent Dani into a downward spiral that she could not handle. Each day led to more trauma, tears, and anger until I had enough. The job was not worth the money or the stress.

I asked Dani to quit her job with a massive promise from me. Scared yet empowered, I vowed to take total responsibility for our finances. If Dani took time to heal and received some mental health support, I hoped she'd get better and we could get back to doing our business together. I didn't know how, but I knew I had to fix our finances quickly.

Making that critical decision, I focused solely on building my business separate from Dani's. I walked into our home office each morning with fear, dread, and determination. Overwhelmed and petrified, I was deeply committed to turning the situation around.

At forty-six years old, I faced over $100,000 in debt plus our monthly mortgage payments and monthly medical expenses due to my wife's physical troubles. I also lived with Chronic Fatigue Syndrome since I was fifteen and Fibromyalgia since I was nineteen. I didn't just have an uphill battle; I had to dig myself out from underneath our growing debt and look after my wife with her physical and mental hardships, plus myself. I felt as though the mountain was growing steeper and steeper each day.

Quickly, I realized I needed to quit my low-paying, full-time job to concentrate on building the VA business. Slowly, clients came forward, and finally, things started to come together. That was a turning point, a testament to my resilience and determination to overcome our current financial situation.

After two years of working our business on my own, my dream was like a fading heartbeat in the distance. While Dani desperately wanted to contribute financially, it was not mentally or physically possible. The toll of COVID-19 broke her heart repeatedly and contributed to her deteriorating mental health. We witnessed the loss of so many people across the world, plus members of my family. Dani loved deeply and empathized with every part of herself; the sadness of the pandemic took everything from her. Yet, I refused to give in to despair. I clung to hope, determined to overcome these challenges.

I began working nearly full-time with a new client in the fall through a friend's referral. This allowed me to concentrate solely on that contract and care for our financial needs — such a relief! That opportunity gave us hope for a brighter future despite our many setbacks. Finally, I seemed to be making progress on the steep mountain climb of debt and from the overwhelming stress of our daily lives.

Unfortunately, the Universe wasn't done testing us. The very next month, after a routine mammogram, I received news that would change my life. I was diagnosed with stage three breast cancer. Facing this daunting diagnosis head-on, I began chemotherapy three short weeks later and resolved to fight the disease with all my strength.

Thanks to a Saturday chemo treatment schedule, I mostly worked Monday through Friday. The company was phenomenal about any time I needed to take off to recuperate or for appointments. However, the reality was that I didn't get paid if I didn't show up or log in. Our financial situation needed me to work, and I was feeling massive pressure.

I had zero time to think or feel in the organized chaos. Days and weeks flew by; working, chemo treatments, doctor appointments, surgery, and radiation treatments. Meanwhile, Dani experienced increased suicidal ideation with ongoing, debilitating depression. Life was a blur of busyness and stress; with no time for calculated steps, I had to *run*. I could not indulge in self-care. Even my favorite go-to of journaling fell by the wayside most of the time. My focal point was helping Dani.

Through this journey, I began to lose myself in the oblivion of Dani's depression. Every fiber of my being had to be centered on something for her. Even through my cancer recovery, I felt like I had to protect Dani from any pain or struggles. Despite having cancer, I knew, without a shadow of a doubt, that I would survive. Cancer felt like a blip. The thought of dying never entered my mind. Where I experienced doubt was how to survive Dani's mental health sickness. As my sadness and frustration increased, I didn't know how her condition was going to get better.

By the following summer, Dani endured yet another mental breakdown. At this point, she wore her mental anguish like a second skin, and it enveloped her with an intensity I did not know was possible. Instead of having suicidal thoughts weekly, they became a daily, then a constant companion. No matter the problem, no matter the situation, suicide was the first and only answer.

As a result of living with chronic illness my entire adult life, I learned many coping mechanisms. However, journaling, listening to music, and simply leaving the apartment were no longer priorities. My focus was entirely on Dani and her mental stability. I would do anything to help her, but nothing made a difference. I felt helpless, alone, and more and more lost by the day.

As a caregiver of a loved one, it was like watching someone scrambling to climb a mountain but continuously sliding backward and being helpless to save them. I watched the pain literally fill Dani's face each day; I heard her sobbing while I was in the other room trying to work. She struggled to find the right mix of medications that helped her mentally, but most had powerful side effects that she could not handle physically. I held her hand and laid heart-to-heart wherever possible.

Instead of being a patient with a cancer diagnosis that has hope of healing and remission, I became a witness to Dani's condition, transforming into a terminal one while my cancer was in remission.

A year and a half after our introduction, my contract client became my full-time employer. I finally could take time off and get paid, which was such a gift and lifted some of the weight off my shoulders. Despite this reprieve of pressure, there was no time to process or appreciate the moment. I still felt the crushing weight of our debt.

Since depression often leads to self-isolation, we fit that mold perfectly. Dani only left the apartment for errands, mental health-related appointments, or emergency room visits. I hardly left the apartment without her anymore. It was not that I was afraid she would hurt herself if I left her on her own. The truth was that I did not want to leave her feeling any more isolated. I felt trapped and paralyzed in a life I had never designed.

I began losing hope, though I kept encouraging Dani to try the therapy suggestions and to keep working towards improvement. Random thoughts of ending the marriage would occasionally pop into my head, but I pushed them away as quickly as I could, knowing that she couldn't live on her own. All I could picture, if I let the thought linger, was Dani finding a spot to sit outside and simply waiting to die. I couldn't let that happen. She deserved love and respect, no matter how difficult it was for me. I would rather be with her each day and support her as best I could emotionally, mentally, and financially, trusting that she was safe and protected. Every thought and decision was centered around the question, *how does this affect Dani?* I could see my individuality paling in the shadows.

The following Mother's Day, Dani and I had a really good morning. Surprisingly good. We each called our respective mothers. While Dani's conversation with her mom was, as always, laced with her depression and suicidal ideation, they still had a nice chat. We treated ourselves by going to the mall and getting fries and hot dogs to bring home. It had been ages since we'd done that, and it was so much fun. Dani even smiled and laughed some. It was a lovely morning.

We enjoyed our lunch, talked a little, and had a pleasant afternoon. At about 2 PM, Dani said she wanted to lie down for a nap. It was perfectly natural for her to go into the bedroom for two to three hours for a nap. Her sleeping was always an escape for each of us in different ways. It gave her relief from all the intrusive thoughts and overwhelming feelings, while it gave me a break as I knew she was safe.

When I went to wake her, I could immediately tell she was different. Dani looked more peaceful than I'd seen her in years, and I could tell she wasn't breathing. There was no movement, no heartbeat. When I pulled the covers back, I could see blood pooling in her legs. I called 911. Trembling from head to toe, I tried to do CPR until the paramedics arrived. I left the bedroom, and after a while, they came back out to confirm that the medical examiner was on the way. Dani had died.

The rest of the afternoon and evening were a blur of police, emergency workers, and the medical examiner taking her away. The next horrible moment came when they wheeled her out on the stretcher. She was enclosed in the body bag and at an angle instead of flat like she would've been if she was alive. Watching her being rolled out like a suitcase was one of the hardest things I've ever witnessed. I couldn't believe this was where we were now. Dani was out of pain, and I now had to figure out what that meant for me in the long term.

At first, I was numb to all the logistical responsibilities that accompany a death. I was on autopilot. There was such a change in the atmosphere of the apartment. Dani had placed cardboard over the glass, as any sunlight bothered her immensely. Her presence was still lingering even in the physical darkness. In every room I entered, I still felt it was filled with her compassion and love. Dani told everyone how much she appreciated them, whether it was a delivery driver bringing meals or the emergency room doctor who spent time listening to her story. She adored humans to the point where they overwhelmed and consumed her. Dani profoundly felt that living in this world was too much for her despite her appreciation and value for others.

The journey of caregiving for a loved one through any long-term illness is exhausting and overwhelming. After prioritizing Dani for so long, I had to figure out how to heal myself. A week after Dani died, I ran the dishwasher, and the unspoken rule was that I unloaded it in the morning. For her, it was a task that couldn't wait. I hated the guilt of her emptying the dishwasher when it was one of my few chores. When I opened the dishwasher to unload it, I thought, *Yes, I could do this right now, but do I want to? Do I have to?* The answer was a resounding *No! I didn't want to or have to!* It was such a big moment for me to step away from doing something that pleased Dani and *only* because it pleased her. I didn't care if the dishes got unloaded immediately. I didn't need to do it out of obligation. It felt amazing and freeing to be in charge of something as simple as a household chore. For the first time in almost eight years, I was deciding for *myself*.

My best friend and I were out doing some errands a month later, like we did before Dani's depression took such a firm hold on my life. The days were getting longer, so the sun was still shining beautifully. It was warming up, spring was in session, and summer was approaching. We were both getting hungry for some dinner. Previously, I'd have rushed home to have dinner with Dani so she wouldn't be alone for more than two hours. But, on that lovely crisp day, I realized I didn't have to go home. I could have if I wanted to, but this time, going home was not *required*.

Wow! What an *impactful* moment, an Ignite Moment, and a quenching taste of freedom. I could choose for myself, and I was choosing *me*!

Looking back, I realized throughout my journey with Dani, I was heading in a dangerous direction. I had blocked out the importance of caring for *myself* mentally. I had forsaken the things that mattered to me. While I don't like 'should' thoughts, there were things I could have done better, and now I am redesigning my life.

Sticking with my mental health routines, like journaling and meditation, could have eased some of my stress. I wish I engaged a therapist for myself. While it made me feel guilty to leave the apartment without Dani, if I had done that more, it could've helped me cope. Saying all this, the most critical missing piece was to give myself more grace. I realized that self-care is not selfish but a necessary, loving gift for yourself.

As the months passed, I started making decisions I wanted, ones I couldn't do before because they had impacted Dani's health. I took all the cardboard down from the windows and brought light into our apartment. I slowly reignited my life. I cleaned out unwanted possessions with the patient help of my best friend. I felt brighter. While I sometimes felt guilty for making so many changes, I needed to finally put myself first. I needed to reconnect with who I am and feel free.

Whether it's a mental, physical, or a combination condition, I learned that things can change over time. Typically, the change is for the person to get better, but sometimes, the condition is terminal. Regardless of how the change occurs, it's possible to survive while still achieving goals for yourself and liberating to come out the other side a better, more rounded person.

Today, I enjoy life more, embracing silliness again and bringing play into everyday things. I'm even bringing fun back into my work life by reintroducing myself to the world as a writer with my childhood nickname, Mickey. I remember now how to find joy in the simple things of life, like a lovely warm coffee on Sunday morning and watching the sun rise gently on the horizon of the beautiful Rocky Mountains where I live. I chose *life* and am excited for a bright, amazing, interesting, and remarkable future.

It is easy to get lost in caring for someone else, but balancing that with self-care is critical. With support and inner strength, it is possible to persevere through hardships and challenges. Taking incremental steps toward a brighter future by journaling and holding a few minutes for yourself regularly allows you to keep moving toward the top of that mountain. Movement is movement; when done consistently, momentum toward a goal will get you there. Take care of yourself, you matter. YOU deserve love and respect.

Ignite Action Steps

- **Carve out some time to evaluate your current situation.** *Are you taking care of yourself the best way you can? Are there small things you could change to care for yourself better?* Pick one thing and work on that, then pick another as your habits develop.

- **Create a self-care routine now that is simple and easy to adapt to your life.** For example, journal daily for fifteen minutes, go for a short walk regularly or listen to your favorite music on your own. Pick something fun!

- **We all need support.** If you or someone you know is in mental distress, contact mental health professionals as soon as possible.

- **Set a small, achievable goal that you've been putting off.** Set a due date, and then tell a friend or accountability buddy to help you stick with it.

Mickey Forsyth — Canada
Author, Productivity Coach, Speaker,
CEO of Step, Step, Pick Systems and Design
mickeyforsyth.com
 mmforsythwrites
 mickeyforsyth

Joe Kavanagh

Joe Kavanagh

*"It is when you speak directly from the heart you make the
most powerful and profound impact."*

I want to remind the reader that if you truly want to be successful, you need to be who you are at your essence. We are conditioned to think that men should hide their emotions and be stoic and that we should chase money over love. I hope that you, as the reader, especially male readers, know that it is okay to express your emotions. What I hope you get from my story is that when you speak directly from the heart, you make the most powerful and profound impact.

The Exposure!

I can't believe this just happened! Here I am, standing in the men's room, choking back tears. Men don't cry. I don't cry. I cannot cry! I am a successful salesman, a VIP at an iconic event, sitting in the front row, and a leader and mentor to so many. I've been at the front of numerous rooms in my career, teaching, training, etc. I love being the center of attention. When the moderator selected me as a 'volunteer' for an exercise she wanted to demonstrate, I thought, *Yes, this is my moment to shine. To be seen.* My ego was in all its glory…until…she dug deep enough into my subconscious. I was getting emotional. Tears wanted to come out more than my words did. My ego was embarrassed. There was nowhere to hide.

Striking up conversations, connecting with others, and selling has been my life. It seems I've always had a knack for knowing what to say to convert a lead into a sale. I was told I could sell ice to an Eskimo. But I didn't sell just any ice. No. My ice was imported, caffeine-free, diet ice. The best in the world. The real estate world. Selling it this way justified selling it at a premium price, making me more money. *Did I care that my prospect got the best deal?* Maybe, maybe not. In many cases, deep down, all I really wanted was that commission. Like Jerry Maguire said, "Show me the money!" After all, I had a family to take care of. I felt I could not face my peers unless I was successful. Making as much, or more, money than my colleagues was priority number one to me. I wanted to be the best and have everyone tell me so. *Stroke that ego, baby!*

In the mid-nineties, I started a real estate appraisal business from scratch in a city I was new in and grew that business into one of the most successful firms in the area in just a few short years. All my hard work paid off. Business was booming. We finally owned the home on the golf course, with the pool in, the country club, with all the trappings that go along with it. I played golf two to three times a week. I got myself down to a seven handicap and took up tennis, also. I took my family of five on a European vacation, as well as a domestic one, every year. Our children went to private schools. We dined with friends and clients at the best restaurants. Life was a party. I had made it! We were happy.

Then came the decline in March 2007, and the balloons started to deflate. As residential appraisers, we noticed a shift in the real estate market. Property values didn't seem to be going up anymore. Initially, we assumed some outliers skewed the data. Over time, we reluctantly had to admit the market was softening. Our lender clients didn't want to see this reflected in our appraisals as it would raise red flags with the processors and underwriters, thus killing their loan deals. A dead loan means zero pay for the banker. Homeowners would be angry if we reported their property values were dropping. We did our best to limit the disclosure of this in our reports.

As the months went by, the evidence was clear and overwhelming. The market was crashing! I lost clients because we started reporting the truth and wouldn't fudge the appraisal values. Orders slowed to a crawl. I wasn't worried, though, as I had several rental properties with positive cash flows. This was Plan B. *Yes, they would carry me through this financial slowdown in appraisal work.* Well, we all know what happened to the housing market in 2008. The sh*t hit the fan! Some of my tenants stopped paying rent due to job losses. I had to evict several of them. The problem was there was no one calling to replace them. I experienced a roughly 75% drop in my business, and half of my rentals were vacant. I had to resort to Plan C. *Every successful entrepreneur has a Plan C, right?*

I had a substantial line of credit I could tap into. *Yeah, that will carry me through.* The bank didn't agree and said they were calling in the line of credit and would not renew it. I felt sick to my stomach. All the pleading in the world could not convince them to allow me to continue carrying it. That spelled disaster for me as all my financial resources had stopped producing. Eventually, I had to let all my staff go, let my office lease lapse, crawl home with my tail between my legs, and work from there. Soon enough, I received foreclosure notices on several of my properties. *I was a failure.*

I felt embarrassed to be seen around town, fearing people would ask me how things were going. For months, I had difficulty sleeping and went to a doctor to get some pills to help. Instead, he diagnosed me as depressed and prescribed anti-depressants. This label of a pre-existing condition would come back to haunt me when I was applying for life or health insurance. Life was spiraling out of control as far as I was concerned. We eventually had to sell our home. I was in my fifties, and everything I worked so hard to achieve had disappeared. My ego was crushed. In hindsight, it was also the beginning of the end of my thirty-seven-year marriage.

At fifty-nine years old, I was separated, living in a one-bedroom apartment and just making enough money to get by. To say I was pissed off at the world, especially the banking industry and the government, for ruining my business was an understatement. I was blaming everyone. Life was miserable. To think that life was happening *for* me versus happening *to* me was bulls**t in my mind!

I needed something to lift my spirits, so I decided to check out a local festival a few weeks later. *Blessing of the Fleet* is the official name, yet we commonly refer to it as 'the local shrimp festival.' It celebrates the opening of shrimp season, during which clergy from multiple faith-based religions bless each shrimp boat as they pass by the end of the pier in a single file. A parade of boats, if you will. I love most seafood, with shrimp among my top three or four favorites. I had never attended this festival in the past. Because my ex-wife was allergic to shellfish, she had zero interest in attending such a festival.

The day was beautiful and sunny, a perfect spring day in Charleston, South Carolina. I thought, *I would stay and listen to the music if I saw someone I knew.* As a musician myself, I love and appreciate live music. I ventured around for a while and finally ran into a guy who used to work for me. We decided to get a beer and hang out for a bit. Walking out of the beer pavilion, I held the door for a couple of ladies coming along behind us, and *there she was.* A mysterious-looking redhead with a broad-brimmed floppy hat that many southern women wear to shade the sun from their faces. She had the most magnetic, loving, captivating smile. I couldn't take my eyes off her. My ego piped up and said, *Look, she's smiling at you. She must really like you.* Naturally, I struck up a conversation. We talked for a couple of minutes. I asked if she would like to get a cup of coffee sometime (feeling cliché), gave her my business card, and asked her to call me. *Guess what she did!*

We started dating and often discussed our values and what we wanted out of life. It was clear she was into spirituality as she studied Sanskrit and had traveled to India on pilgrimages. She loved lighting candles and incense, 'pulling cards,' and interpreting them. *Not me.* I was more interested in how to start making money again. I was not into spilling my guts and sharing my feelings with her. After all, *I am a man, and men don't do that. Men want to talk about sports or cars and talk about nothing. We don't get emotional and share our deepest, darkest secrets. We don't get all teary-eyed. That's for women to do. Women are emotional; men are stoic.*

Recognizing I was suffering internally and desperate to be (financially) successful again, she sat me down for one of our talks. She said, "If you truly want to be successful, you need to be who you are at your essence." *What was she talking about?* I don't even know where my essence is. *How do I get there? Give me directions.* She recommended I attend a guided group meditation. I had never done any guided meditation before and resisted. However, redheads, especially beautiful ones, can be very persuasive. Off I went. Little did I know that would change my life.

With zero expectations, I arrived at the local retreat center. Twelve of us sat in a circle. At the heart of the meditation, we were guided to visualize a deep, pitch-black hole in the ground with stairs sticking out of it. We were told to notice our fears and to think of someone or some entity who we knew loved us and who we trusted and loved, someone we could take into the darkness to keep us calm and our fears away. After the meditation, we went around the room to share our experiences and who we took with us. I heard the typical answer from the group: spouse, mom, dad, and best friend. I even heard one say Jesus and another Ghandi. My reaction was, *I screwed this up.* Being the last one to share, I explained I must have misunderstood the assignment, as I didn't have anyone like that. The person I took with me, who I knew I loved and who they loved me, was me as a six-year-old!

Unexpectedly, I noticed that most of the other attendees were teary-eyed and *emotional* (there's that word again: *emotional*). They thought taking my younger self with me was so profound. *Really?* It was just what my subconscious had pulled out. When asked to explain, I told them that life up to six years old seemed simple, filled with protection and love. I didn't know hate. I felt any problem could be solved by simply discussing it and agreeing on a mutual solution. Even with world problems, there would be no fighting or wars if we just listened to each other and accepted our differences. Up to that age, I only experienced love. Then, what happened around the age of six? I went to school and started to integrate into society.

I noticed that not everyone thinks the way I do. There are rules to be followed. Rules in school, rules of social etiquette, rules of social behavior. Without realizing it, I was being 'conditioned' to get along with others. Classmates would laugh at me sometimes when I expressed my true feelings. We all know that uncomfortable feeling when we are laughed at. At that point in my life, I stopped being me at my core and my *essence*. I wanted to be liked by my friends and teachers, so I started being the person I thought *they* wanted me to be, not my true Self. The real me was stuffed into a closet, never to be seen again. That changed me and ruled my life for nearly six decades!

Back up on stage, thinking it was my moment to shine, the moderator kept prying deeper and deeper, asking me what I was feeling in my heart. *What message did I want to convey to the audience?* Every time I thought I gave the 'right' answer, she kept asking, "Why?" Prying deeper with each why, like peeling an onion and slowly unraveling the layers, removing the ego. Finally, I succumbed to the challenge. She asked me to take a minute or two and look at each person in the room (about two hundred people) and tell her what I saw. It hit me like a tidal wave. *Where was this coming from?* I checked in with my ego and agreed on what I would say. So, I took a deep breath and said, " LOVE! I see nothing but love!"

*Wait. What?! That's not what I was going to say. That's not the right answer. Where the f**k did that come from? It certainly didn't come out of this mouth. This is a macho male leader, trainer, and mentor.* "Aha, finally," I heard her say. "Sounds like we got to your core, the real you. Your essence. What's in your heart." Holy sh*t! I had completely forgotten about that version of me. The closet door that I thought I had locked when I was six years old had just been re-opened. *But how? How did she know the code? I had forgotten the code. Too late for that,* I figured. The real me had been exposed, yet I felt ignited. I then told my story of the group meditation and how I had re-discovered who I really was at my essence. *Wow, what an impact that was!*

My 'exposure' was now done, and it was time to break for lunch. I couldn't wait to get out of that room and be alone. I felt embarrassed, so weak as a man.

As I left the stage, a couple of men approached me to thank me and wanted to hug me. Before I knew it, about twelve to fifteen people, mostly men, were lining up to thank me for sharing my true feelings and speaking from my heart. A couple of men had tears in their eyes. I felt shaken, not fully understanding my impact on the audience. As I finished talking to each of them, I found the exit and started towards the men's room to be alone with my thoughts. Along the way, attendees, both women and men, continued to stop me, telling me what I said was profound and very moving. Several asked for hugs and told me, "That's the message the world needs right now, so get out and share it!"

As I composed myself and started to leave the men's room, one of the attendees who I knew a little about (I did know he was a multi-millionaire) but had not met him yet, was walking in. He had been looking for me. He shared that he had not spoken to his dad in over nine years. After hearing me share my emotions and true feelings on stage, he went outside and called his dad to tell him he was sorry and that he loved him. He then asked me for a hug, and I obliged. Teary-eyed, he thanked me profusely and said my sharing moved him. I was surprised by his vulnerability, but at the same time, I thought I was onto something. Maybe the Universe knows what it's doing, and this happened *for* me, not *to* me. *I finally got it!*

Everything happens for you, not to you. I reflected and realized all those struggles, losses, and everything I went through was for a reason. Without all those lessons and blessings in disguise, I wouldn't be where I am. I struggled to accept *why* everything happened to me for the longest time. Those tears I shed in the bathroom were tears of truth and finding the real me. *Me at my core.* It was no longer about money or sales. It was about integrity and genuineness. *Being my true self is being the best!* Now, I have a new message because everywhere I turn, people, especially women, tell me that men don't need to be stoic; they should share their emotions and they can be their authentic selves.

A few months later, I was to give a talk on stage at an event in Las Vegas. I was told I should talk about my successful career in sales and share some motivational quotes or ideas. *You know, the typical motivational stuff.* I started preparing my sales speech about six weeks before the event. While I wrote a good one, it didn't feel quite right. About ten days before the event, I woke up, and a voice said, *Screw this! I'm going to tell the story of my life prior to that fateful group meditation and how it has changed since that time.* I threw my original speech in the trash and sat down to rewrite it. It was as if I was downloading information, and God was dictating what I was to say (that's another story). I wrote from the heart and knew it would make an impact.

At the end of that talk, most of the people in the room came up to thank me for being so raw. So vulnerable. So emotional. Oddly enough, this time, it was mostly women. They all said in some form, "You need to get this message out to the world, especially to men. They need to hear this from you and know sharing emotions with others is okay." I have since discovered that women prefer men who can be vulnerable. *Yes, ladies, we men don't realize that. We think 'men are men.' We don't show emotions. It would be a sign of weakness if we did.* That was what I used to think. Now, I know better. I have a new heart-centered purpose, not just running after the money but becoming truly successful, an inner success: sharing vulnerably, making an impact, and changing lives. I have the most outstanding redheaded woman by my side to thank.

My message to you is to be your *true self,* who you are at your core. *Your authentic essence.* Not who you think others want you to be. Be willing to share your emotions freely and with heart. Not only will you feel better, but you will also have that ripple effect that ignites lives and creates an impact. Know that when you speak directly from the heart, you profoundly affect others positively. Living in true integrity is the meaning of love. After all, this is why you are here in this lifetime…to experience all that life has in store *for you.*

Ignite Action Steps

1. Trust your gut and listen to your heart.

2. Your true essence is love. Tap into your six-year-old self and share with others.

3. Learn how you are showing up to others in less than 90 seconds: https://codebreakerglobal.om/crackyourcode?code=kavanagh

4. Reach out to me directly to learn more: savvycal.com/candjcoaching .

Joe Kavanagh — United States of America
Successful Entrepreneur, Certified NLP Coach, Certified Trainer &
Coach in the BANK Personality Method
joe-m-kavanagh
joe.kavanagh.395
joeknowscharlestonrealestate

Karla VandenBerg

"Walk in wonder, and goodness will come to you."

I hope for my story to spread sparkles and dreams. My wish is that you elevate your self-esteem and never give up. I know that when you walk taller and smile brighter, you feel better and can accomplish anything. The world seems easier when you believe in yourself. Chase your dreams, and goodness will come to you.

Chasing Sparkles and Dreams

As I sat in the dark corner quietly watching the joyful smiles and awkward dance moves, my eyes were glued to the golden clock hanging on the wall. It was like I was in a trance watching this joyous party celebrate New Year's Eve before I would be escaping to a journey of my own. The next day, I was leaving Canada.

I didn't sleep much that night as the excitement in my heart had my thoughts racing. It was a chilly, dark New Year's morning when I carefully placed my last piece of luggage in my small trunk. The roads glistened with ice, and looking back, I should have been scared, but I wasn't. I didn't even think. Fearlessly, I began to follow the signs that would take me away from the city I was raised in and had spent the last twenty-two years trying to make it work. I had only fond feelings for the prairies, but it was the idea of the desert sunshine all winter long, lots of golf courses, resort-style homes with outdoor pools, and the possibility of a new beginning that pulled me. I wanted the chance to clear the slate, vanish from the past, and start anew!

To be clear, I had no idea where I was going to live, nor did I know anyone in Scottsdale, Arizona. I was planning to work as a golf pro as that was a sport that I had spent years perfecting. Little did I know once I arrived that the idea of actually being employed was legally impossible. I found a two-bedroom place advertised in a tiny apartment finder book located in a local grocery store. The next morning, I woke up deliriously happy in my partly furnished, roach-infested apartment. Each day was a new struggle of endless opportunities! *Think positive, walk in wonder, and goodness will come to you*, I told myself. I believed that, and it helped me to survive and thrive!

The next day, I decided a reward was in order, so I bought a very expensive, navy blue and white striped short dress that fitted just right. A friend of mine recommended the dance club *Studabakers* as the place to check out. I still remember looking at my matted orange lipstick in the rearview mirror, encouraging myself aloud, "You can do this, Karla," before walking in.

I watched the door as if I knew someone special would walk in. Then, a handsome, six-foot-seven, tanned Dutchman suddenly appeared. It was an instant attraction, a feeling I was not familiar with. He sat down beside me, we danced to the words of Meatloaf, and six months later, I found myself living on an Arizona dairy farm. I believed in love, not cows, but for him, I would have moved anywhere.

Two years later, we decided to build a dairy farm of our own in Washington state and pursue the American Dream. We had no idea that we had just purchased deeded land on an Indian Reservation and didn't have control of our water rights. But what we did have control over was endless, filled with fulfilling hard work. There was no time for fun; we even forgot about Christmas until we received a box of juicy oranges at our front door.

The following year, we got married, and soon after, we had a daughter and then a son. My daughter was a gift, a little doll, and my closest friend. She and I would take trips to the mall, play with toys, color, and sing as we drove down country roads. The dairy farm grew, and the money flooded in, but I was playing less of a role in the business. I wasn't included in the day-to-day operations, which now felt secretive. *I was no longer important.* Slowly, I became more detached from things, slipped into a depression, and lost my sparkle.

One day, I found myself watching The Oprah Show™, and that day, she was talking about finding your passion. I began reflecting that for as long as I could remember, I have had an infatuation with sparkles. I love how they glisten and shine like pretty colorful diamonds. I remember my Dad telling me how he vacuumed sparkles out of the carpet for years after I left home. I decided while watching that show, little girls should have the opportunity to shine bright, and *what if I could give them 'sparkle makeovers?'*

Inspired, I decided to open a children's salon. I called it Monkey Dooz™ and designed it so that boys could sit, drive a jeep, and get a haircut while girls could get a sparkle manicure. I created the most spectacular sparkle glitter station, and during birthday parties, I would offer princess makeovers. I can still remember the tiny little feet hanging down from the pink furry stool, the Disney™-like dress, and the precious little eyes that would close as I applied the shimmery eyeshadow. Trying hard to sit still with eyelids closed, the little girls would fidget in anticipation and wonder what they would look like when I was all finished. Once I held up the mirror for them to see, their eyes would widen with surprise, and their smiles would light up the room!

The feeling that I had when I saw their joy was one that cannot be replaced. To have helped a little child to feel so good inside and happy helped me to understand more about my own life. I thought, *if I had had a chance when I was younger to have my self-esteem elevated, I surely would have felt better about myself! I would not have cared about people watching me or worrying about what they thought. I could have felt better inside if I had believed in myself.* Creating Monkey Dooz felt like I had finally found my mission, and I was going to help inspire young girls and spread *self-esteem, sparkles, and dreams*!

Magic graced the salon I had created; parents would walk in holding hands with their children. It was a moment of unique bonding. I came to realize that I had created much more than a regular salon; I had built a magical place where children would walk through the doors in wonder and leave feeling like a real live princess!

Clients loved Monkey Dooz, and I felt accomplished. I knew inside that I could franchise the salon with locations across the country for everyone to enjoy! Yet, I could also feel some resentment brewing at home for my desires and ambitions.

Doing my daily routine of office banking, I called the bank to update our account. It was my usual morning call, only this time the assistant was in shock and informed me that $580,000 from our account was gone. *How could that be?* I still remember that day when the world around me froze. I was stunned. *Why had my husband removed the money?* The impact was beyond words. There were no tears, no answers, only disbelief. I never knew I had any marital issues; he was my partner and my best friend, yet something had changed.

After attempting to call my husband in an absolute fury of madness, I drove to pick the children up from school. After loading them in the white suburban vehicle, I drove ten hours back home to Canada to my parent's house because I didn't know what else to do. The next day, as I was walking outside, I heard my name being called as a stack of divorce papers was thrown from the window of a black Mercedes™. The war had started, and I hadn't even asked for one.

Statements from the teachers filled the papers, saying, "I worked too hard," "I didn't care about my children," and "I didn't answer the phone on Sundays." I felt betrayed and blindsided. I drove back to Washington State with my kids to try and reconsider. More times than I can count, I thought about turning off the highway to go and hide. My eyes flooded with tears; my sweaty hands gripped the steering wheel as I turned down the gravel road to the house that was my home just a short time ago. I knew I would be alone in the fight for what was right. The not-so-wonderful part about divorce is that it favors those who have the money. Our money was now his money, leaving me with no money. Life changed immediately.

As I approached the house, I saw my husband and two other men standing and looking at me. These men used to be my friends; in fact, I hired the tall one with brown wavy hair staring directly at me. Letting my children walk into that house without me that day was one of the most heart-wrenching moments I have ever endured. I was told that I would now be residing in the guest house, which was actually an enlarged shed we built for our parents when they would come to visit. My vision of sparkles and dreams had been banished, replaced with betrayal and the feeling that my whole world was slipping away.

When I opened the door, still feeling as if this was some type of movie, I bumped into many large cardboard boxes with details of my belongings etched on the outside. I later found out that the nanny I hired to help with my children had been directed to pack up all of my personal belongings. I fell to the floor sobbing and realized that when faced with such emotions, your body reacts without asking you for permission. The sorrow was overwhelming, and I was in utter disbelief.

Looks of concern and confusion from the dairy employees who passed by the guest house for the next months were in abundance. At night, when darkness fell, I would make my way to my daughter's window. It was easier to see her alone in her room at night, and I would stand next to the roses I planted, tapping on her window in the hope that she would see me. The thorns on the rose bush cut deeply into my skin, but I never felt pain because my concentration was on my daughter. I wanted to show her Mommy was here.

My employees at Monkey Dooz were aware of the tragic situation I was in, and they decided to help me by working for no pay for the next two weeks! That simply doesn't happen, and I was so grateful to have such caring souls work for me. They became my family, along with our customers. Meanwhile, I was barely holding it together. I didn't even have enough money for a toothbrush.

Feeling hopeless and without a strategy to regain my dreams, the universe stepped in to help me. I applied for a loan and was nominated for an award without my knowledge. Shortly after, I received a call telling me I had won the *Enterprising Woman of the Year Award.* I screamed with joy! Sparkles of magic had descended. Pooling all my resources, I went to New York to accept my award. They told me I was getting nationwide coverage and advised me to open more stores in 'up and coming' locations.

A lifelong friend from back home graciously lent me the money I needed to open a flagship salon. The idea was to have three successful locations, and then I would create a franchise. Monkey Dooz became the talk of my not-so-sleepy little farm town and soon, people from California were interested in opening a trademark location. I was so enthralled that my sparkle dream was finally going to be seen on the big stage in California! *Go big or go home*, I thought, determined to not give up.

After appearing on the cover of magazines, Monkey Dooz was built at the Atlantis Resort™ in the Bahamas, the Ritz Carlton™ in Florida, and the Boca Raton Resort™ in Florida. I presented these resorts with the first Kids Spa idea, and they loved it!

Then, the 2008 economic housing crisis hit and affected everyone's pocketbook. Sparkle nails, best friend parties, and Club Spa Pedicures were no longer included in families' budgets. After five years of building Monkey Dooz, I closed the salon and felt deflated. But, ever the entrepreneur, I still had dreams.

Picking myself up, I decided to move to Arizona because of the opportunities and because I was familiar with desert life. Immigration had a different plan for me and wanted to deport me back to Canada. When I first came to the United States, I had a student visa and, later, an investor visa, which I lost after the divorce. I worked hard to receive another investor's visa with Monkey Dooz, and now that it was closed, I was no longer welcome to stay where I had been living for almost twenty-five years.

Once I arrived in Arizona, I found living without a work visa very hard. The old days of earning cash 'under the table' seemed impossible. I started a landscaping company and would spend endless hours at Home Depot™ learning about different types of plants. I would speak to my family in Canada each day, missing them and unable to travel home because of my legal status. I was stuck again, having to survive by trusting the path that lay ahead.

Music helped me forget about the problems that circled around me. The song "Live Like Tomorrow Never Comes" led me to soul-searching. I decided that it might be better to go visit my friend in Alabama by the sea rather than stay in Arizona, where I couldn't afford my air conditioning bill. I am forever grateful for the good friends I had in my life, as they were the people who helped me to survive. If not for the individuals who serendipitously appeared out of nowhere, I would have had to return to Canada. The journey would have ended without the full story, the experiences, the laughter, and the wondrous adventures that I have stored in my mind.

I met one of my guardian angels when he dialed the wrong number, and I answered. A magical synchronicity. I went to go live on his yacht in Florida at the end of a long floating boardwalk with a fun, country-themed bar at the other end. I had one set of clothes, no money, and would shower in the bathroom located beside the bar. While on the yacht, I realized all my material possessions meant nothing. Walking barefoot in the sand, I felt completely at peace amidst the teal-blue waters. "Live Like Tomorrow Never Comes" was becoming my theme song.

Finally, my visa came, and I could work legally in the U.S. I was excited to pursue my real estate license. My Dad always felt I would be a good realtor. Following his recent passing, I thought this would be a good way to honor him. After many hours, exams, and the discovery that almost everyone I had met in Arizona was also a real estate agent, I had to get another part-time job. Deciding a job working in a tree nursery would benefit my landscape background, I endured the hot Arizona sun and pushed a wheelbarrow. Just as I forced myself to like this position, it came to a sudden halt. A month into the job, after closing, I walked up to the chain link gate and eagerly pulled it so hard that the entire ten-foot fence came off the rails, pushing me to the ground. The water source broke, spraying twenty feet into the air and soaking my entire body as I found myself pinned under the fence. It seemed that I wasn't supposed to work that job any longer. That was my last day.

Once more, almost broken, I lay in a dark room with no job or money. Although it had been ten years since the last time I walked into a church, I thought it was time I made an appearance. I needed some sparkling divine intervention from the man upstairs. Miraculously, after the sermon, the church put briefcases on tables in the parking lot filled with twenty dollar bills for each individual who was in attendance. We were told to add twenty dollars of our own money to the first and invest that in our 'inner gift' to create something magical. I graciously accepted the money and quickly put it in the glove compartment of my vehicle. I drove around with that precious twenty dollars in my car for a week before asking my immigration attorney what I should do with the money. *What was my gift?* I wondered. *What impact could such a small amount make?*

Little did I know, my attorney had set up a meeting for me with a non-profit organization interested in doing golf tournaments and said to put the money toward fuel to get to the interview. I was hired on the spot, paid in advance, and given a stunning company beach house to reside in. My job was to organize celebrity golf tournaments, something I was perfect for! I felt like a princess and that my prayers had been heard. My investment in myself grew to be the deposit toward my dreams.

I had no idea how to organize a golf tournament, never mind a celebrity golf tournament. I had no team to help me and didn't know anyone. Trying to start each morning with a routine, I would go to the local coffee shop first thing. One day, I was standing in line when I saw a man in a wheelchair struggle to open the door. I quickly left my spot to assist him and told him he could go in front of me. The man behind me didn't look thrilled. I turned to him and said, "This is the right thing to do." He then smiled and offered to buy me a coffee. That man ended up introducing me to people who would help sell out my golf tournament! Do the right thing, and magic happens!

With those connections, I set up an appointment on New Year's Day with a suggested sponsor. While most were sleeping, I was working, and the sponsor was impressed. He opened his checkbook and wrote me a check to sponsor my event. He then went on to write more checks that helped make my dreams of finally franchising Monkey Dooz a reality! He is also the same person who, after thirty years, helped me become legal in the U.S. He believed in me, allowing me to embrace my dreams once again. The impact of a single conservation, a moment of kindness, and unexpected support have impacted not just my life but my business, my clients, and all the children who get to come and feel the sparkle of Monkey Dooz. I am happily working on franchise opportunities throughout Europe, the United Kingdom, and Dubai to share sparkles globally.

Never give up on your dreams. You never know you are standing beside in a line. Don't be afraid to talk to people, because new friends can have a major impact on your life. Be open to accepting, seeking, and finding who has been placed in your life to help you accomplish your dreams. If you believe in yourself, you will see magic and sparkles everywhere. Be positive, walk in wonder, and goodness will come to you.

IGNITE ACTION STEPS

- **Write your dreams** - You achieve your dreams faster when you write them down. The journey gives you what you need to tell your story. Without a journey, there will be no story. Success is failure turned inside out.

- **Aspire to who you can become** - Never feel fear; walk through every open door, speak to strangers, and visualize what you want.

Karla Vandenberg — United States of America
C.E.O Monkey Dooz Salons
monkeydooz.com
monkeydoozofficial
monkeydoozofficial

The Ripple Effect of Impact

Impact is never just about one person. When we step into our purpose, we inspire others to do the same.

Think about someone whose impact changed your life and how you, in turn, can create that same ripple effect for someone else.

- Think of someone who has deeply impacted your life. What did they do that made a difference?

____

____

____

____

____

____

____

____

- How can you pay that forward and be a source of inspiration for someone else?

____

____

____

____

____

____

Doreen Kilbreath

Doreen Kilbreath

"The Universe will never give more than you can handle."

My intention is to give hope to others who may be struggling or grieving the loss of a loved one. You never know your own strength until you are faced with a challenge. I want you to know that when the need arises, you will find the strength required.

My Everything

My brother invited me over to check out his new place and meet his three roommates. While we were visiting, something about his friend, Dave, intrigued me. I had a feeling, although unsure how I knew he would someday be my boyfriend. The quiet guy sitting over in the corner, enjoying his bottle of beer, and just taking in all the conversation made me laugh. His smile was contagious, and he had such pretty eyes. Then he stood up, and he was my height! I had always been the shortest person in my class through grade school and always the first in line on school photo day. He was only five foot two.

Before I knew it, I was on cloud nine. My first date with a guy who had won my heart from the first moment I saw him. There were butterflies in my stomach from his innocent giggle and angst in my throat when I had to say goodbye. All the feelings blossomed, and 'it' was finally happening.

We had been invited to a friend's wedding and had a terrific evening. We danced, we laughed, and I wished for the night to go on forever. It was the perfect date.

We were both 19 at the time. I was living on my own and loving my new-found freedom of being out in the world. I had been raised fairly strict. Being the oldest, the rules applied more to me than my younger brothers. We were raised to know right from wrong, to respect our elders, and work hard. Dave had been out on his own since he was 15 years of age and quite enjoyed living a single life. I was so attracted to his rebellious ways. He was living a carefree lifestyle. He had a few minor run-ins with the law and enjoyed sociable drinks with his buddies after work. A bit of a bad-boy attitude, if you will.

In very short order, we decided we would do this thing and moved in together to start living the life of our dreams. We both had decent jobs. I was a parts technician for a communications company, and he was an apprentice pipefitter. We had a great circle of friends and enjoyed our social life. Looking back, we may have enjoyed it too much. We would go out every weekend with our friends and spend time drinking, socializing, and genuinely having fun.

After living together for almost five years, we decided it was time to purchase our first home instead of paying rent to someone else. We had big dreams yet were so scared, with no idea what this journey would entail. We found a little fixer-upper mobile home with so much character, and we both loved it! Dave was very handy when it came to renovations and loved woodwork. We spent almost every weekend restoring it and soon had our first home looking exactly like our dream. We enjoyed working together, building our lives, shaping our dreams, sharing ideas, and planning for the future. It was truly our happy place.

Shortly after we moved into our home, we found out that we were expecting our first child. We had never planned to have children, and after living together for five years, we had strictly focused on the two of us. I was so shocked and scared when the doctor first told me the news. I wasn't sure how Dave would take the news…and *what on earth would my parents say?* We were 24 years old and not married. Unlike most little girls, I had never had the dream of a big fancy wedding, looking like Cinderella. I was never one that wanted to be in the spotlight.

When I returned home from the doctor's appointment and told Dave our news, he was excited! I was grateful that we were going to be raising a family together. It was a huge sigh of relief.

Our first bundle of joy arrived in May 1989, and we were so happy and excited to bring her home. In November of the same year, with a little nudge from my mother, we decided to get married. Marriage was not a topic I took lightly. There were rocky moments in my parents' marriage, and I simply knew that if I got married, it would be something I would do once in my lifetime, and that person would have to be very special to me. We talked and decided that we would take a train vacation from our city to the neighboring province and visit Dave's relatives there. We had arranged to stop in a cute mountain town and get married by a Justice of the Peace. It was the perfect ceremony. We were married and then ran back to the train to continue our journey.

Two years later, we welcomed another baby girl, and by the fall of 1992, our third child, a son, had arrived, and our little family was complete. We had moved on to our second home, three little ones in tow, and life seemed to be magical.

In the spring of that year, our world as we knew it was turned upside down. With a newer house and a family to care for, my husband took on a part-time second job. The job required him to have a security check and a complete physical exam. The exam revealed to us that Dave was a Type 1 diabetic who required daily insulin injections. We were shocked. I knew we were pretty darn good at accomplishing anything we set our minds to, so there was no question we would figure diabetes out.

We took the suggested training with the local dietician and had a practice session at the doctor's office on how to do the daily insulin injections. I figured we were golden. I soon realized that Dave was drinking more beer, more often, and I knew this had to change. I would drop subtle hints and comments that the drinking needed to stop or, at the very least, slow down in order for his sugar levels to get better.

My comments and suggestions went on for years. I did not want to 'rock the boat,' so to speak. When I would go out and leave Dave in charge of parenting the kids, he would have a few beers and pass out. Later, I came to realize he was not drunk; his blood sugars had gotten so high that he was literally experiencing unconsciousness.

Trying to boost our finances, my husband decided it would be great for him to purchase a semi-truck and start hauling crude oil for a local oil company. The work was great, the money was good, and he worked very long hours. The drinking continued, and I was starting to notice the onset of other health issues. He had lost so much weight; he was just a piece of the person he used to be. His vision was getting worse; his temper was shorter. He was having run-ins with co-workers and losing his patience with his bosses. I was so scared. We upgraded our home a few more times, and we lived in our absolute dream house. We had purchased an acreage just out of town; the kids loved the open space. They had a dog and all the outdoor toys. They were all so happy, but I was scared.

I finally had reached my breaking point after years of watching him waste away. I could not live like this anymore. I was in constant fear that his sugars would spike and he would pass out while driving. *What if he hit someone else while on the road?* He would never forgive himself. I had to say or do something to try to save him from himself. We sat and had a discussion, and I told him I had noticed all these changes in his health and outward behavior. I asked him to stop drinking because I was afraid he was going to die.

"I CAN'T STOP! WHY THE HELL DO YOU THINK I WORK SO MANY HOURS?!" He shouted.

His words shook me to my core. He continued to explain to me that when he was driving the truck, he knew he could not be consuming alcohol, or he would lose his job. Therefore, if he worked long, hard hours, he had more hours sober. I was absolutely beside myself. *What did he mean he could not stop? Why did he not want to be at home with us? With his children?* I knew those kids meant the world to him. *Why would he not want to spend time with them?* The alcohol had such a hold on him that it was pulling him away from all that he loved. I sat for a few moments, trying to sort out the conversation we were having. I looked at him as tears rolled down my cheeks, "I am giving you until the end of summer. If you do not stop drinking by then, the kids and I will be leaving."

What had I just said? I was telling him I was going to walk away from our marriage. *How could I do that to him?* I had to protect our kids; I just knew somehow, this all had to stop. Slowly, my husband lifted his head, looked at me, and said, "Don't worry, I will look after it."

We had such fun times with the kids for the next couple of months. We booked holidays; we spent weekends at the acreage sliding down the super slide in our yard and spent quality time together. I recall thinking to myself, *Now, this is the way life should be.* The drinking had slowed down a lot. He would have a couple of drinks in the evening, most often after the kids had gone to bed. I thought we were on the right path, and life would only get better from there.

On a typical Thursday in October, my husband was up bright and early to start his work day, as per usual. He left home around 3 AM. At around 8 AM, I was busy getting the kids ready to head out to school and heard our semi-truck pull into the yard. My husband came in, but he was not feeling well. He was likely experiencing a touch of the flu. He had been vomiting and had diarrhea, so he was going to go rest for a couple of hours and then head back out on the road.

When I returned that afternoon after picking the kids up from school, I found him still sleeping in bed. I tried to talk to him, but he said he didn't feel well. I carried on with supper, then homework, and then got the kids settled into bed for the night. I went into the bedroom to check in on my husband, only to find him unresponsive. *What is going on?* I felt a surge of panic!

I frantically called 911, then quickly called my parents to come sit at the house with the kids so I could go to the hospital to find out what was wrong. The paramedics arrived, and I could not even make myself go into the bedroom. I knew…deep down in my absolute core, it was not going to be good news.

Upon arriving at the local hospital, they informed me that they were going to airlift my husband to the larger city hospital as they were not equipped to offer him treatment. At 11 PM that evening, my dad and I drove 2.5 hours to get to the hospital where the air ambulance had taken my husband. We sat in a private waiting room for about five hours; the minutes ticked by so slowly. No one was telling me what was going on. I could hear all the hustle and chaos in the hallway outside the door. I did not want to go out there; I did not want to be in the way.

Finally, I could not take the uncertainty any longer. I went out to the nursing station and asked what was going on with my husband or if I could at least see him. The nurse took me into his room, and as I looked at my husband lying in the hospital bed, wires running everywhere, monitors beeping, I knew my husband was not in there. I just looked at him, and my body went numb. I turned around and went back to the waiting room.

After what seemed like hours, the neurologist came in to inform me that my husband had been declared brain dead and shockingly asked if I would like to donate his organs. My mind was reeling….*What?*

I was so sad, angry, confused, and horrified. *What am I going to tell my kids?* My dad sat with me, looked at me, and shook his head. For 2.5 hours, all I could think was, *"What am I going to tell my kids?"*

That day was the hardest day of my life. The pain of losing someone I loved with all of my heart felt numbing. I then had to sit down with my three children, aged 13, 11, and 10, to tell them that the man they adored was not coming home ever again!

I knew life would never be the same. I had no idea what I would do or how; all I knew for sure was that I *had* to figure life out for my kid's sake.

Dealing with death is so bizarre; you are required to make so many decisions and so many plans at a time when you can hardly remember even to breathe. Dealing with insurance companies, banks, funeral arrangements, and running our business was very trying. However, *you do what you have to do*. Life had dealt me with a situation I could never have imagined, and I had to find the strength to get my kids and myself through it.

Once the funeral was over, family and friends returned to their everyday lives. I got the kids all settled and back into their school routines. Sitting at home alone, I spent long evenings pondering *what exactly we should be doing*. I was so uneasy and scared to be living out of town on my own. The insurance company had declined the life insurance policy due to life choices, which contributed to Dave's death. I was horrified! I had to make the mortgage payment and feed the kids. Many sleepless nights of sending prayers and asking for guidance on navigating everything.

About two months later, I received a phone call from a friend. He knew of a couple interested in my acreage and wondered if I would be open to trading their home in the city for it. We looked at the house; it was beautiful, exactly what we needed, and much easier to afford. Our prayers were answered.

Dave's death had such an impact on me I decided I had better start taking better care of myself, or my kids would not have anyone to look after them. I was having chest pains from high blood pressure and stress, which frightened me. That started me on my health journey. I began yearly physical exams, started a weight loss program, and focused on myself and self-care.

Dave's loss impacted me so much that I decided to put all of my faith and money into opening a weight loss center and became a business owner and health coach. The Universe provided an opportunity for me to provide for myself and my family and allowed me to help others turn their lives around and lead healthier lifestyles.

Looking back, some twenty-two years later, my husband's passing still saddens me. I can still see the faces of those three kids as I told them that Daddy would not be coming home, that he had gotten sick and gone to heaven. However, the place in my heart where nothing but pain and sadness lived is now replaced with love, strength, and a deeper knowing that our lives impact so many. We can touch the lives of others, but we don't realize the impact we are making until we *begin* to make it.

Every challenge and opportunity shapes us into who we are. It is important to be grateful for all of life's lessons, regardless of how they unfold. Life doesn't always go as planned, the Universe has a bigger and better plan for you! Realize the strength you have and use it to create a positive impact on your life and those around you. Know that everything you do has the potential for impact, so decide what that impact will be.

Epilogue: I now have a very special man in my life who treats me like a queen every day. We have built a beautiful world together and enjoy all that the universe has to offer. This year, we will celebrate twenty 'impactful' years together.

Ignite Action Steps

- Surround yourself with amazing, positive friends who will support you in your darkest moments.

- Prioritize your health and schedule yearly physical exams and checkups.

- Gratitude! Always be grateful for all you have. Remind yourself daily of what's great in your life. You woke up this morning, which is a lot to be grateful for.

- Words are very powerful. Speak positive words and think positively to keep your days filled with positivity.

- Follow your intuition for guidance; it knows you best.

- Trust and have faith. The Universe always has your back.

Doreen Kilbreath — Canada
Business Owner / Coach
justforyoulloyd.com
Just For You, Health & Wellness
just_for_you_health_wellness

Chantelle McFarland

Chantelle McFarland

"The light is a beacon of hope, guiding us home to ourselves and each other."

To my fellow truth-seekers, I dance with the fear of being seen by sharing the wisdom within my story. When we stand in our integrity and vulnerability, we offer our gifts to the world. May my truth guide you and ignite the light within. The journey into the dark is how we reclaim ourselves — discovering treasures within the deepest parts of our being. By shining love and light on ourselves, we illuminate and heal the darkness in our world.

My Heart Whispers

My father loved his Panasonic™ video camera. He purchased it the day after I was born, bringing it to the Regional Hospital to record his pride and joy. He remained devoted to capturing our family holidays and celebrations, creating a home video cassette collection. Within these cherished tapes is one that makes the greatest impact. I slid it into the VHS player and pressed play.

With only a few minutes of film remaining on the tape, the scene of my little sister's third birthday party came to life on screen. The visiting room in unit 37 was full of family and neighborhood friends back in the same local hospital where I was born. The camera lens pivoted toward my mother, who was catching her breath after a terrible coughing fit and sipping water. I was sitting next to her, the tip of my tongue stuck out to the left of my mouth while I solved a puzzle.

I remember the constriction I felt in my body listening to my mother wheeze and gasp for air like that. Her hands would shake as she placed her palm against her chest. The other hand often made a fist against her mouth as if she was fighting to make the coughing stop. She looked fragile, and I moved around her like she could break. The IV in her arm pumped morphine into her veins, and the oxygen tube ran from her nose to a cylinder tank. She would try to hide the pain and smile when I was there with her. I also pretended as if her pain didn't bother me either.

My mother stared through the camera lens, unnaturally flashing her teeth, an exaggerated response when asked to smile for the camera. Her dark brown hair was dull and straight, and she wore an oversized t-shirt. She hunched forward weakly to drink from a straw. The dismay she felt being recorded was communicated by the exhaustion and pain in her eyes. Her skeletal hand raised in protest, shaking badly like she was subtly waving goodbye. The final words, "Quit it already," came off loud and clear. As the television screen turned a cobalt blue, it pained my eyes to readjust to the brightness. The cassette tape clicked and ejected from the VHS player. *The ending was abrupt and final.*

She passed away in June, two months later, from stage four lung cancer. I was almost five years old. My sister would be too young to remember her mother. I have always carried in my heart the impact of not getting to know who she was before she had been taken away. My father's impression was that she had chosen cigarettes instead of us. I always believed my mother shined the most radiant inner light, and she loved me and my sister dearly. I would rewatch the home video VHS tapes as if I was collecting evidence. The woman smiling back at me proved the heartstrings connected between a mother and daughter stay connected forever.

On the night she died, I crept out of my bedroom after hearing my dad walk through the front door. Peering down the flight of stairs, his eyes met mine. "Mommy died, didn't she?" I questioned.

His response carried the weight of his words, "Yes, baby, she did." With a nod, my body moved down the hall and back into my bed. Later that night, his feet cast shadows underneath my bedroom door. I had turned to face away as quietly as possible before squinting my eyes closed, pretending to be asleep.

Fluorescent light emanated through the open crack of the door. I froze like it was a game of hide and seek. Darkness consumed the room once more, and I held the pain in my chest until he walked away. It felt safe to cry again.

Remaining tethered to the past was my way of holding onto control and protecting memories to keep them vivid in my mind and alive in my heart long after they were gone. As a child, I was often lost in daydreams. It felt like an unspoken family agreement to contain both my grief and the love I had for my mother. My father held her responsible for leaving him a widower with two young girls. His pain and anguish were buried under layers of resentment and blame. While my inner world allowed my imagination to run wild and free, I adapted, dimming myself on the outside for safety.

Some memories hold onto us. The details are fragmented; I recollect raindrops falling and the smell of fresh dirt. My little sister was nearby while my dad was a few steps ahead, facing a gravestone. He unzipped the fly of his blue jeans and turned his head to glance in my direction. I heard him say, "And you are so much like her," as if I missed what he'd initially said. He returned his gaze as he began urinating on the jagged edge of the grey stone. I crinkled my nose in disgust. Something grabbed those words and pulled them deep within me, like a lock and chain. *I was too much like her. I was too much like my mother, and he was peeing on her gravestone.* There exists no evidence to support that this moment in time ever happened, yet my body holds the trauma, the weight of his words.

She is never coming back. I will never see my mother again in this lifetime. A mental lightbulb moment circuited directly into my heartstrings. Screaming in the highest pitch into my pillow, a grief-stricken silent scream. The dead of night was my safe refuge while my family slept peacefully in their bedrooms upstairs. That was when I stopped tucking her into bed beside me, and I stopped praying that she would appear in my dreams. She felt lost from me in a way she never had before. My father demanded I act like a young woman should. With maturity, my dream world was fading, replaced by a painful reality check out of my control.

On the day after my thirteenth birthday in October, my grandmother passed away. My father loved and respected his mother so much that he referred to her as his best friend. He grew up in a small rural farming community with eight siblings in a poor Christian household. Home life tested his mental health. His father beat him every chance he could, and he didn't understand his father's hatred toward him. At seventeen, he was expelled for punching his teacher to the ground. He drove home to confront his old man, fists raised. To escape the turbulent abuse of his father, he moved three hours away.

When his mother passed away, it did much more than dim the sparkle in his eyes. He had too much grief and anger for any amount of Spiced Bacardi Rum to drown out, though he continued to try. He was running from a past he was tethered to, and it was all catching up to him after many years of avoidance. It was my mother's fault he had to face parenthood alone. His Jekyll and Hyde coincided whenever I reminded him of her. Walking on eggshells no longer predicted safety, and nothing felt more trustworthy than the belief that something was inherently wrong with me.

The turbulence of his rage amplified as time went by. *What did I do wrong?* Without warning, his fist drove into my upper arm. My marshmallow-thick winter's coat barely sheltered the impact of the blow. My bicep muscles screamed as I suppressed a whirlwind of madness within, exasperation wanting to cry out of me and tears threatening my eyes. It wasn't like him to leave bruises, they left evidence. I pretended to listen intently to every word he said next, calling me names no father should ever say to his daughter, but I felt worlds away. The shrinking sensation dulled my senses while my adrenaline remained on high alert. I struggled to regulate my breathing against the heaviness in my chest.

My journal was my safe place to express my broken heart. *Grief held onto her shoulders. She fell to her knees in despair.* I looked for love in all the wrong ways, but I needed someone to care. The one person who loved me unconditionally was taken away. When I experienced pain, I felt alive. It was better than feeling numb and dead inside. The high was something I'd never felt before: what an adrenaline rush! Nothing I did was ever good enough. My soul was so tired I almost gave up trying and battling between fighting to die and to survive. I felt alone and misunderstood and questioned why I should care if no one else did. *With arms stretched wide, she cried, for the world had left her there.* Poetry brought my feelings back to life.

I almost gave up in that low moment when I was around fifteen years old. The turbulence of my mental health in those years is heavy to witness within the words on my old journal pages. At a rapid pace, I started attaching myself to anything that made me feel free. I became unrecognizable, no longer the shy honor roll student with the same circle of friends. Rumors quickly spread around my middle school about the cuts I was hiding on my body, my virginity, suspected drug use, and an alcohol-related school suspension. My eyes stayed down as I walked the hallways, misunderstood. I dreaded weekends when I was stuck at home. My father shamed my sinful choices as if they were a personal attack against his reputation and God. It became a vicious cycle that affirmed I was a burden, and I opted for more reckless abandonment to fill the absence of love within myself.

I prayed for mercy that God would not give up on me. It took years to truly recognize the blessings that would reignite my inner flame at a time when it was nearly extinguished. One afternoon, my ninth-grade teacher stopped me as I walked through her classroom door. Her hand extended towards my shoulder, and my eyes met hers in complete surprise. When she asked if I was okay, my guard instantly broke down, tears falling. For the remainder of my last year of middle school, we passed a journal back and forth. She taught me about silver linings, and she became my first silver thread of hope.

I was introduced to my high school Learning Strategies teacher at the start of tenth grade. Redemption stories inspired many of her classroom projects. Her heart was wrapped around the guarded, hypervigilant kids, the hardest to love, those who needed it the most. This remarkable woman has been a beacon of hope, piercing the darkness for many students. Her unwavering belief rekindled my broken spirit, and her impact reignited the dreamer in me. *I will see the beauty in my wings when I become the butterfly.* To this day, Mrs. Smith remains a light in my life.

I entered high school pregnant and gave birth to my oldest son when I was sixteen. He was worth fighting for and gave my life a refined sense of direction and purpose. My story became one of resilience. My rebel heart would fight to survive from that day forth. I did not walk the straight or narrow path. When I fell to my knees, I would get back up. I had overcome being kicked down so many times; it was how I persevered. Inner strength was the core foundation of my ability to keep going. I was a fighter, battling against my inner demons and sabotaging behaviors.

Still, the powerlessness of depression felt like a deep hole. Although I tried to get ahead, my past always caught up and knocked me off guard. That is when shame imposed to question why I continued ending up in the depths and dancing with my inner demons. Desperation wanted me to climb back out, but I couldn't sink my nails into the hardened clay. It tested my faith, wondering why God had never supplied a ladder. The fear was that the world would dismiss me as a broken mess. I protected myself by keeping the world at arm's distance away and found myself isolated in my perceived hell. My hypervigilant mind tried to help me regain control, attempting to fix what was wrong with me to escape the anguish of that six-foot grave I called depression.

Inspired most by the empowering women in my life, especially my mother, I felt called to be a light in the darkness for others. As I strived to make a difference, I started building momentum, two steps forward and one backward. I immersed myself in self-growth and self-development work. As a busy mom of three, I inspired people by sharing my journey. I prioritized myself and supported other women in creating healthy lifestyle habits. When my accountability group encouraged me to turn my hobby into a business, I became a dual-certified life and health coach. I never imagined myself in a leadership role, yet it ignited my passion! My life flourished with new possibilities from my empowering self-love journey. *The caterpillar games are over, and I now have wings.*

The honeymoon phase of my spiritual awakening felt like hitting a magical lottery, rekindling my child-like wonder of magical possibilities. I became curious about a deeper spiritual meaning when recurring numbers and owls appeared everywhere. I was learning to trust the wisdom of my intuition for the first time.

In hindsight, the spiritual journey forward was divinely paved. The backward steps illuminated my subconscious programming. They revealed the perpetual loopholes I was stuck in and the toxic patterns I repeated. I wanted to impact the world, but imposter syndrome haunted me, endlessly returning me to the same limited belief: *I have to measure up to be worthy.*

My father passed away when I was thirty-three, on the last day of November. That previous July, I broke four years of silence after his health declined to ask him in-depth questions about his life. He confessed he was petrified after my mother died. "I did not feel good enough to be a parent, and I didn't know how to parent because of my old man. I did it all by trial and error. I have made a lot of errors, but my love for either of you never stopped."

Standing against the railing of my back deck, I could not believe my eyes. Three bald eagles were soaring in circles in the sky above the river, symbolizing my dad's soul was free and that my soul deserved to be free also. That truth ignited my healing journey. It was time to stop running away from my past and allowing self-doubt to hold me captive. It was time to discover my true identity by embracing the beauty in my darkness. I would meet my inner child and allow myself to feel safe, to feel it all. I had unintentionally allowed my fear of being seen to make me believe I did not belong. The darkness held the key to my transformation, and I hadn't slowed down long enough to notice that it was the portal home to my soul. I was the light at the end of the tunnel I was searching for. *Surrender, my heart whispered.*

My continued journey of self-reclamation is my mission to make a lasting impact in the world. As I move forward, I can feel the weight of the old stories loosening their grip on me. The beliefs I once carried — about not belonging, needing to prove myself and measure up — are slowly being replaced with a deeper truth. Love and safety are nurtured from within. I am learning to honor myself by no longer attaching a need for external validation. My heart, which once feared connection, now desires to be vulnerably witnessed (seen). I release the unhealthy attachments to my past identity by shining my radiant light, a flame rising from the ashes. I create the life of my dreams by taking aligned action toward my heart's vision.

Your integrity is a gift to the world. Embrace the beauty in your darkness to discover deeper truths about who you are. Create a safe space to surrender to the fear and discomfort and allow emotional release. Trust that your heart can clear the density while visualizing love and light illuminating the shadows. Notice how to begin shining your light, and reflect on how you can light the way for those in need. Acknowledge your wounds, meet your inner child, and provide the love and safety they need from you. Free yourself by following the whispers of your heart, taking one inspired step at a time toward your expanding vision. Your inner light is a beacon of hope, calling you home to your soulful essence, igniting the path forward in service to a brighter humanity.

Ignite Action Steps

- **Call back your power by untethering from the past.** Release the attachments to the past, the identity, the beliefs, and the behaviors adapted to survive. Be the author of your life and create a new story. The past never meant anything about the truth of who you are.

- **Hold onto your power.** When you seek validation, you seek belonging from something or someone outside of yourself. Do not abandon yourself in fear of being abandoned by someone else.

- **Embrace your inner child.** We can only grow to the threshold of our inner safety before we turn around and run toward our familiar sabotaging comfort zones. Ask your inner child what they need to feel safe and provide love and validation.

- **Replace judgment with curiosity.** Invite a greater understanding of *why* you ever dimmed your shine in the first place by sitting in discomfort. Embrace the beauty of your darkness by loving the fragments you have felt ashamed and afraid of within yourself.

- **Express your emotions.** We are meant to feel the highs and lows. Emotions are energy in motion. Tears and healthy emotional releases are healing.

Chantelle McFarland — Canada
Mom, Certified Habit Transformation Health Coach and Certified Life
Coach Soulpreneur of Soulful Emergence, Author, Truth-seeker and
Free-Spirited Woman
soulfulemergence.com
chantellemcfarland90@gmail.com
chantellep1990
chantelle-mcfarland-soulfulemergence
chantelle_soulfulemergence

Overcoming Challenges to Make an Impact

Many of the stories in this book prove that our greatest impact often comes from the challenges we have faced. The moments that tested us the most: the setbacks, losses, and hardships are often the very experiences that shape our strength and define our purpose. Growth is not always easy, but it is through adversity that we discover who we truly are and what we can overcome.

The struggles you have endured have impacted you, and that story can inspire others. Your experiences hold the power to guide someone else through their journey, offering them hope, perspective, and a reminder that they are not alone. Every challenge you have faced has prepared you to make an impact in ways you may not even realize yet.

- What personal obstacle have you overcome that has strengthened you?

- How can your experience help others going through a similar struggle?

Dave August

DAVE AUGUST

*"People are going to give you an opportunity in life,
and it's up to you what you do with it."*

My story is to remind you that no matter what your background or what struggles you have been through, you can always do better and turn your life around. Life's a journey, and you choose what you make out of it. If you are given an opportunity, run with it. Don't ever stop dreaming. With hard work, if you put your heart and soul into something, you can create whatever you want. Along the way, as you lift yourself up, remember to give back by helping another with a warm hug or a few kind words. You never know the life you may save or the impact you may make.

THE DOOR OF OPPORTUNITY

A collection of the world's best athletes paraded before me. I was seated in one of California's fanciest, most stunning restaurants for a big ceremony dinner. Tears welled in my eyes as my name was called to come up on stage. Clutching the iconic *Don't Give Up* Award, I noticed the beaming faces of my sister and my mom, and my heart filled with pride. Only ten people have ever received this award in its history. 'Have faith and hope. Fight through it, there are always people that care for you.' My message was of perseverance. Never did I think that someone like me would be inducted into the Multi-Ethnics Sports Hall of Fame, someone who at a young age got involved in gangs, became a drug dealer, failed at school, and battled for years with alcohol. It was one of the pivotal events in my life, and in that moment, I realized that I was a testament to never giving up on my dreams, to no excuses, and to the possibilities that lie in all of us to become a better person.

Even though I was raised by good parents who loved me and provided me with a wonderful home, I ended up hanging out with the wrong crowd. Drawn by flashy cars and motorcycles, selling drugs seemed like a quick way to make money. *It was fun*, I thought. I was intrigued and didn't think about the repercussions. I didn't know how to say *no* and make better choices at the time. I was weak-minded and somewhat of a follower because I didn't like the person I saw in the mirror. What I thought was the easy road led me on a downward spiral and a world filled with pain, self-destruction, and jail.

From a young age, I loved playing with cars and spent hours detailing them in our backyard. Without school certificates, I made up for what I lacked in education with determination and dedication. I knew I was good with cars, and with support from my dad, when a local lot became vacant, I grabbed the opportunity to set up my own shop detailing cars. My career began by washing the hoods, getting down on my hands and knees, and scrubbing hubcaps. I learned that it doesn't matter how small you start out, if you don't give your all, you will never know what you are truly capable of. Anything less than 100 percent means you are not giving it your best; you have to put your nose to the grindstone to know what you can achieve.

I was excited to grow my business and keen to try out new ideas. One of my early clients was a former Raider™, a professional American football player. I set up a football-themed car detailing event with food, beverages, and music and asked if he would help by signing autographs. He agreed. That one initiative was such a great success that it connected me with more players, which led to me being offered the chance to work for the Raiders, looking after their vehicles as a full-time gig. Spotted as a hard worker, all sorts of exciting offers started to come my way. *I realized that people are going to give you an opportunity in life, and it is up to you what you do with it.* I grabbed the bull by the horns and stepped into a whole different world, including organizing a PR stunt for former American President Bill Clinton and meeting the head of the Secret Service, who was a huge football fan. Mixing with such inspiring athletes and influential people felt like a dream come true. It shifted my focus toward a more positive group of people to hang out with; yet, like a yo-yo, I found myself pulled back to my old negative behaviors, seeking what was familiar.

On the outside, it looked like I had turned my life around. I was becoming a better person and creating an impact. I had managed to leave drugs behind.

However, I still couldn't ditch the crutch of alcohol. I found myself giving in to the irresistible urge to stop by the bar before heading home. I would then hop in my car, sometimes driving over the speed limit. Once, I bashed into a light pole, and another time, I almost hit a cop. Predictably, I ended up with repeated charges of Drinking Under the Influence (DUI). This became a regular pattern. I would spend four or five days in jail and then swear that was the last time. And maybe it was, for a bit, perhaps even a year, but then I would inevitably relapse. Only when an ankle bracelet and longer prison time became a real threat did I know something had to change. I wasn't giving 100%. I still wasn't doing my best or using all the tools God gave me. I was making excuses and not doing the right thing. At that moment, I realized that if I wanted to have a true and lasting impact on the lives of others, I needed to become a real role model and a true leader.

It was time to be honest with myself and start leaving my own legacy. I knew I could do more and be more. Without faith, there's no hope; without hope, there's no faith. I believed in myself. I acknowledged that I had spent too much idle time in bars. I was now strong enough to say *no* to hanging out with people who negatively influenced my life. Ready to be the kind of leader that I wanted to be, I knew that if I threw myself into being busier in the community, I would be able to keep my inner monsters at bay and have a more positive and greater impact.

Being involved in the athletic world, I saw up close the great impact sports can have on young people and the community. As a representative of the Raiders, I helped them with a project called *One on One Against Hunger*. During Christmas and Thanksgiving, we would go into schools with boxes filled with canned goods and turkeys. The kids' eyes sparkled with excitement when they spotted famous football players showing up and helping out. I saw a different side to humanity and what it means to care for other people, and I wanted to do more of it and make a bigger impact. My focus shifted from cars to sales and fundraising. Soon enough, I was raising money for kids' football camps. The camps allowed me to see the kids in action and what it meant to them to have such an experience. When I saw the impact the money I had raised was making, it changed me. The work spoke directly to my heart. I enjoyed standing on the sidelines and cheering those children on. I wanted them to know that I cared.

Even now, years later, I get choked up when I see the familiar face of someone I had coached tell me that my words mattered or that I made an impact on their life, a much bigger impact than I realized. It makes my heart thrive to hear how the kid that I supported playing football, who was stuck at school, got an education and is now the CEO of a big company. To witness how a child has thrived in life and be a part of that transformation lights me up. Being there for them has taught me that we never truly know how a few simple words of enthusiasm and kindness can impact another. Experiences like that showed me that our influence is often much greater than we realize. It shows me that no money in the world can put a price tag on helping a person in need when you do it with genuine intention.

Driven to keep lighting up children's lives, I kept saying *yes* to more opportunities to work with kids and make a difference. After ten years in sales, I found myself each year pushing to do better than the last. When a new door opened, I stepped forward and earned the title of 'Executive Director of Marketing for the NFL™ Alumni Northern California Chapter.' Going from cleaning hubcaps to running the alumni was a monumental achievement for me. It all stemmed from hard work, dedication, and belief in myself.

That Christmas, and for the last twelve years, toy drives have been a huge part of my life. They are a collaboration of many months of hard work to deliver Christmas presents to impoverished children all over the local community. As Christmas approaches, we work sixteen days straight as thousands of presents are covered in sparkly wrapping paper, the work of real-life magical elves. I helped coordinate this massive project. My favorite part was at the end when I dressed up as one of thirty Santas who have the honor of riding in the front seat of a fire truck and delivering Christmas joy and gifts to hundreds of kids. It has been the best job in the world because there was a time in my life when I was so wrapped in hurting myself I avoided joy and happiness. Not being a father myself, this event allows me to feel like I have so many kids I can give to.

The moment I opened the first door and saw the tiny faces beam, I felt the difference I was making. Sometimes, I walked into one-bedroom homes with four kids eagerly standing around me in hopeful anticipation. With screams of joy, I could see how much this simple act meant to these precious little ones. My heart swelled. I truly feel that I am making a difference for these families. It was a moment they would never forget, and I was grateful to be a part of it. I was becoming a better version of myself because I had moved beyond what I once thought was a limitation in my life.

Another time, as I looked around a bare room to see just one small toy on the ground, I felt a lump rising in my throat. As I reached out with a toy train wrapped in red and gold Christmas paper, I saw the gratitude in the eyes of the little boy before me. When I wrapped my arms around this tiny child, I received the most genuine hug in return. I knew inside he was just crying out for love. My heart melted as I could give him such unconditional love.

My body had been through a tough ride after years of drugs and alcohol, and while I was focusing on helping others, I was neglecting my health. I was first diagnosed with cancer around the age of twenty-seven. Thirteen surgeries later, my cancer was in remission, and my passion for helping sick kids in hospitals was ignited. Through my struggles with my healing journey, I became stronger and learned how to better look after myself and how to love myself more. Ever the opportunist, I recognized the chance to help in hospitals and became part of an organization that donated money to buy bags filled with stuffed animals to give to sick kids. These children got a warm, cuddly creature to cheer them up, and they also got to keep high-quality bags to put their clothes in when they went home. It was just a small act with a lasting impact.

I had the privilege of helping one very ill boy who I met at the hospital, extending his life for an extra two years. Giving him nutrients that had supported me on my path to wellness and infusing him with hope, I cared. Sadly, this young boy passed away at an early age, and the family struggled financially. I wanted to contribute, so I helped raise money for his funeral. I recognized that there are many children and families out there who need our help. I have found that every little bit helps; *every effort makes a difference.*

Word got out in the local community that I was positively impacting the kids in the neighborhood. I was asked to speak by the Raiders at a local school and present a child with an award who was blind in one eye and had become a state wrestling champion. As a person who had struggled with dyslexia and had limited education, I was hardly an eloquent speaker and was extremely nervous, but I had passion and conviction in my message. With only a few notes, I knew the only way forward was to speak unscripted and genuinely from the heart. As I gained confidence, talking before an audience became easier. I found that after a few lines, the butterflies in my stomach disappeared, and the fire in my voice rose. I spoke that day that *no matter what you go through in life, you can prevail if you are willing to persevere.*

I told my story. Who I am and what I have done. I spoke to those young people about what I had learned explaining that we are not living in an easy world and are surrounded by lots of temptation. We all have crosses to bear and struggles to pass through, but sometimes, hurdles make us stronger. Going through rough patches teaches life lessons. Many kids dream of an athletic career, but I warned them that this was just borrowed time. I advised them of the importance of an education and that you could always turn your life around. "Sure, you may make a few mistakes. You may get into trouble. But resist peer pressure," I said, as the pain of my past decisions fueled me onward. "Listen to your gut, and don't be a follower. Be a leader. Not everyone is going to be great, but if you don't give 100 percent, you will never know." I reminded them, "Do the right thing every day. Give life your all, and make no excuses."

I finally felt that I was slowly becoming that leader. Being nominated for the Multi-Ethnics Sports HOF *Don't Give Up Award* was a very proud moment. My parents taught me that if you do something from the heart, the 'man above' will give back in abundance, maybe not tomorrow or next week, but at some point, in some place, no matter what. After many years of failure and disappointment, it felt rewarding to finally be doing good in the world, good work from the heart, God's work.

I began to spot the many opportunities right on my doorstep. All around me, there were chances to give back and connect with people who needed a helping hand and to be treated with grace, understanding, and compassion. I took warm meals to neighbors across the street who were on their own. I became a board member at the senior center. On one particular occasion, I was asked to speak at a dinner to a large Arizona crowd and raised $60,000 for prostate cancer. I talked authentically from the heart about my journey with cancer and how I battled the disease. It surprises me to witness what someone with little education has been able to achieve with willingness and determination. My business partner, who was at the event, heard me talk and was inspired to get a medical check-up. He found out he needed urgent medical treatment immediately. He later told me that if it wasn't for me, he would never have seen a doctor. My words changed his life. It proved to me that our words have an enormous impact.

Now, I strive to live my best life and to help my family, friends, and those around me live that best life. I finally love the person staring back at me in the mirror. I know I am no longer a follower and have become the leader I aspired to be. I want my mom and the incredible people who gave me a foot up in life to feel proud of me and the work I have accomplished. I feel abundantly rich in life, love, and generosity. I want to be an example of what a great legacy looks like and to inspire someone else to give it their all, their full 100 percent. I have turned my life around, and you can also. No matter what struggles you have been through, don't ever stop dreaming. Your legacy will follow your journey. Take action today and see what you can achieve.

Be willing to help someone and create betterment in *their* life. We all go through struggles, yet we can use those struggles to inspire us to make a difference in our lives and the lives of others. We all can do 'good work'. Humanity depends on us to create a positive impact and make the world a better place. *Our success is only built on the success of others.* When you give to those around you, you receive more in return and that success multiplies. Find something you care about and make a difference. You then become a role model for others who want to do the same, and that, my friend, is the true impact we each have within us to ignite *impact* around the globe.

Action steps

- Love yourself. You can't love anyone else until you love yourself. First, you must take care of yourself and your mental health. You are no good to anyone else if you don't make this a priority. There are times and places to help others; otherwise, you can wind up forgetting about yourself while helping them.

- Look for simple acts of kindness on your doorstep. These acts are everywhere when you open your eyes. *Does a neighbor need a hot meal? Could you sit beside the bed of a sick child in the hospital? Can you carry someone's groceries to their car?* Kindness can happen anywhere.

- Give someone a hug. You might save someone's life by reaching out and giving them a hug and showing you care. Everyone needs to know they matter.

- Talk kind words to others. In just listening to another, you could be changing their life. Use words of encouragement, especially to children. They need to know what they're capable of, and even if they have been through rough patches, they can turn their life around.

- Share your story. Share the lessons you have learned. Remind people of the good in themselves and how they, too, can live their best life. Be willing to share your story and inspire a positive message.

- Get involved in your local community. *What can you do in your local community to make a difference? Is a local charity looking for volunteers?* Too much idle time for kids or adults is not a good thing. Volunteer, keep yourself busy, and give back.

Dave August — United States of America
Executive Director of Marketing
NFL Alumni NorCal Chapter
Dave-August

Lynda L. Sullivan

Lynda L. Sullivan

"Everything you are looking for, you have to create within yourself."

My wish for you is to understand that the most important relationship you have is with *yourself*. When you are nicer to yourself and strive to become the best version of yourself, the people and connections you need in your life will fall into place. I want you to discover the best version of you has always been there, patiently waiting. You already have the power within you to create the life you want. Go within yourself to transform your outer world.

The Journey Back to the True Me

"How does it feel to be an orphan?"

Those were the words spoken by the Deacon at my mother's funeral, the same Deacon who had delivered my father's service when I was just sixteen years old. Now, they stood before me, in my forties, asking a question that cut straight to my core.

At that moment, the weight of those words settled over me like a heavy blanket. I realized there was no one left to call when I needed advice and no familiar voice on the other end of the phone to guide me through life's uncertainties. Both my parents were gone, and no one was there to be my safety net for all my life experiences, including raising my son on my own.

The lessons my parents had taught me – responsibility, family, and kindness – were all I had left. I will forever love and cherish those lessons since the comfort of my parent's presence and the reassurance of their wisdom were gone in a physical way.

I was an adopted child, and my adoptive parents shared that information with me since I was very young. It was a beautiful adoption, and my adoption day was celebrated in the same way my birthday was. We often thanked my biological parents for the family they helped create. It was never a negative thing for me, and my adoptive parents were always my mom and dad.

Until that moment when the Deacon posed that question, I had never truly felt orphaned either by my biological parents or my adoptive parents. But, as the Deacon's question echoed in my mind, I suddenly felt orphaned not once but now twice.

My adoptive parents, who had loved and raised me as their own, were gone. It was a sharp, undeniable loss, and for the first time, I felt utterly alone, as though the foundation I had always relied on had been completely taken away. I had never thought of being orphaned by the two people who raised me, nor did I ever consider being an orphan by the two people who gave birth to me until that moment.

The feeling of not having parents is a tough realization, one that most people face at some point in their lives. I felt the weight of loss more than I ever had before, like I was spiraling out of control and unprepared to handle the situations I would now face alone. As time passed, I came to understand something profound: *I could look at life in two ways: through the lens of what I've lost or through the lessons I've gained.*

One of the greatest lessons I received was watching my mom navigate the loss of her father just a few short months before the passing of my dad. Her navigating grief, taking care of me and my brother, and overcoming challenges she had not endured before gave me a sense of knowing that I can do anything I put my mind to. During that time, I learned the strength of taking care of myself, the lesson that, although people are physically gone, they are always alive in my heart and the value of never taking things for granted.

However, being sixteen, I didn't truly understand the lessons that she was showing through her actions until after I lost her. It took me years to realize, but when I look back upon that time, I see the courage and faith she had. I knew that was inside me as well.

With both my parents gone, I let the loss define me. I felt alone, untethered, and unsure of what came next. For months after my mother's funeral, those words echoed in my mind: "How does it feel to be an orphan?" I couldn't shake the weight of them. Even though I had wonderful friends, family, and a supportive community, I felt abandoned. My mother had always been my anchor, the one I turned to for advice and comfort. Without her, I felt adrift and directionless.

Once her house was sold and her possessions were tucked away, I realized I needed something to ground me again. A friend whom I looked up to suggested some books for me to read: *Think and Grow Rich* by Napoleon Hill and *The Strangest Secret* by Earl Nightingale. The lessons I learned in those books inspired many new thoughts and ideas. That led to another recommendation from my friend to join an online mastermind group. The growth I saw in myself through reading the personal development books was extraordinary, so I decided to give the course an honest try.

The six-month course was called *Thinking Into Results*™, a program created by Bob Proctor and Sandy Gallagher of the Proctor Gallagher Institute™. The program promised to help participants 'unlock their potential,' but I wasn't entirely sure what that meant. All I knew was that I needed a change. I needed clarity, to believe in myself again, and something to take my mind off the heavy burden of loss I was enduring.

I threw myself into the course. At first, it was overwhelming — facing myself, my habits, and my limiting beliefs in such an honest way. But as I kept going, something shifted. I began seeing patterns in my life and understanding how to reshape them. It wasn't about fixing what was 'wrong' with me; it was about discovering the best version of myself that had always been there, waiting. I stopped focusing on what I had lost and embraced the gratitude for what I had. I understood that I could create the life I wanted and didn't have to simply accept what life handed me.

When I joined *Thinking Into Results*, it wasn't just about learning tools or completing exercises. It was about connecting with a group of people who were striving to be the best versions of themselves. The person who suggested the books for me to read and a few of my other friends I also admired greatly had already gone through the program, and I'd seen firsthand how it helped them achieve their goals and break through barriers they once thought impossible. I thought to myself, *If they could do this, there's no reason that I can't also.*

Coincidentally, while going through my mother's things, I found the book *The Secret,* which I knew also contained writings from Bob Proctor and other great thought leaders. Reading through that book, I saw that my mother highlighted different text areas. I was impacted to discover that she was reading the same words that I was! I felt closer to her and that I was going in the right direction. It was like a sign from her that this course and my studies were the right path for me.

The tools I learned during that six-month process taught me how to shift my thinking in ways I never expected. What stood out the most was the people: their stories, their determination, and their willingness to face their challenges head-on. Being part of that community inspired me to dive deeper into myself, to truly believe in my abilities, and to overcome what was holding me back.

For the first time, I learned how to look inward, to truly understand who I was and what I needed; it wasn't easy, but it was transformative. The growth I experienced wasn't just about achieving results; it was about realizing the power I already had *within* me to create the life I wanted. Little by little, the work began to show results. My relationships grew stronger, not because I was giving more of myself to others but because I was giving more to *myself.* I set boundaries, prioritized my needs, and learned to embrace quiet moments alone. I slowly began healing and embracing the orphan inside me.

In my career, things began to click. My momentum in my real estate business grew, and I found myself surrounded by incredible clients, supportive colleagues, and a network of professionals who uplifted one another. For the first time in a long time, I felt like I was on solid ground, working toward my purpose.

My son, JT, also started thriving. He excelled in school and explored new hobbies with a confidence I hadn't seen before. It was as if my growth was creating a ripple effect in the people closest to me. Watching his growth became my proudest moment, and together, we found happiness and security in our growth.

Yet, I'll admit, it felt as if there was still something missing. That question from the Deacon still lingered in my mind. "How does it feel to be an orphan?" The words had once symbolized loss, but I began to wonder if they could mean something more.

A few years before my mother passed, I got a letter in the mail one day. It was from the adoption agency who wanted to inform me that my biological family was looking to connect. To say that I was hesitant is an understatement. I wasn't sure after all these years why they wanted to find me. I'm not going to lie, my first thought was someone in the family must have needed an organ or something. I spoke to my mother about it. She shared her thoughts and feelings and was very supportive and open to my meeting with them.

As the days went by, curiosity got the best of me, and I responded to the letter. Shortly after, I met the maternal side of my biological family. Pleasantly, I was wrong about the organ; they ended up being extremely wonderful people, and we instantly felt a familial connection. I learned that my birth mother had passed away in her early twenties when I was still a toddler. She was in a car accident, and since that time, my biological grandmother had been searching for years to find me. After hitting many dead ends, she eventually received help from my cousin, and they were able to reach out to me via the letter.

Once we were reunited, we visited throughout the years. I learned more about my birth mother: her joy, zest for life, and generosity. I also learned my birth father was a very nice man. The two of them were very young when I was born, so they made a courageous decision to make sure I received the life they didn't feel they could provide for me. Being with my biological family gave me a sense of where I came from and solidified the fact that I was never considered an 'orphan.'

My maternal biological family and my adoptive mother formed a wonderful relationship. They shared photos and stories over the years. It was amazing to see the unity between them. When my adoptive mother passed away, they all came to her funeral and showed their support and gratitude for the woman who took care of me for my entire life.

For the past few years, I've had a photo of my birth father given to me by my grandmother on my nightstand. When I look at the picture, I would think about what it must have been like for him. *Did he have a good life? Did I have any siblings? Did he think of me?*

A year after my adopted mother passed, someone suggested I search for my biological father. I knew that neither my biological mother nor father had ever truly wanted to give me up. They wanted the best for me and felt adoption was the only way to achieve that. My adopted family gave me a wonderful life full of love and opportunity and a great older brother. For that, I am forever grateful. Yet, I still carried questions regarding my biological father. So, I began the search. I wasn't sure what I would find, but I knew it was time to take the step. Within two hours, I had found him.

Knowing where he was and how easy it was to find him was incredibly emotional for me. Without my studies and the support of friends and family, I may not have made the decision to search for him. I used my intuition, had many moments of prayer, and gained the strength to follow through before I decided to reach out.

Within a week, my biological father and I met for the first time. I honestly thought it was going to be a quick visit of "Hi, how are you?" and "Nice to meet you." Driving there, I was excited and nervous. Sitting in the parking lot for a few minutes to gain strength, I knew it was time. I got out of my car, walked through the door, and saw a man staring, waiting for me to walk through it. I instantly knew it was him, and I hugged him and cried. What I thought was going to be a quick meeting turned into hours of talking and reconnecting with one another.

That moment hugging my father was profound — one of those turning points in life that leaves you forever changed. At the time, I didn't know the full story of my biological family. However, I did learn the best parts. I was an older sister to two half-siblings: a younger brother and a sister. I also gained a caring stepmother, who was very welcoming to my son and me. She was a huge support to my father throughout the years as he dealt with my adoption. I also have extended family in the form of cousins, aunts, and uncles.

There's so much more to that part of my journey. I could write an entire book on it alone, but finding my father marked the beginning of a new chapter in understanding *myself*. Knowing him was a moment of growth and a realization that my story was far from over despite all of the hurdles I had to overcome.

Meeting him was a reminder that life is a series of discoveries, each one teaching me more about myself and my capacity for connection, love, and understanding. This journey of uncovering my past is still unfolding, and it's one I will write more about someday.

This journey wasn't just about reconnecting with my family or finding success in my career. It was about learning to honor *myself*. When I stopped focusing on the pain of what I had lost and shifted my energy to becoming the best version of myself, everything else began to fall into place.

Now, when I think back to the Deacon's question, it is no longer a mark of loss but a symbol of growth. I'm not an orphan; I'm a person who has learned to stand on her own and embrace the lessons life offers. There is no final destination. Our lives are a journey to our best version, and the ups and downs are all part of it. You just have to keep your eyes, mind, and heart open.

I have discovered that focusing on myself and learning about who I truly am and what I need is the key to transforming my perspective and my entire life. I am forever grateful that I decided to invest in myself and my growth. As Bob Proctor said, "Change is inevitable; personal growth is a choice." I'm thankful that I made that choice.

Life is not always an easy journey. There are moments when the loneliness creeps in or when doubt shows up, and we question whether the work was worth it. Each time I start to feel that way, I return to the tools I have learned, the tools that remind me that the journey begins *within* and is mine to create. We are all in this human experience, and it is not always going to be sunshine and rainbows. Life is meant to help us learn and grow into the best versions of ourselves If you want to impact your life, be willing to do the work, invest in yourself, and grow into the best version of yourself.

Ignite Action Step

- **Shift Your Focus.** Instead of dwelling on what you've lost, ask yourself what lessons you've gained. That shift in perspective can open doors you never imagined.

- **Honor Yourself.** Prioritize your needs and take time to invest in your personal growth. It's not selfish—it's essential.

- **Trust the Process.** Life doesn't always go as planned, but when you let go of expectations and embrace possibilities, incredible things can happen, things that are better than you expected.

Lynda Sullivan — United States of America
Realtor, Senior Business Development and Acquisitions Revolution Group
Lynda.sullivan.52

Brenda Gerling

Brenda Gerling

"We all have wisdom deep in our soul that is longing to be shared."

Each of us embarks on a unique journey through life, one that is shaped by love, loss, disappointment, and triumph, all bringing valuable wisdom. My hope is to revive the tradition of the elders sharing their wisdom through storytelling. I wish that through my story you recognize that you also have a story that your family longs to hear.

Preserving Wisdom

I was born with a curious mind and an insatiable desire to learn. I was that inquisitive child who always asked, "Why?" And books helped me find answers. I questioned everything and sought a deeper understanding, particularly when things felt unclear. And truth be told, many aspects of life often seemed very confusing.

I've always had this inner knowing, an uneasy feeling in my gut that warned me when something wasn't right. I witnessed numerous behaviors that didn't feel aligned, yet everyone else seemed to embrace them. I have often said, "Just because everyone is doing it doesn't mean it's right." To fit in, I tried drinking and smoking, but none of it ever felt authentic, leaving me disconnected and self-conscious. The connection I longed for was found in my books. They became my steadfast confidant, always there to comfort me and provide an escape from the confusion around me. Through their pages, I could embark on incredible adventures and satisfy the deep curiosity within my soul.

Growing up on a farm on the Canadian prairies in the 60s and 70s, my world was quite small. I attended a small country school during the week, church on Sundays, and helped with chores around the house and farm. With limited channels on TV, most of my time was spent immersed in books, rushing through my homework and chores so I could retreat to my room and curl up with my favorite stories. The *Little House on the Prairie* series by Laura Ingalls Wilder transported me to a simpler time when life seemed more certain. I would get lost in Laura's adventures for hours, and as soon as one book was finished, another was waiting to be devoured. It's no wonder I eventually became an elementary school teacher, eager to share my passion for reading with my students.

I was overjoyed when I landed my first teaching job, instructing grades 1 and 2 at the same small country school I had attended as a child. It felt like a dream come true to return to the very classroom where my own love for the written word had been nurtured. Teaching quickly became my passion, and I poured my heart and soul into it, arriving at school by 7:30 AM and not leaving until around 5:00 PM. Teaching filled a deep desire of mine to share my knowledge and ignite a spark for learning in the next generation.

As the years passed and I became a parent, I found myself questioning the actions and behaviors I was witnessing more deeply, especially as I struggled to balance my roles as a teacher and a mother. Most mothers I knew were working outside the home, yet I questioned why I was rushing my children to childcare while going to school to nurture someone else's children. While teaching remained my passion, my heart truly belonged to my own children, and it became increasingly difficult to give 100 percent to both my students and my family. I longed to stay home and focus on raising my own kids. After several years, I decided to leave my full-time teaching position, instead choosing to work as a substitute teacher, allowing me to enjoy the best of both worlds.

Just as I had fully dedicated myself to teaching, I poured all my energy into raising my children. While I no longer had time to read for my own enjoyment, I treasured sharing my love of reading with my four little ones. Snuggling up for their nightly story time became one of the highlights of my day. I also loved being there when they got off the school bus, eager to hear all about their adventures at school. I cherished those moments, but as they got older and became busy with activities, we didn't have many opportunities for our after-school chats or bedtime stories.

My days were consumed with cooking, cleaning, helping with homework, and driving kids from one activity to the next. I also worked as a substitute teacher, served as president of the Figure Skating Club, and helped my husband on the farm. Early mornings and long days had me falling into bed each night overcome with exhaustion. Feeling trapped in an endless cycle of busyness that was draining and depleting me, not only did my books become a distant memory but so did my dreams and desires. I had unknowingly created a disconnect between myself and my needs, no longer knowing what I wanted or how to enjoy life. Deep down, I couldn't shake the feeling that life was about so much more than this tiring routine. I loved my family, but deep inside, my heart was aching, longing for the part of my story that felt like it was missing.

Driving home one dreary, cold winter day and feeling completely exhausted and overwhelmed, Reba McEntire's song "Is There Life Out There" came on the radio. As I listened to the lyrics, tears welled up in my eyes, "She doesn't want to leave; she's just wondering, is there life out there?" Realizing I had lost myself in all my responsibilities, deep sadness engulfed me. In that moment of being overwhelmed, I surrendered to the Universe and said to myself in desperation, *"There must be more to life than this. This can't be all that I am here for."*

Soon after, as if the Universe had heard my plea, incredible mentors appeared in the form of the written word. Books found their way back into my life like the return of a long-lost friend, but this time, they weren't just my companions; they were to become my greatest guides. Rather than the storybooks I was drawn to in my childhood, I was eager to dive into more inspiring non-fiction books, seeking wisdom and guidance.

Remarkably, a collection of incredible insights by new authors began to find their way to me. The works of Wayne Dyer, Louise Hay, Anita Moorjani, and many others soon became powerful catalysts for change in my life. As I eagerly devoured their words, my mind was opening to new possibilities. Whenever they mentioned one of their mentors, I also sought out those titles. I yearned for a deeper understanding and started reading texts that were centuries old and rich with ancient wisdom. For the first time, I was finding answers to questions that had lingered for years and began to view life through a completely new lens. That deeper understanding I was longing for slowly came to me.

One of the first books to profoundly impact my life was Wayne Dyer's *Change Your Thoughts, Change Your Life. Could I really change my life if I changed my thoughts? Was this the answer I was seeking? Was it really that simple?*

I had attended church most of my life but felt a deep disconnect from God. The God I had been taught about felt like a judgemental old man sitting in the clouds, watching my every move, determining whether I was being good or bad, and punishing or rewarding me accordingly. At the same time, I was taught that God was loving and that He was all around us and within us. This felt so contradictory and confusing. *If God was truly this all-loving presence within and around me, why was He judgmental, and why didn't I sense Him?* But, honestly, I didn't want that critical old man inside or around me because I was afraid of him! I could never understand this, but Wayne Dyer's teachings transformed everything. He introduced me to the concept of a loving God, a presence full of pure, unconditional love. This resonated deeply with me, and once I changed my thinking from that judgmental God to a loving God, I began to feel and see this presence everywhere. It was the sparkle in my grandchildren's eyes, the spectacular beauty of nature, and the goodness within my own heart.

One of my favorite quotes from Wayne Dyer is, "When you feel good, you feel God." So it became quite simple: I felt God's presence if I felt good. I had found a space to offer my prayers without fear of judgment. My connection with God was not just on Sundays but every day, all day. This loving God became a powerful presence in my life, and that's when I started receiving the answers to my prayers, which guided me toward a deeper sense of meaning.

Around the same time, Louise Hay's book, *You Can Heal Your Life*, came to me and deepened my understanding of the power within me. It taught me that we create our lives through our thoughts and words, reinforcing what I had already learned from Wayne Dyer. She showed me that everything I needed was already within me and that I could become my own healer if I learned to love myself. After reading, "You've been criticizing yourself for years, and it hasn't worked. Try approving of yourself and see what happens," I began paying closer attention to my thoughts and words and started doing her mirror work and affirmations. Gradually, I became kinder and more loving toward myself and others. The shield I had put up as protection from the chaos and confusion in the world began to soften. Her message had a huge impact on incorporating more self-love into my life.

Another book to appear as if divinely guided was Anita Moorjani's *Dying to Be Me,* providing even greater clarity and insight. Her story removed my fear of death and gave me a renewed appreciation for life. The miraculous healing she experienced solidified my belief in the power within us to recover from anything. Her message to "love yourself like your life depends on it because it does" verified what I had learned from Louise Hay and renewed my commitment to honoring my needs and desires. I began to recognize the divine essence within myself and developed a clearer sense of purpose. I discovered that we are co-creators with God, capable of shaping a beautiful life for ourselves and those around us. The messages she received to "treasure your magnificence" and "go back and live your life fearlessly" ignited my courage to chase my dreams and embrace the guidance I was receiving, leading me toward a more fulfilling life. As self-doubt began fading from the pages of *my* story, I gained the confidence to step out of my comfort zone. I began taking courses, attending conferences and retreats, and learning how to truly nurture my mind, body, and spirit and reignite my passion for life.

After acquiring many new insights and discovering an entirely new way of living, I decided it was time to get all that wisdom down on paper. My newfound knowledge had me waking up an hour earlier each morning to write down my thoughts and questions about everything I was learning. I committed to writing every day, and as I continued, I kept seeking answers. Soon, guidance began to flow through my pen. It was as though the more I wrote, the more wisdom emerged from deep within me. I wished I had known this all when my children were growing up so I could have passed it on to them. After writing for several years, I felt compelled to share my new perspective.

I was inspired by a book my great-great uncle had written when I was a child about his journey immigrating to Canada in the early 1900s. Learning about his tenacity and perseverance to travel to and settle in a foreign land had a huge impact and planted a seed of how precious sharing life's journey can be. Having always felt that the history of our elders was fading, I thought that one day I would write a book for my children and grandchildren. Every Christmas, I gave my children a book. That year, I decided it was time to write my own book to give to them, one that shared the lessons I had learned on my journey through life.

Each morning, while continuing my writing ritual, I began reviewing all my journals and noticed recurring themes. I carefully chose the most meaningful insights I wanted to share, and gradually, my book began to take shape. I wrote about the divine, magnificent beings we all are and the immense power we hold within. I spoke of the importance of following our dreams and making life exciting. I also shared my views on aging, the insights I gained from my detox and healing journey, and so much more.

Trusting the guidance in my heart, I organized the chapters, incorporating my favorite quotes and concluding with a list of what I know is true for me now.

I created a table of contents, wrote an introduction, and crafted a conclusion. For the cover, I selected a beautiful sunset photo from my first trip to Hawaii. After countless hours of proofreading and editing, my book was finally ready.

After printing enough copies for my family and a few extra, I headed to a stationery shop to have them bound. Handing my books over made me very nervous, as I had poured my deepest thoughts and feelings into these pages, and it felt incredibly personal to me. When I came back later that day, my anxiety increased because my books wouldn't be ready until the following morning. I felt like I was leaving my new baby with strangers for the night! To my relief, they were all bound and ready when I returned the next day. It felt so good to have my baby back in my arms! Cradling my books warmed my heart as I flipped through the pages, relishing the insights I had shared and the comfort they brought me.

Once I had the books home, I wrote a heartfelt message in each one, wrapped them in shimmering silver paper, and tied them with a ribbon. As Christmas approached, the nervousness crept in. I felt incredibly proud of my creation, yet I was still very anxious about presenting it to my family. I was on the verge of sharing something deeply personal that felt like exposing my heart and soul. My family could never understand why I had been waking up so early every morning, and I was about to reveal why. Not even my husband knew what I had been working on!

I decided to wait until all the gifts had been opened before giving them my special package. My stomach was in knots, and I had to make several trips to the bathroom! With excitement in the air and paper scattered all over the floor, I took several deep breaths, trying to calm my nerves. With trembling hands, I presented them with my book, *What I Wish I Would Have Known*, explaining the journey I had been on and my desire to share it with them. I told them how I had always felt we were losing the wisdom of our elders and decided to write a book about the wisdom I had gained. I wanted to pass on these new perspectives about life and the insights I had acquired.

It felt like I was handing them an intimate piece of my heart that holiday season. Whether they chose to read it or not, I knew it marked the beginning of sharing wisdom I felt had been forgotten. I believe my book will have a lasting impact on my children, grandchildren, great-grandchildren, and anyone else who reads it, just as Wayne, Louise, Anita, and my great-great uncle's book profoundly affected me.

Life is truly an incredible journey, and as I look back, I realize my book became a reality because I listened to the subtle nudges of my soul, guiding me to keep seeking answers to the questions I'd carried for so long. Through those books that seemed to appear in divine timing, offering the perfect message, I was inspired to write a book to share all the divine wisdom I had received.

You are meant to live in a profoundly glorious, expansive state that empowers and enlivens you. When you follow the little nudges of your soul, life unfolds as a beautiful journey, an incredible adventure waiting to be explored. As you continue navigating life, you will continue learning and growing, gaining fresh insights and perspectives. The wisdom you acquire loves to be told. *We all have wisdom deep in our soul that is longing to be shared.* I encourage you to begin sharing those insights with your family and those you love. You never know the impact of your story; you just need to trust that someone is eagerly waiting to hear it.

Ignite Action Steps

- Look closely for books that inspire you on the shelves of friends or at a local library or bookstore.

- Spend some time each morning writing down your thoughts and questions about life and watch the wisdom begin to flow through your pen.

- Know that your journey through life has brought a lot of experiences that your children and grandchildren are eager for you to share.

- Interview your parents and grandparents and begin to share their stories.

Brenda Gerling — Canada
Spiritual Teacher, Author, Wellness Coach
inspiredwellnessandwisdom.com
Brenda Gerling

Kerstin Pelletier

Kerstin Pelletier

*"Breath is the key that opens your heart to
unconditional self-love and wisdom."*

**My wish for you, the reader, is that my story brings you hope and a belief
in new possibilities. My intention is for you to find comfort in knowing
that even in the darkest moments, your breath is always there for you; it
is your lifeline, connecting you to Spirit and the light within.**

Breathing the Light of Spirit

On a bitter January night, I sat in the warmth of my home office, hands trembling as I pressed 'send' on an email to my family containing my last will and testament. The weight of finality pressed heavily against my chest as I finished packing, and the darkness within me felt inescapable. I was trapped in a place of unimaginable despair, what some might call the 'dark night of the soul.' In mere hours, I would board a plane to Mexico with one haunting purpose; to find someone, a Cartel member perhaps, or anyone desperate enough to end my life for a price.

Physically, I was broken. My entire body ached as though I was constantly battling a high fever. Some days, I could barely make it down the hallway to the bathroom, let alone dress myself. Work had become impossible. After countless appointments with doctors and specialists, I was diagnosed with fibromyalgia, chronic fatigue syndrome, irritable bowel syndrome (IBS), and a list of other ailments. The pain was relentless, often keeping me confined to my bed.

The suffering wasn't just physical; it cut deeply into my heart. The man I had married just over a year before seemed like a stranger to me now. What had started as a storybook romance and fairy-tale wedding felt like a trap, and the person I once cherished seemed unrecognizable. I was embarrassed and filled with regret for having remarried for a second time. *How had I let myself get swept up in the fantasy?* I thought I knew better. Every fiber of my being was urging me to leave, but I was ashamed. I had an overwhelming guilt for ignoring all of the yellow flags, which continuously waved at me along the way.

Dark thoughts raced through my mind in an endless loop. *How could I have let this happen? What was I supposed to do now? What would people think if I went through another divorce? How could I face the humiliation of admitting I'd made another mistake?* And, even more daunting, *How could I support myself?* I was too ill to continue working as a self-employed massage therapist, and my physical and mental health left me incapable of taking on any other job, especially one so physically demanding. The business I'd built, which once provided for me, now felt like a memory slipping through my fingers.

Relentless, negative thoughts spiraled in my mind, one feeding into the next until each one multiplied into a dozen more. My suffering felt endless. Every joint and muscle in my body throbbed with pain. Sometimes, the intensity was so overwhelming I would black out. The medications I had been prescribed for pain management barely took the edge off, and their side effects were brutal. Among the worst was the surge of suicidal ideation, a side effect that was slowly engulfing me. Thoughts of ending my life crept in constantly, vivid and unrelenting.

I was drowning in the depths of my agonizing thoughts. I pictured myself locking the garage and sitting in the car with a hose running from the exhaust until I succumbed to asphyxiation. Other times, I imagined downing bottles of alcohol and wandering into the snow, hoping the cold would take me as I passed out. I envisioned slipping into a warm bath after taking a handful of sleeping pills or driving off a cliff in the Rockies. Twice, I had checked myself into the hospital, aware of the danger I posed to myself. Yet each time, the thought of how my death would devastate my family and friends — especially the person who found me — stopped me from executing. But recently, my mind had turned to a new, desperate idea: hiring someone to end my life. I naively hoped this decision would shield my loved ones from the truth of how I died.

Eradicating my suffering was the real reason for boarding that plane. At one point, I thought Mexico could have been a belated honeymoon for me and my husband. We'd missed that celebration due to COVID-19. He said he was too busy when I asked him to join me. I resolved to go alone and decided to use the trip to end my life. I told my family and friends it was a vacation to heal, to find peace under the sun, but secretly, I had other intentions.

Boarding the plane on my own was no small feat. My body struggled with even the basics; managing luggage felt Herculean. I couldn't bear the thought of juggling my bags and my pomeranian dog, Marley, in my condition, so I decided to leave him behind. As the plane lifted off from the cold winter landscape and headed toward warmth, I focused on deep, diaphragmatic breaths. I tried to soothe my body, reach inward, grounding myself against the pain and silencing the torrent of thoughts, if only for a moment.

Stepping into the darkness, I arrived at the vacation rental alone. Anxiety started to creep into my stomach, heart, and throat as I punched in the code to the key box…it didn't work. *What would I do if I couldn't get inside?* I was in a foreign country, unable to speak the language, and the shuttle bus was long gone. Fear surged, but I reminded myself to breathe, to reach inward, and the panic attack that had been building began to dissolve. I tried the code again; this time, it worked. I retrieved the keys and stepped through the gate to where home would be for the next month.

I could make out a beautiful yard, even in the dim light. Trees swayed gently, and despite the late hour, birds were still singing. In the distance, I could hear the ocean. Though thousands of miles from home, I suddenly felt more at peace than I had in months. I let the warm air embrace me, inhaling the scents of flowers and the sea. For a moment, everything felt beautiful, and the pain lifted from my body and soul. I unlocked the door and stepped inside. Suddenly, my dark thoughts returned, flooding back like a storm. *I was here for a purpose—how was I going to find someone willing to end my life? Who would take the little money I had to spare?* My mind spiraled back into the shadows, and the physical pain returned just as sharply.

After a long, sleepless night, I stepped outside to explore in the light of day. The yard was breathtaking, with vibrant colors and lush greenery. I spotted a hammock chair and settled into it, slowly spinning as my thoughts mirrored the motion. Though I was surrounded by beauty, the sadness and loneliness felt sharper than ever. Yet, something about being in this place stirred a small glimmer within me, like an ember in the winter cold, a faint sense that maybe — just maybe — life could get better.

I sat as tears spilled down my face, flowing like a river that needed to reach the ocean. *How could there be hope when I felt so trapped?* My life felt like a nightmare with no escape. Every part of me was suffering: my health, my marriage, my finances, my career. As if that wasn't enough, my young adult daughter had recently gone through an intense trauma. As a mother and empath, I could feel her pain almost as if it were my own. It was all too much. I didn't know how to escape the agony except through my breath, an innate coping mechanism I used to manage the pain of fibromyalgia. And so, as my mind raced, I took a deep breath, connecting within.

At that moment, I did something unfamiliar — I prayed. Out loud. I reached out to Spirit, God, the Universe, and said, "Please, Universe, please help me. I don't know what to do anymore. I can't go on like this. I feel so alone and lost. I don't want to be here if this pain is all that's left. I need clarity. I need to know what to do next, or I don't think I can continue. Please, help me." After I spoke those words, I fully surrendered to the Universe, closing my eyes and breathing deeply. What happened next is something I will never forget.

It felt like a soft, soothing blanket of love or the wings of an angel wrapped around me. Unlike anything I have ever felt, a sensation of profound warmth and comfort enveloped me. I breathed into this feeling, letting it expand, allowing its gentle embrace to hold and love me. I felt lighter like all my troubles had dissolved with each exhale. The darkness in my thoughts had been drawn into a brilliant light, and I realized I no longer needed to fear it. I felt supported, cradled, and unconditionally loved.

As I reclined in the hammock, soaking in these radiant feelings, I sensed something in me had shifted. Looking back, I believe this was the temporary death of my ego, a reset of sorts, leaving my mind a serene, blank slate. This was the beginning of my spiritual awakening — a deeper connection with Spirit than I had ever experienced before. From that moment, a calm came over my nervous system like I had never known, and my healing accelerated. Within days, after months of barely being able to walk due to pain, I found myself riding a bicycle, taking long walks, and even carrying groceries in a backpack.

Small miracles graced each day as I basked in the sun's warmth and took long, soul-nourishing walks along the beach. Although my ailments had not completely vanished, I found myself in a state of peace I hadn't known before. I made beautiful connections with others and began studying to become a certified life and health coach. A voice within, clear and steady, guided me toward this path, telling me that I was meant to help others find healing. With my mind quieted, I could finally hear my inner voice, sharp and certain. Whenever thoughts or emotions surfaced that didn't serve my highest good, I acknowledged them, observed them, and took a deep, cleansing breath to connect. I knew that my breath was my connection to Spirit, and in using it, I found peace, love, and joy within myself.

I instinctively understood what I needed to do about my marriage, but I sought more clarity. I asked my Spirit Guides repeatedly to help me see clearly, hoping for concrete evidence to support my decision. Though I had received intuitive messages before, I was waiting for something unmistakable.

Three weeks into my stay, the clarity I had desperately longed for finally arrived. After ending a video call with my husband, an overwhelming sense that something was amiss gripped me. An inner nudge compelled me to reach for my phone and check the app for the security camera I had instinctively reactivated before leaving home. The camera revealed a live feed that took my breath away like a harsh wind on a bone-chilling day. Pulses of dread coursed through me, and bile rose in my throat. The heart-wrenching images of what my husband was 'busy' doing brought excruciating pain, yet they also delivered the clarity I needed to move forward with my decision to separate from him. Sometimes, life's most valuable gifts come wrapped in the ugliest packages. And though this discovery was brutal, the gift it carried was priceless.

With one week left in Mexico, I desperately tried to find an earlier flight home to confront my husband and personally escort him out of my house, but I couldn't. So, I stayed, using the time to meditate deeply, center myself, and prepare for what lay ahead. Though I was dying inside, trembling with sadness and fear, I video-called my husband and calmly asked about what I had seen displayed on the camera. His response was a web of lies. Finding a sense of self-worth buried deep within me, I asked him to leave my home. From my vacation rental, I ended my marriage.

Throughout it all, I reminded myself to embrace the present. I had a choice: let this painful discovery eclipse the beauty around me or remain in the moment, free from the grip of past pain and future worries. With every thought that tried to pull me away, I chose, again and again, to come back to *Be Here Now*.

My ability to reconnect through breath, release what no longer served me, and stay grounded in the present illuminated my path and saved my life. I felt a newfound sense of unconditional self-love, the courage to prioritize my well-being, and a deep trust that the Universe supported me every step.

When I returned home, I began preparing my house and belongings for sale. Although the stress was overwhelming and the physical pain intense at times, I managed to carry on with the guidance of Spirit and the support of many beautiful hearts who appeared to help me. I closed my massage therapy business, sold my house and most of my possessions, and negotiated a settlement to bring my marriage to a peaceful conclusion.

I moved into the countryside into an old fifth-wheel trailer generously loaned to me. I could never have managed this without the kindness and support of my family and friends, to whom I am eternally grateful. Though my body was on the mend, the process of moving and managing everything brought painful flare-ups. With the equity from my house sale, I was finally debt-free and had the resources to begin a true healing journey and the freedom to live life to its fullest.

Now, I live the simple life I once yearned for, working both online and in person as I live a nomadic lifestyle. I am deeply grateful for the soul lessons I've learned. I understand now that these experiences didn't happen *to* me — they happened *for* me. Without those challenges, I might never have made the changes needed to live an authentic, simple, peaceful, and soul-centered life. I have looked within, connected with something greater than myself, and learned to love myself unconditionally.

The impact of hitting rock bottom, of being willing to end it all, awakened my greatest internal knowing. Connecting with Spirit brought forth my authenticity, leading me to the truth of who I am and guiding me to the wisdom of my intuition. Trusting in the Universe has provided me with small daily miracles; through breath and self-love, I am healed and whole.

Maintaining a conscious connection with my breath and heart has become my anchor, grounding me emotionally, mentally, physically, and, most importantly, spiritually. This profound healing journey has led me through deep inner work, energy healing, inner child connection, and reprogramming of my subconscious mind. I am beyond thankful to share that I have fully healed from fibromyalgia, chronic fatigue, and IBS. In less than two years, I now live medication-free and embrace a life rooted in holistic wellness.

Today, my work centers on guiding others to connect with their inner Spirit through breath, releasing limiting beliefs, embracing forgiveness, and cultivating self-love and transformation. My heart and soul are devoted to igniting change and inspiring impact, helping others discover the love and light within themselves. No matter how dark the shadows may seem, you can always connect to your Spirit — through your lifeline, your breath. With each breath, you can bring light into the darkness, heal, and love all parts of yourself. As you do, may you find the strength to walk your unique path of self-love and bring more love and light into the world.

Ignite Action Steps

1. **Breathe deeply.** With each breath, ground yourself in the present moment. Allow your breath to open a connection within – to the true essence of who you are, and feel centered in this presence.

2. **Acknowledge your pain.** Bring awareness to your painful emotions, honoring them as part of your journey. Unreleased emotions can manifest as 'dis-ease' in the body. Allow them to flow through you with compassion.

3. **Practice forgiveness.** Release thoughts and emotions that no longer serve you. Forgive yourself and others. Forgiveness is a gift you give yourself, freeing you from the weight of the past.

4. **Embrace self-love.** Choose to love and accept all parts of yourself, including the shadows. Recognize that every aspect of you is worthy of love and kindness.

5. **Cultivate gratitude.** Give thanks out loud or in a journal for every step of your journey, including the challenges. These experiences bring you closer to your Spirit, the truth of who you are. Here lies infinite peace, love, abundance, and the beauty of the present moment.

Kerstin Pelletier — Canada
Transformational Self-Love Therapist, Certified Life & Health Coach,
Certified Teacher for the Stanford-based emotional intelligence/mindfulness
programs - Clarity Catalyst, Culture Catalyst, and Insight for
Life for kids/teens, Certified Teacher of Presence through
Eckhart Tolle's School of Awakening, Author, & Speaker
metamorphicwellness.ca
Kerstin Pelletier
kerstinpelletier
kerstin-pelletier-a54576b

K·3825
71 OHIO
33643
SEE VERMONT 63

Ann M. B. McIntyre

"We create our own applause. Learn to applaud yourself."

Know that there is life and living after physical and/or mental abuse. It is possible to change the cycle. I want you to know that there are people who can help. Call on them.

It Will Make Me Feel Better

"You used to be such a good girl. What happened? Why are you so bad? I don't know what I'm going to do with you." Before starting kindergarten, I remember my mother asking me these questions daily. Sometimes, she yelled. Sometimes she didn't. Recalling her tone and the cracks in her voice, I know now that there were times when she was trying to appear stern while hiding helplessness. I cringed at the impact of those words. Like any child, I wanted her love, hugs, and approval. I recall wishing I had never been born because I thought that would make my mother happy.

My earliest memory of this time was in the bathroom of our 1950s, ten-acre country home. When I was a toddler, my mother would yank down my panties. With purpose and force, she lifted me and put me on the pastel-pink toilet. My legs dangled as I leaned back against the cold porcelain. She bent over me and, using her stern voice, said, "Look at me." With sad eyes, I raised my head to see her shaking her finger as she spoke. "You know what to do. And you know what you're going to get if you haven't done it by the time I get back."

Oh, I knew. Knowing what would happen wasn't going to change the result. Instead, I stared down at the mosaic linoleum floor from my throne to ease my fear. It was pretty…yellow, pink, turquoise, white and black. I could see beautiful butterflies and flowers, much like we see shapes in clouds. All kinds of little patterns came to life, made me smile, and calmed my nerves.

Her sudden return ended my daydream. She lifted me slightly to check. Nothing. "Well, here we go again. When are you going to learn?" she yelled as she reached for the hard plastic bristle hairbrush behind me. She then beat the top of my thighs. They turned red as I screamed, and tears fell on them, increasing the sting with each contact of the brush. She shook her head while exclaiming that this hurt her more than it hurt me. *It didn't feel that way.* She removed me from the toilet, pulled up my panties, and, with one last swat, sent me to my room. Defeat took over, and I would sob into my pillow so no one would hear.

On my first day of kindergarten, my mother decided to pick me up rather than have me come home on the bus. Crayon drawings, except for mine, lined the walls of the small classroom. As the three of us stood there, my teacher described the assignment as she handed my drawing to my mother. "I asked everyone to draw their house, and I thought that you may want to have Ann's drawing to hang on your refrigerator!" she exclaimed with the same admiration for kindergarten talent that she knew my mother would mimic. To her surprise and my dismay, my mother shook her head, replying, "This doesn't look like our house. Huh, she'll never be an artist."

As the words hung in the air, my head fell in disappointment. The smell of the crayons had been intoxicating. Drawing had been the highlight of the day, and I loved it! We had learned to print our names at the bottom of the paper. I felt like a real artist!

In the car, my mother asked why I was crying. "If you don't stop, I'll give you something to cry about when we get home. If you think I will hang some crayon sketches on our refrigerator, you're quite mistaken. We have a nice home, and it's going to stay that way. That drawing belongs at school with the others."

A week before my sixth birthday, Dad dropped me off to live with my first-grade teacher while Mom was in the hospital. I was about to become a big sister. Mom and Dad were hoping for a boy. I was supposed to be a boy named Alan. I was told the first child should always be a boy. I wondered if this was the reason why I was such a disappointment to my parents and if I hadn't been born, they could have had their boy. On the day of my birthday, I was watching cartoons when they arrived home with their bundle of joy. "Would you like to hold your birthday present?" My mother said. "This is your baby brother." I wanted them to celebrate my birthday, not give me a brother! When I asked about my birthday, all I heard was, "No birthday for you this year!"

Years later, we moved to the DC suburbs. Families on all sides suddenly surrounded us. There were girls my age with which to play. I loved spending time at their homes but rarely invited them to mine. Their mothers smiled. Their mothers and fathers were kind and laughed. Like most kids, I wanted to join the 'in' crowd. Instead, I was taunted for being too short, too fat, and too bright. I asked my mother if I was fat. She replied, "You could be pretty if you weren't so chubby." *I'm ugly,* I thought.

When my friends got in trouble, they would comment, "Boy, am I gonna get it." I knew exactly what they meant, or at least I thought that I did. I was wrong. I later learned that all they 'got' was no TV or were grounded. They weren't beaten. Evidently, both my brother and I were horrible, misbehaved children. The beatings continued. "You and your brother are lucky," my parents said. Mom explained that her mother and grandmother beat her with a cat o' nine tail. Dad said that he was tied to a pole in the basement and whipped.

"If you can't do something right, don't do it at all." I still hear Dad's voice echoing this advice in my head. It was decided that I would learn to play piano, despite my request for singing lessons. As I practiced, Mom shouted with disapproval, "Stop making the same mistakes." To prevent upsetting her, I avoided playing when she was home. For twelve long years, I loathed the involuntary chore. The only tolerable part was the applause of approval I received at the end of a recital. It filled my soul in a way I longed for as I tried very hard to please my parents, especially my mother. *If only they would applaud me.* My inability to meet my parents' expectations kept me from fully pursuing many of my passions. After all, if you can't do something right, don't do it at all!

"As long as you live under this roof." I had a goal to get out from under their roof. All I needed was a plan. Due to what my mother had told me, here's what I knew: I was too stupid to devise a plan. I was too fat and ugly ever to have a boyfriend, which meant I would always be alone. I was bound to fail at everything because I couldn't do anything right. I was only a girl. I was afraid. Afraid of them. Fearful of everyone and everything. Afraid of being beaten "within an inch of my life."

Later, my parents demanded that I go to college. Either that or get a job and pay rent. I thought, *what do I want to do, and who do I want to be?* I wanted to be an actress and an entertainer in the theatre. That was my escape. *I could be someone else. I could be liked. I could be loved. I could receive applause, acceptance, and even awards!* When I suggested to my parents that I was looking at schools with theatre programs, I was shut down completely. "Do you think that this is a joke? College is serious. You are lucky to be going and even luckier in that we don't expect you to pay for your education, but we will not pay for you to become some type of floozy. Pick something else."

They agreed once I explained the career options available if I majored in art. As I researched schools, my mother informed me where my peers had been accepted: Johns Hopkins, Cornell, and other prestigious institutions. I was admitted to Kutztown State College's School of Art. "Kutz what?" she said. And so it happened! For eight months out of the year, I was out from underneath their roof. *Freedom at last*, I thought.

"You can't do anything right. What makes you think that you can be on your own? You don't know how to do anything without being told. You're good for nothing."

They were right. I didn't know how to be alone because I hadn't been given the opportunity. *Or was I supposed to have taken the opportunity?* That would have meant more consequences. I needed to learn quickly, but I didn't.

Before I knew it, I was nominated for Homecoming Queen. *What? Me? I wasn't pretty. I wasn't thin.* I called home and was thrilled to share my latest news. "That's nice, what about your grades?" A month later, I was elected to the Student Government Council. Again, I shared my news with Mom and Dad. "That's nice; what about your grades?" they asked again. Soon, the first semester was over, and it was Christmas vacation. I heard about so-and-so making the honor roll. I heard about someone else being on the dean's list. I showed them my drawings. "Nice. Why did you get a B- instead of an A?" I heard about someone else receiving an academic award or recognition. "Why can't you be like our friends' daughters?" Wanting my parents' approval, I tried to shine in any way possible. But it wasn't good enough. All they cared about were my grades.

Late that following May, I suddenly became ill with a fever of 105.2. I was taken to the hospital, and by the time I was released, the semester was over. I had missed my finals, and every course read incomplete, counting as an F. I had lost my full-time status. I couldn't return in the fall unless I agreed to take a lighter course load and see a counselor twice weekly. Since I couldn't tell my parents about this latest development, I had no choice but to agree.

I wasn't going to be analyzed. I was not about to be 'shrank.' *Oh no, not me.* I knew how this was done. Sure, I would attend every session. I would answer questions when asked, but I would not let some Kutztonian counselor get into my head. *No way.*

The college counselor was quite personable. Let's call him Dr. Know. He was handsome, with dark hair and a hint of gray. I remember how his eyes danced when he smiled. He seemed interested in me. At our first appointment: my grades. The following session: my hobbies. *This isn't so bad*, I thought, he's not here to *shrink* me after all. Another time: how did I choose Kutztown? And then: my childhood. *Very sneaky, Dr. Know.* And so, it continued week after week. He talked less, and I talked more. One day, he asked, *"Why do you think that you failed last semester?"* I explained that I had been hospitalized. "Oh, that's right," he said. *"And how were your grades before becoming ill? Would you have passed all of your classes? Do you think that you would have had any 'D's?"*

"Maybe," I mumbled. *"Why were your marks so low? A 'D' means that you would have to repeat the class. Did you tell your parents you were failing before getting sick?"* He was firing questions so fast that it was hard to keep up.

I answered him as though he should already know his questions and answers. "No, I can't tell my parents that I'm failing. There would be hell to pay. Yet, they expect me to fail." He paused. "I'm sorry. Let's slow it down. Why do you think that you're failing?"

"I don't know. I'm supposed to, I guess." The tears started to fall. "Do you think that your parents are right? Did you fail in order to make them right?" With a firm desire to reveal the truth, he continued. "You said that you were supposed to fail. And so you did. You made your parents right. What would happen if they knew for certain that you flunked out of school?" My voice was barely audible as I wished that I could vanish. "They would hurt me," I revealed. "They would yell and scream. They will tell me what a disappointment I am to them… that I'm an ungrateful child… that I deserve to be beaten." Dr. Know got up, walked around his desk, and sat beside me. "Ann, not all parents beat their children. Maybe a wack on their butt now and then. And I can tell you that we feel horrible afterward when we do. Abusive parents don't feel bad. They feel good, and then they feel guilty. *Hitting a child actually makes them feel better*. That's how you know. That's not how it's supposed to be. You must know that now, right? You're a beautiful and talented young lady. You brought your grades back up to where they need to be. If you want to stay at Kutztown, you can! From what you've told me, your parents were abused — much worse than you. Often, the abused become abusers. You would think the opposite, but that's usually not the case. Abuse isn't just physical. You know that, too, right? You are here. You haven't missed a single appointment. Deep down, you wanted the answer, and you figured it out. I didn't *shrink* you. You did it yourself. You're stronger than you know. I'm going to give you a phone number. It's a hotline. If something happens when you return home, call and get help. And I'm here. If you want to continue our sessions, you can."

A part of me had been awakened. Dr. Know was correct…deep down, I had always known something wasn't right. *What was I going to do with my newfound information? How was this discovery going to impact me going forward?* They would undoubtedly deny any accusation that I made. It didn't matter. I felt empowered. I felt new.

I made it home in time for dinner a few days before Thanksgiving. As my brother left, my father reminded him of his 12:00 AM curfew. Hours later, after midnight had come and gone, I lay in bed, listening to my parents' conversation in their room. The squeak of the rocker was almost as loud as the sound of my father's leather belt being snapped harder and harder. I went to my door to hear their words. "You know it's not going to do any good hitting him," she said. "I know," he replied, *"but it will make me feel better."* With a hand over my mouth to muffle my gasp, these were the same words that had been predicted days before: "It will make me feel better."

I heard my brother enter the house around 3:00 AM. My father, still awake, raced down the stairs in one swift motion. I followed him as fast as I could. The two were facing off, with the kitchen table being a small barrier. I jumped on my Dad's back, and he flung me across the kitchen floor. But it was enough diversion for my brother to flee and fly up the stairs. My father, his face red with rage, shot me a look that let me know I was next. While he was attempting to break down my brother's bedroom door, my mother was making her way to the kitchen. With a voice so calm that it surprised me, I stood my ground, "It stops now — no more of this. You've abused us long enough. It's over. It ends tonight."

"Oh really?" she managed, "and what are you going to do about it?" With resolve, I lifted the phone off the hook — the dial tone seemingly louder than usual, almost beckoning me to silence it, "I know who to call." I rattled off the number that I had put to memory. "Shall I make the call?" In a whisper, she said no and fainted.

At that moment, I realized that my superpower was standing up for others. My counselor guided me to see what I didn't want to grasp. Although up to that point, I thought that my parents could do no wrong and that I could do nothing right, I learned that we all need a little 'fixing.' My parents had a profound impact on me. Discovering my 'self' was the next step, and that growth is ever-evolving.

Writing this chapter has been a part of that discovery. These two thousand-plus words aren't meant to air dirty laundry but instead to provide hope to those of us who have been bullied, used, and/or abused. This chapter is for you and me.

Three decades after the incident around the kitchen table, my mother and I had a deep talk through tears and pain. Her validation wasn't nearly as sweet as the veil lifted to reveal a new resolve. I made a promise to myself to never become jaded and to always be there for others. Sadly, my father and I didn't have a talk before his passing.

I chose to have a life, and it has been anything but easy. There are going to be times when you want to give up because it is hard, because of the negative voices in your head, or because you doubt your own self-worth. Persevere. It is worth doing, even if it is challenging. You matter. Be brave! You can stop the patterns from your youth. There are people who can help. Reach out and learn to live, love, and take back your life. Be kind first, and take a moment to give. With compassion and understanding, we can impact our own lives and the lives of others.

Ignite Action Steps

1. Ask yourself if your reactions are how you are feeling in the moment or if they are residuals from the past. Learn how to recognize the difference between the two.

2. Be yourself and not what someone else puts upon you. Follow *your* heart.

3. Learn to recognize the signs of abusive behavior. Help where you can, offer a hotline number, listen, ask caring questions, show empathy, and be supportive.

Ann M. B. McIntyre — United States of America
Artist, Creative, Designer, Author
arlegacyart.com
arlegacyart

Jennifer Pascoa

"We are placed in the throes of the unimaginable because our stories are designed to become the survival guide for someone else."

My hope is that by reading my story, you'll come to know you aren't alone, no matter what you are experiencing. Struggle and suffering are not your enemies. If you fight against the battle, the battle wins. Moving with the ebb and flow of the pain, and eventually through it, helps you find the other side of it. I promise you there is that 'other side!' But the only way is to persevere. Go with bravery, even if it means some ugly crying along the way.

A Mosaic of Threads

The theme of my story isn't original. I'm not the only woman who has experienced what I have. Millions of women have been in the same scenario. I always say I'm nobody special, but I can't do that anymore. We are all here on purpose for a purpose that is greater than ourselves. It's no mistake that we have endured the riptide of grief because our stories are designed to become the survival guide for someone else. We are placed in the throes of the unimaginable so that when we come out the other side, we can help someone else who is going through it, too.

My story is special because it's mine: filled with twists and turns, the roller coaster, the ashes turned beauty, the reckoning after the decimation, and how everything was woven into a harmonious mosaic by threads I did not see at the time. It's the lost and found: being tossed aside, left behind, then picked up, and placed somewhere else where I could be found. What I learned, though, is that I wasn't lost at all. I just hadn't been found…*yet*.

CRASH.

"Do you know what's going on between your husband and my wife?" he asked on the other end of the line. "Maybe you'd better sit down." Everything I knew to be true about myself and my husband was gone with one simple phone call. Slow motion set in. I was outside my body, listening to the conversation with *her* husband, and my world spiraled in all directions around me. I was in the garage, sitting on a crate. It was a Friday afternoon in October, and I shivered but not because of the chill in the air. Adrenaline flooded my soul; my heart raced so fast it took my breath away. Her husband read me the emails he'd exchanged with my husband. My husband denied it, of course, even though the truth was obvious. The phone call lasted less than ten minutes, and I had no idea that life could *crash* so quickly.

I sat in the garage after the phone call ended for what felt like hours, but only minutes passed. I had to pull myself together because just inside the house, the walls rang with laughter from my assistant and the daycare children whom I cared for in my home. I could hear the playful giggling of my toddler playing with her friends. My daughter was blissfully unaware of the breakdown I was in. Grace was only two and a half years old, and her life was also about to break. *How would I hold my emotions when my soul was screaming?* In a zombie-like state, I walked back inside, and my assistant knew something was wrong. I could barely get the words out, and all she could do was wrap me in her arms.

My husband would be home in a few hours. *Had he been with her while telling me he was working?* Probably, based on the evidence in the emails. *Had he driven two hours from our home while she drove three hours to meet in that spot?* Maybe. Or maybe they rendezvoused somewhere close by. It didn't matter. He was coming home soon, and I had to figure out what to do. I left my assistant in the daycare downstairs and went upstairs. Grace wanted to come with me, but I convinced her to stay with her friends. She's an old soul. She had a look on her face that told me she knew something was different with her mom.

The afternoon whirled by, the daycare children got picked up, and my assistant went home. Grace, my heart and soul, my safe space, my 'why' for having my life, needed me to be her mom. When my husband finally came home, my emotions were so raw that all I could do was be stoic, sitting on the couch while he tried to sit next to me. The only thought in my head was to keep hold of myself, or my behavior might cause some unwanted legal problems. I did not know how I could think so rationally, but not looking at him, not speaking to him except in one or two-word answers, and not acknowledging his presence in our home while my entire foundation was crumbling was all I could muster.

I processed the chaos as best I could. My mind tried hard to understand what was happening, *but it made no sense.* There had been no signs. *Or were there?* Nothing had happened that would lead me to believe I would get a phone call like that. *Had I missed what now seemed obvious?* My mind was whirling, and in my confused state of disbelief, I started to take responsibility for his actions. I made his betrayal *my* fault. *I must have done something that made him do this.* I kept asking myself. *What did I do?* I didn't know, but I convinced myself I did 'something' bad. Guilt showed up, and so did remorse and shame. I desperately wanted to apologize for my actions, unclear of what they even were.

It took a few days, but I was finally ready to talk about the phone call I'd received. I asked a neighborhood friend to play with Grace while my husband and I went for a walk. I told him about the phone call I received and about the email exchange. I told him I knew about *her*. He told me there was nothing to know because nothing had happened. I asked him what I did to cause him to step outside our marriage, and he denied any wrongdoing. My guilt increased, fed by his words of denial and anger. It felt as if it was all my fault. I still didn't know what I had done, but whatever I did, the damage was irreparable.

Weeks went by, and our marriage was broken. He left early and came home late. We barely spoke, and it was terse and tense when we did. Our love was sand slipping through my fingers. I tried desperately to hang onto it, but the tighter I held, the more he let go of me. My father had passed away a year prior, and now I was losing my husband. Inertia was laughing at me as it sped forward, and I was powerless. He made plans to move out but didn't share those plans with me, only that he was leaving. Then, two months after I received that fateful phone call from her husband and twelve days before Christmas, a U-Haul™ was parked in our driveway, and he began to empty the house of his things. He closed the front door and left me in *our* home, where I thought we'd be forever. I was tossed aside into my new life, a life I didn't want and hadn't asked for.

SHATTER.

Grace was deeply confused. She knew her world was suddenly different, that Daddy wasn't home anymore. She saw her mom howling in the agony of the shattering, and her tiny mind couldn't understand how her world would be forever shaken. All she could do was cry with me.

Life began to ebb and flow in a way I could not wrap my head around. Grace was going between two houses, being picked up and dropped off constantly. A new language formed of being parents together but not being together. The woman had left her husband and now was with mine. He became someone I didn't know. Twenty-one years we'd been together, and the colors he showed me weren't those of the man I'd been in love with. The animosity. The rage. The yelling. The lies. The threats. The name-calling. "You're stupid." "You're so retarded." "I'm going to take our daughter away." "You're selfish." "You only care about yourself." My new life became surviving with delusions of getting back together, telling him I'll do better, and convincing him that it'll be different and that I wanted him to return. Throughout our interactions, hatred was spewed at me; I was called horrendous names and yelled at from the street for all the neighbors to hear, with Grace standing beside me. Every day, I felt my life being shattered into pieces that were even smaller than the ones that had already been broken.

I remember being curled up on my knees with my head on the hard, cold tile floor in the downstairs kitchen and sobbing so violently that the tiles would surely break. I remember being huddled up against the bathroom cabinets and wishing I could pour myself into the pipes under the sink so I could flow with the water from the taps and the pain would wash away. I remember so needing the warmth of a father and curling up into the arms of someone else's dad because I didn't have mine. I remember the only day I ever asked someone to take care of my toddler because I had no emotional or physical capabilities to ensure her safety. The pain consumed all of me. It was eating me from the deepest part of my core, and I was no longer me but simply a shell. Something had to change because if I stayed on this path, I surely wouldn't make it.

CHANGE.

In the months after he left, I was drowning in grief and trauma, shattered and broken beyond repair with his hateful words ringing in my head and my self-worth destroyed. I longed for peace. I was still in our marital home running my daycare business. Grace's presence gave me a reason to get up every day, but I desperately wanted to feel rested. The home's walls enveloped me, the home we'd made our life in, and I was engulfed by all the memories. Being in the neighborhood surrounded by people I thought were friends but who chose sides only reminded me of what more had been taken from me. I was constantly afraid of being in his presence when I didn't know who he would be that day, and I always wondered what he said about me to others. Being in the primal state of needing to protect Grace from the trauma only added to the chronic stress. My existence was ebbing away. I wanted to run away and go where we knew no one, and no one knew us.

There is a valley on the other side of two mountain passes that we'd been visiting for years, and it always felt like home. We'd dreamed of what life would be like when we lived there together one day. While I knew I wouldn't be making the move with him, I needed a new life for Grace and me. My faith led me to my knees with my hands up, begging for mercy, grace, and direction. *God, what would you have us do? Where do we go? Do we stay here or do we leave?*

I started researching communities in different areas and eventually settled on a city I knew would be perfect for us to start over. Although it felt like magic, God's grace and hand sold our marital home in ten weeks. I found a place to live, a preschool with an opening for Grace, a church, and a job. The pieces came together so quickly and seamlessly that I knew with a deep, fierce, and unrelenting knowing that I was doing the right thing. God was putting the fragments of my life together, and all I had to do was say *okay*. There I was, standing on the edge of a cliff to take the leap of faith, and there was no other option except to go. There was no promise of a soft landing, but I felt hope and a tinge of excitement for the first time since he'd moved out! I thought we just might be okay! I regained some inner strength, which felt good, and I wanted more of it! Some of the weight lifted off my soul, and I discovered the peace I'd longed for in its place.

Two months later, the moving truck pulled into the driveway, and my heaven-sent team of angels emptied the home that I thought I would be in forever. They lovingly packed up the seven-ton moving truck full of our furniture, hopes, and dreams, and we drove away from the life that was taken from us. It was December, five days before Christmas, and only one year since my husband had a moving truck of his own. I was weighed down in my inner storm AND an actual snowstorm as we drove over two mountain passes. The wind yelled. Snow littered the roads eight feet high on the sides, and the beautiful trees glistened with winter. Grace, singing and playing in her car seat, was excited to be on a wild adventure! The back of my car was so full I couldn't see out the window, but I didn't want to look backward, only forwards. The fog was dense, and I couldn't see twenty feet in front of me.

With eighty-seven kilometers to go (because that's what the sign told me), we pulled over and got out on the side of the highway to take a picture. We had come so far in that snowstorm, in a *life*-storm, and our new life was a mere eighty-seven kilometers away! My soul was electric with the intense excitement of a new beginning. The storm wasn't over yet. We still had the hardest part of the drive to endure: the summit of the second mountain pass.

That summit is notorious for its bad weather. Even in the summer, when temperatures can reach 100 degrees Fahrenheit, the summit holds true to its reputation. I'd driven these mountains many times over the years so I wasn't afraid, but my body was wracked with nerves anyway. For the remaining eighty-seven kilometers, Grace and I were quiet. Slow and steady, white-knuckled and praying to God for Him to drive the car with me, we meandered along the highway to the summit through a blanket of fog and snow. I couldn't even cry because my emotions were buried too deep while we drove. I knew we'd make it, though. We had no choice! If we wanted to get to the other side of the summit, the only way to do it was to go through it. *Isn't that true of storms?* Sometimes, they pass on their own while we are still; other times, we must forge through them to find the sunshine on the other side. I had all I needed: Grace; she had saved me through the *crash, shattering,* and *change*. Without her, I'm confident I wouldn't have made it.

Finally, we passed through the summit! Slowly, surely, and with a newfound confidence I didn't know I had, the summit became a part of the rearview mirror, and the descent down the mountain to our new life began. With each kilometer down, the fog lifted, the snow slowed, and the wind silenced. The storm settled. My soul relaxed, and my breath filled my lungs again. I started to feel a rush of something in my body I didn't recognize! I felt alive again! I'd become so used to being in the darkness that I wasn't used to the light, but I felt it!

As we descended the mountain, the light got brighter. It greeted us and welcomed us to our new life! At the bottom, I realized that not only was the sun peeking through the clouds, but the light was igniting my soul! At the foot of the mountain was the glorious lake I longed to live by for years, and we pulled over at the lookout point. We got out of the car with the sun pouring out of the afternoon sky. I took Grace by her hand and said, "We're home." I cried as many tears as I had for the past year, but this time, they weren't from pain but a triumphant feeling of joy! I had made it, and the impact of all I'd been through helped me find myself again.

Our lives are a tapestry, a mosaic of threads woven together. When the storm engulfs us, when the mud drags us down, when we gasp for breath despite the air around us, and when we long for the earth to swallow us whole—those are the moments that plant us. We aren't buried. It might feel like it, but we aren't! We are planted! A reckoning happens when we move through the pain and find ourselves. It's in those very moments that the ashes become beautiful. The *crash* is temporary, and the *shattering* is followed by picking up the piece and putting it all together. Everything is made new.

Ignite Action Steps

Grief is chronic. It doesn't go away. We learn to move forward with it rather than moving on. The waves will continue to crash, but we learn to move with the waves rather than fighting them. The days and nights can feel endless, so be gentle with yourself. Treat yourself with care and grace; give yourself time and patience. A hot cup of tea and a soft blanket often help.

Find someone to help you, whether another adult, friend, counselor, or parent. Find someone who will let you tell your story to them repeatedly. Talking about the situation and your feelings is a release! It's healing, even if it doesn't feel like it at the moment.

Finding a new hobby or new activity is incredibly freeing. Go back to activities you let go of that you had once loved. You don't have to move away physically! Or maybe this is your opportunity to have a fresh start in another place.

Be with people who bring you joy and make you feel you are valuable. For me, it was Grace. Being in a community is vital. Find those who lift you, listen, and love you no matter what.

Jennifer Pascoa — Canada
✉ *pascoajennifer@gmail.com*
f *Jennifer Pascoa*
⊙ *jenniferpascoa_sharpenyourfinances*

Summer Bozohora

SUMMER BOZOHORA

"Our children are our greatest gifts and our master teachers."

It is my intention this story stirs your soul and ignites faith in you that everything in life is in service to a higher purpose. I hope you feel this truth, not just think you are an integral thread of the Universal Tapestry and its purpose. My writing is meant to serve as a bright emergency flare, illuminating your path like a guide for a traveler who has lost their way. May it inspire an implicit trust in a higher purpose that brings everything in your life into a divine, perhaps even magical, life-giving perspective.

RELATIONSHIPS ARE ASSIGNMENTS

There is a saying that goes something like, *"Your children are your greatest gift from God."* Yet, despite our best efforts at raising them, our sons and daughters can seem to cause us the greatest stress and, at times, the most pain.

Why, then, does the greatest gift come with such stress and pain?

My journey to finding the answer to this question began on a very specific day in one of the most unexpected and unforeseeable ways. It was a day nothing could have prepared me for. Despite my age– fifty-one– and the unique and challenging experiences I had resiliently arisen from, I was not prepared for THIS day. It was the day I found myself standing in a doorway through which I would then pass into a wasteland of despair, disbelief, confusion, and loss.

I was standing on the landing below the entrance to the kitchen of my ex-husband's house and had come seeking support to help me with the undeniable pain and grief I was experiencing as I read our daughter's angry texts that I had been *'abusive.'*

It was the day my daughter, the one dear soul I had spent the last sixteen years raising — primarily on my own — and whom I loved more than anything, would enter a portal of her own becoming, her own strength, her own truth. And it would not include me.

I came seeking his support because he was both my daughter's father and my friend. Together, we successfully divorced without lawyers. Initially, we had lawyers because that's what you do, but eventually, we got so frustrated with them, fired them, and found our way together using a mediator and notary instead. For the last ten years, we've been successfully co-parenting. All of a sudden, everything felt like a shipwreck, and I was drowning.

Having visited his house many times to eat dinner, play cards, and enjoy birthdays and Christmas celebrations, I had no reason to believe this was the last day I would ever enter it. As I came in, he greeted me coldly and abruptly, his six-foot frame standing on a landing three stairs above me. My world spun in confusion, and my knees were like Jello™. I was gagging on my own tongue while I looked up at my friend and also my ex-husband, sobbing and hyperventilating out of desperation and confusion about my daughter's accusations that left me in utter disbelief.

As I fettered a whelp crying out for my daughter, who was at home with him, he looked down at me with his arms crossed and said, "Get out!" As her Dad ushered me out of the doorway, I was stunned and confused. I couldn't breathe; it was as if my breath had been completely drawn out of my lungs like I were vacuum-packed.

After he closed the door behind me, I stood on the porch outside and imagined it was a bridge from which I could plunge myself into the river. In that moment, I understood how someone could have the urge to take their own life and end the unbearable pain and confusion this world can bring us to face.

Devastated, I felt an unbearable anxiety rise within me. I felt as if I were dying. I felt lost and utterly hopeless. That day and the events that unfolded since led to a year and a half of *'estrangement'* from both my ex-husband and my daughter. I learned later it is what professionals call *'parental alienation.'* I reached out to a variety of professionals — including dear friends who were family counselors — made appointments with psychologists and intuitives and hired a mediator.

Honestly, I thought I could easily figure out the conflict's cause. I had resources. I had much of the same education and therapeutic training as many of the professionals I sought help from. I thought I was a good parent and a forward thinker, and I earned my livelihood and life path by helping others navigate extreme storms in their lives. And, mistakenly, I thought this challenge would take skill and that it would be smoother sailing toward reconciliation than it was.

What I realized was that this voyage was a little different. I found myself adrift in unfamiliar waters, and the wind had been taken out of my sails. With egotistical self-righteousness, I focused on the stormy seas my daughter seemed to bring with her and how she did not navigate them the way I would.

As I was the 'captain' of the family ship, I believed my daughter should listen to reason — to what I thought was reasonable. Not many would argue with me that parents want their children to listen, if not 'obey' them. It makes sense. Young children lack the basic skills to navigate busy roads or sharp kitchen utensils. Beyond the toddler years, there are tough times and dangers in life we want to protect our children from: drugs, violence, crisis, unexpected death, family conflict, accidents, and illness. That's what I was brought up thinking.

Becoming angry, annoyed, or frustrated with a teenager who either doesn't listen or seems disrespectful or ungrateful is not uncommon. On the other hand, and equally true, when children reach their teenage years, they are intensely frustrated with their parents who do not listen to or understand them.

Let's just say by the time my daughter was fifteen, she was less and less receptive to my point of view. I wasn't that receptive to hers either. I had a lot of judgments about her behavior. Little did I know how heartbreaking and hurtful something I said had been in an argument during our last New Year together. It was her sixteenth birthday, and something I said sent her into despair. Any attempts I made at a deeper communication or connection afterward failed. I hadn't realized it, but she had jumped ship and began treading the stormy seas of resentment. She distanced herself and went to live with her Dad. In the following months, we spent some time together, but as unresolved pain and conflict goes, it leaks into new situations. I can look back and see how it culminated on that painful day.

In the days after the excommunication from the doorway of my old life, my daughter did try to communicate with me. She sent long accusatory texts, and, admittedly, I would respond in kind. I didn't realize she was drowning, screaming, reaching out for a lifeboat, and I didn't offer her one. I was so focused on telling her to get back on the ill-captained ship that she just blocked me, shutting me out completely. She got a new phone and a new phone number; I was completely disconnected.

Of course, I tried to rationalize with my ex-husband through email. I was often aghast at his answers to my pleas and, more often, at his lack of response. Despite being completely engulfed in a fog of panic, at times, I was aware enough to realize I was actually so desperate I was manipulative. Clinically speaking, some would say I was 'anxiously attached.'

Eventually, I got the insight to hire a mediator, and he contacted my ex-husband directly. It worked, sort of. Hearing my daughter's complaints and her long list of ways I had failed her made me even more desperate. It was as if I was her enemy, the one who undermined her or deliberately caused her pain. I could only reel in shock and disbelief. After two exhausting conflict-reinforcing sessions, my ex-husband was overwhelmed, and my daughter was even more justified in her rage.

As a facilitator of communication strategies and relationship dynamics myself, I realized the mediator may not have known how to navigate the seas he found himself in. Ours was a fleet of ships filled with unique, 'neurodivergent' minds and highly purposeful souls that collided under a culmination of unusual stressors. It was at that moment, I set my ship in reverse to back out to gain perspective. Disengaging the mediator's services, I realized I had the tools and the skills to navigate our families' collision; I just needed to apply them!

During our three-way collision, the shock wave sent off a signal and opened new pathways for us all. Parallel to the devastation, a new soul-led partnership simultaneously entered my life. Dre and I found ourselves continuously crossing paths, meeting each other in shared social circles. He was over a decade younger than me, so I often ignored his subtle advances, but as time elapsed, we had some meaningful conversations. In one of our first phone chats, he asked me a question, which was also a lesson he learned as he navigated his relationships with his siblings: *"Do you want to be right, or do you want to be connected?"*

As Marianne Williamson says, "Every relationship, every situation is part of a divinely created and highly specific curriculum for your soul growth." It now appears, in hindsight, that I was given three very important and overlapping assignments: my daughter, her father, and Dre. Together, they created a specific curriculum that reconnected me steadfastly to my soul, God, and Love and ultimately deepened my authentic path of service.

Some miraculous sequence of events led all of us — my daughter, her boyfriend, my ex-husband, Dre, and I — to celebrate my birthday over dinner. I was relieved and elated. Shortly after our dinner, my daughter and ex exited my life again.

Another year passed. Although at times it was agonizing, I slipped into trusting the universal design of my life, I learned patience, acceptance, and a profound new level of trust and love. I waited for this new sense of peace within me to show itself in the world by giving me an opportunity to test my new resolve. That day came. My daughter called me to tell me her dad was in the hospital; he had had a stroke. I immediately went to visit. I recall the day clearly. As I walked into his room, he was with a rehab nurse, barely able to stand and shaking to hold himself up. I must have appeared concerned because I remember him saying, "It's okay, Summer, I'm okay."

The nurse questioned me, "Who are you?" I replied, "I am the mother of his daughter, his ex-wife, and his friend." My response seemed to satisfy her. As he lay back in his bed, he reached out his hand, and with what strength he had, he pulled me in for a hug. For the very first time, I saw him cry. He thanked me for being there despite the trials of the last two years. His gratitude was palpable, and in my heart, I thanked God for the time I had to embody my answer to the question Dre had posed to me: *Do you want to be right, or do you want to be connected?"*

After her father's stroke, my daughter moved out of his home, wishing to individuate and initiate herself into her own life. She separated from him, from both of us. Without explanation or warning, she left and moved to another town. He was devastated, and I was astonished. Although all 'relation-*ships'* are sacred, I do believe the assignment children are given regarding their parents is unique, holding the potential to dissolve ancestral lineages and bring about a profound transformation of consciousness.

Although we had not seen it then, my daughter had gifted her Dad with the same opportunity I had: to evolve. Six months after she moved away, she and I started conversing via Facebook Messenger™. There seemed to be some development in our 'relation-*ship'*, and she shared more of her life experience with me. Some things became clearer, and I thought we were making good progress. That is, until she blocked me again!

Abrupt disconnection is always shocking. This time, however, felt very different. I had learned to steer my ship around inner obstacles of self-doubt and recrimination with great adeptness. My 'relation-*ship*' with Dre and our shared knowledge was a well-made chest full of divinely-timed treasures that elevated my skills. It allowed me to master my anxiety and reset my tongue as a powerful rudder to navigate high-stakes relationships. I easily honored my daughter's need for space. My ship had gained new sails with a consistent wind of self-respect and inner peace. I *had* turned a corner.

A couple of months later, my daughter sent me a little message about my favorite chocolates, of all things. The gesture was meaningful; it indicated she had also shifted course. I sent her a little emoji response without any further dialogue, and a couple of weeks later, she sent some photos of what she was up to. I let her know how much I appreciated the pictures and being a part of her life, and she expressed her desire to have me in her life, also. She said she "missed my mom," using the word *mom* for the time in two years. With patience and honest dialogue and through the power and wisdom of Conscious Communication — derived from Non-Violent Communication — my daughter and I ended up spending a blissful day together. It was the fourth anniversary of the moment that had set her painfully adrift.

The voyage of estrangement is a painful, psychological, emotional, and spiritual trauma, a longer-than-necessary, drawn-out, unresolved triggered state between people. Although these prolonged traumas can come in many forms, I know that they stem from a distorted view of our relationships with Self, Source, and others.

What my daughter has taught me is this: *Our children are our greatest gifts, as well as our master teachers.* The greatest gifts come with the most stress or pain because, with every birth, there is a force, in essence, a trauma that transitions us from one way of being to another. Relationships inspire transformation; they are a transitional force of great impact that pushes us to emerge into a new, more aligned path. Relationships are assignments; both parties are sacred mirrors. Souls are drawn together with those who can teach us the most, allowing us to evolve and embrace the wisdom of our own souls. Our children are the greatest gifts from God.

If you are facing a difficult situation, you may want to ask yourself this question: *Do you want to be right, or do you want to be connected? Connection* is the gift we receive when we learn to *trust* that our life is in service to a higher purpose and give up what we thought relationships were supposed to be. In order to experience the deepest form of love, we need to accept, honor, and trust that 'relation-*ships*', specifically with our children, have a sacred purpose that is an essential part of God's beautiful, divine, interpersonal tapestry.

Ignite Action Steps

- Research communication strategies such as Authentic Relating or Non-Violent Communication.

- Read books or listen to podcasts about relationships, triggers, estrangement, or living an authentic life. Podcasts are some of the best places to find very powerful forward-thinking education. Look for unique, experiential healing therapies, courses, or programs on emotional mastery, communication, or family dynamics. I highly recommend looking for a well-designed, community-based course or program. Family Constellations is an engaging and insightful option.

- If you are looking for a mediator, I highly recommend looking for one with in-depth knowledge and application of non-violent communication and/or conscious communication, which overlaps with the wisdom of positive intelligence. Let go and be willing to ask for help.

Summer Bozohoura — Canada
Author, Speaker, Soulful Educator, & Relationship Alchemist
courses.mindbodymedicinetherapy.com
summerbozohora
getresourced

Marion Andrews

Marion Andrews

"True healing begins in the spirit and radiates outward in a physical form."

This story is for you. It is a story of hope, gratitude, and healing. You may face some things in your life that bring you to the point of feeling helpless. My desire is that this story will show you that you can survive, thrive, and experience a whole new, empowered life.

A Spiritual Journey of Survival and Transformation

It started with a strange feeling in my stomach, a pain but more like an ache or cramping. I felt off, just not quite right. Then there was this whooshing noise in my abdomen, so loud, like Niagara Falls. I could physically see it undulating like something moving in there. I was very concerned because my stomach never usually grumbled from hunger.

I went to my family doctor, who suggested it might be an ulcer. He prescribed a change in my diet, tests, medications, and more tests. Nothing we tried made any difference. Then, I began to vomit after eating. I hate vomiting and was seriously worried. That had me going back to my doctor. Nearly six months had elapsed by this time. Fortunately, I was working from home, so when the pain became unbearable, I could just lie down. I knew there was something wrong and trusted my instincts. Finally, the doctor ordered an endoscopy, but it revealed nothing.

I then went to a specialist who wanted to do a colonoscopy to check for colon cancer, but I just didn't see the point. Colon cancer was so low on my list of possible options. I am the youngest of eight children and have a very large extended family. There has never been a case of colon cancer with any of my relatives. My last test, two and a half years prior, showed nothing unusual in my intestines; no polyps, sores, or anything unusual. However, my primary care physician insisted that a more thorough examination was the next logical step since nothing was conclusive. With much resistance, I finally agreed to the test.

My friend drove me to the local clinic. I was annoyed and grumbling. It felt like such a waste of time. On the way there, I excitedly discussed where we would go to eat after the test. I just wanted it to be over so that I could enjoy a tasty breakfast of belgian waffles with whipped cream and fresh, juicy strawberries. It was strawberry season in my area, and I was looking forward to the taste and a foamy latte to top it all off.

The doctor was waiting for me, capped and gowned, and the nurse got me settled and prepared to inject the drug to make me drowsy. As she came near, she dropped the syringe onto the floor, and it rolled away. Ready or not, the doctor began the colonoscopy, and a TV screen near my head showed the procedure. I saw the tube with the camera moving inside of me. I saw lovely pink tissue, which I *thought* was perfectly healthy, and nothing was wrong with me. When the nurse was finally able to administer the drug, I began to feel woozy. That's when I saw an ugly, dark sore on the TV screen. *Oh,* I thought, *that's awful.* I then saw the doctor snipping some tissue from it using his probe. My last thought before I went to sleep was, *Yuck, why is he cutting pieces of that off?*

When the doctor came in to give me the results, my head was still very fuzzy. He quietly told me that there was a sizable mass in my ascending colon. In my drugged state, I didn't understand what he was saying. I smiled and said, "Great, thank you." He told me that I would need an immediate CT scan and that his office would be calling me with the time and place that afternoon. I smiled and said, "Thanks! Thanks," not fully understanding what he had shared with me.

I went in for the colonoscopy with the firm conviction that it was pointless. My previous colonoscopies had always been clean and clear. I always took good care of my health. All the fuss over getting a CT scan was not registering in my drugged-induced mind at that point. I quickly dressed and raced to the restaurant for my yummy waffle breakfast.

While at the restaurant, I got a frantic call from my husband saying our Primary Care Physician (PCP) had called and left a message for me to call him back A.S.A.P. I assured my husband I would call the doctor when the office opened. When I eventually talked with our doctor, it hit me that this might be serious. He began by saying that I would most likely need surgery, and soon! The doctor asked if I wanted him to start the process of scheduling an appointment with a surgeon. I started to feel worried, wondering whether this might be cancer, and asked my doctor for his professional opinion of my case. He was very frank, saying they wouldn't know for sure until the tests were back, but in his experience, there was an extremely high chance that I had colon cancer.

Whoa! That news hit me like a ton of bricks. The fact that our doctor was fast-tracking my appointment was terrifying. I was shocked. It is hard to describe the emotions that surged through my body from head to toe. Even more shocking was him booking my appointment with the surgeon for the coming Wednesday. That was only four days away!

The next few days were tense. I refused to admit that it was cancer until I had the results, but that little nagging voice inside my head was saying, *you know it is*.

My husband accompanied me to the surgeon's office. This was a first for him, as he tends to panic easily and considers every negative scenario possible. He calls it being prepared. I find it unnerving. We approached the appointment with a great deal of anticipation and dread. The surgeon was straightforward and kind, discussing possible scenarios and speaking frankly. I appreciated his candor as I am the type of person who likes the facts and information laid out. I need to know what is what, and then I can deal with it. The reports of the biopsy samples from the colonoscopy have not been returned yet. I was trying to keep things low-key for my husband's sake. Some of my attention was on facing the situation head-on, while the rest of me was trying to keep my husband calm. Concentrating on him distracted me from thinking about what I intuitively knew were the results.

As we were about to leave, the surgeon checked again to see if the results were in. Yes, the report was there. Yes, it was a tumor about 4 cm wide and was *malignant*. Until I heard that word conclusively, I still clung to the hope that it was all a big mistake. But the actual words, *malignant, cancer*, hit me like an eighteen-wheeler. *Whoosh!* It was as if all the air had been sucked out of me. I could scarcely breathe. I have no idea what my husband was feeling or how he was reacting. My focus was now 100 percent on me! Yet, I didn't want to deal with it. I grabbed my stuff and left there as quickly as possible.

Cancer! The Big "C." This was a word that I *never* thought I'd hear applied to me. I had mammograms, colonoscopies, and regular tests. I was healthy. Yet here it was: *Loud, Intrusive, Unexpected, Unwanted*, and many more words came to mind. All I could think of was, *What's next?* Before I knew it, my surgery was scheduled within the week.

While lying in the hospital, I had time to think, asking my spirit and my heart many questions. When I was younger, I was a deeply spiritual *being*. I had to remind myself of that person, reconnect with them, and trust my deepest thoughts. I have always had a glass-half-full attitude and looked at everything that happened as a way of learning and growing. In profound self-reflection, I saw how much my life had been filled with 'being busy' and that I had been on the path of least resistance, ignoring spirituality. To my dismay, I realized that I had spent the last twenty-five years drifting. I was floating along, no longer seeking my purpose. I had buried and suppressed so much.

I knew in my heart and have said it a million times: *Thoughts are things; guard yours carefully*. Yet here I was, ignoring my inner being. I took myself back to that young person and knew this was a pivotal moment for my soul. I asked myself, *Was this it? Was I going to die soon?* The answer I heard in my heart was NO.

Should I take chemotherapy and hope to rebuild my life? I had watched as chemo ravaged other friends and swore that I would never take it. Putting poison into my body to kill the cancer cells and a lot of the healthy cells (collateral damage is the term) was *not* something I wanted to do *ever*! But, and it's a big *but*, when the time came to face my opinion of chemo to save my own life, things looked a little different. The doctors gave me the stats based on the diagnosis: colon cancer that had already metastasized to some lymph nodes. I had a 20 percent chance of surviving a year with no treatment and an 80 percent chance of being alive in five years with it. I didn't like those first odds; I had so much more life to live. Without hesitation, my spirit said, *YES, let's do this*.

Chemotherapy is hard. It is very difficult, challenging, and exhausting, and it takes every bit of fortitude to get through it. After surgery, I began six months of chemo, which meant every two weeks, I was at the cancer clinic for a five-hour infusion, then home with a pump to continue for another forty-two hours. I suffered almost every single side effect that I had heard about.

I had sore feet and sore hands and lost my hair. But in facing those various trials, I also looked for the little glimmers of joy. I tried to find something to be grateful for every day. I knew I might not make it through if I gave in to the nasty feelings.

Deep within my heart, I knew I had been given an amazing opportunity to live and learn. Through the calm and quiet of meditation, my purpose became clear. I understood I could help people overcome their difficult issues and discover a more spiritual path to life. I knew that this experience was the catalyst for awakening the teacher and healer in me to help others grow more spiritually.

When the chemo was done, I had another CT scan. That scan was clear. *I was free of cancer.* The next directions were to go home, start living again, and come back in a year. The only follow-up I did was a colonoscopy about six months later, and it was perfect. I had my infusion port removed because I wasn't going to need it anymore. It had been a constant reminder of the previous year's trials and tribulations. I thought I was cured.

After the follow-up CT the next year, I went to the doctor expecting positive results. In my mind, nothing had changed, and there was nothing wrong. To my surprise, this wasn't the case. Some cancer had spread to different lymph nodes in a different area of my abdomen. *Okay, chemotherapy had worked before, so let's do it again.* The regimen restarted six months every two weeks at the cancer clinic. Strangely, it was familiar and comforting. I was so busy finding ways to heal physically that I let my spiritual practice become mundane. My deepest belief is that the body reflects the illnesses of the spirit, which is why I started trying to become more spiritual. I thought I was on the right track. *So why was I back here, doing this all over again?*

Wake up, call number two! I doubled down on my spiritual practice every morning, which soon became routine. I meditated, chose an Angel card, and recited positive affirmations. I was trying to do everything that I believed would make me cancer-free. Another year went by, and another cancer showed up. In the treatment of this one, my body rebelled in different ways. I had a staph infection in my port and a twisted bowel that kept me in the hospital for ten days, near death. Many things showed up in my body that indicated that I was not yet on the right path. I had radiation, and that appeared to have killed any cancer cells that had escaped the chemo. Again, I was told that I was cancer-free.

Over the next five years, each scan every three months was clear. I celebrated my five-year anniversary on April 10th, 2022. I was ecstatic. According to the hospitals, the research, and every indicator that keeps track of this, *I was now absolutely cured.* Yay!

Just two weeks later, I went for the usual CT scan. I told everyone I met that I had just made the huge landmark of five years cancer-free. Each person at the hospital was delighted, and strangers high-fived me. A week later, I was at the clinic for the results. As I sat in the doctor's office waiting, I felt an uneasiness — my instincts were on high alert. My doctor's face was serious as she entered. *Oh no,* I thought, *it can't be....* The news was there was a very large cancer growing again. *What??? Wait!* I had just celebrated five years clean and clear. I thought I was done with this disease. Talk about shock and dismay. *NOOOOOO!* I screamed in my head. A new tumor had grown around a main vein, squeezing it until it was no longer working. Through the amazing miracle of the human body, the small essential veins around it took over and did the work of the main vein. I couldn't have any surgery in that area as it was too risky. The next step was nine months of chemo. That was the hardest of all, the chemo. I was disappointed, angry and upset. *Why did I deserve this again?!*

That was a turning point. This time, I was going to get better and stay better. I knew I needed to make some changes, which needed to be *bold, drastic,* and *impactful. How would I start?* My thoughts turned to, *Okay, what am I supposed to learn now? What is this going to teach me?* I accessed everything I had in my spiritual toolbox. I began meditating, journaling, and studying about angels. I received Reiki, a healing energy, from my friends and gave it to myself daily. In meditation, I listened to my inner spirit and the angels surrounding me. I heard loud and clear that I had to put my whole heart into my spiritual journey for recovery this time. I needed to be 100 percent committed. No more lip service. This time felt different. To make a life-changing impact, I knew that true healing would begin with my spirit and radiate outward in my physical form.

Every time I went for a CT scan, it showed the tumor was shrinking. That had never happened before. In fact, after nine months, it shriveled to nothing. *I am now cancer-free. Finally! I feel healthy and healed.*

This journey has profoundly changed me. I no longer see my battle with cancer as a punishment or an endless struggle. Instead, it has been the greatest teacher of my life. It taught me that healing starts within and radiates outward. The healing journey is the ultimate gift.

I now am mindful of choosing to be centered on gratitude, joy, and service. Each morning begins with spiritual practices of meditation, journaling, and connecting with the divine energies of angels and Reiki. My home and life are uncluttered, filled only with the people, energies, and objects that uplift and inspire me. My story isn't about just surviving; it's about thriving and awakening to a life filled with love, gratitude, and profound meaning.

Whether or not we acknowledge it, we manifest our experiences and environment. I invite you to start or deepen your connection with yourself and your surroundings. Remember: be present, be joyful, and above all, be grateful for *everything* you have. Life's trials may challenge us, but they also allow us to transform and live gloriously. The power of our divine spirit is limitless. Take that first step toward your own transformation and discover the miracle within.

Ignite Action Steps

- **Advocate for your body:** Trust your instincts and speak up.

- **Be grateful:** Find time to enjoy small things as they add to a glorious day.

- **Journal daily:** Release negativity, embrace positivity, cultivate gratitude.

- **Seek spiritual growth:** Explore, learn, and be open to the divine in everything and every person that appears in your life.

Marion Andrews — United States of America
Author, Speaker, Healer, Reiki Master/Teacher
marionandrews.com
shellshakers
marionauthor2020

Claire Valiquette

CLAIRE VALIQUETTE

"You have the strength inside you to make change; it requires finding your voice."

My intention is for the reader to feel inspired and supported and know they have the power to get through devastation and defeat. Many times, when you lose something so dear to your heart, you can feel hopeless and alone. You can find support and freedom for those who feel trapped and helpless. I hope my story encourages you to reach out to somebody and find the tools that are there to help. Believe that it is possible to be empowered and to overcome.

ANGEL VOICES

There I was at the age of twenty-nine, working any job I could get that paid well. I spent most of the last decade in the oilfield without formal education. Exhausted from working away from home for long periods, I needed a change. It was time to obtain a career, so I applied for college to do some upgrading.

I was excited to pursue my new education and ready for college life. A new guy crossed my path two weeks before my fresh start. He asked me out straight away, but I kept putting him off. I tried to avoid him by telling him I had no phone, but he was persistent. I was moving to a new town and had a strong inner feeling of staying away from him and not getting involved. Yet, he wore me down.

Eventually, I ignored my gut instincts and let him charm me. He was the perfect gentleman at first; he was great with kids and spoiled me. I warned him about my upcoming move to return to school, and he said he was okay with that. I thought *I wasn't going to let a guy hold me back.* But, I quickly developed a strong connection with him, and despite the seven-hour commute, we decided to try. I was falling head over heels for this man and thought I had finally met my soulmate.

The plan was that I would travel every other weekend to see him. It was the beginning of the school year, and I moved in with a longtime male friend, who was like a brother to me and his girlfriend. My friend worked in the oilfield, and I never saw him, but living with another man caused problems with my boyfriend. I started to see changes in his behavior. Initially, he was sober and a total sweetheart. But then, the mask slowly came off, and things began to go downhill. Soon, my living arrangements went sideways, and I had to find a new place. Things quickly became very stressful as I started feeling the effects of his continued verbal and mental abuse. Still, I always believed the apologies and promises he made to be better.

A month after starting school, my period was late. I took a pregnancy test, and it was positive. My heart stopped, and I felt as if everything started crumbling. I was petrified!

I was very sick throughout my pregnancy and eventually stopped traveling to see him. As he began working further away, he had no time for me. We never saw each other. I was distraught, lonely, sad, and confused. Eventually, his calls stopped.

Shortly after, I discovered I was carrying twins. I felt ecstatic yet extremely terrified at the same time. Many emotions and thoughts ran through my head like a million voices at once. *What would life be like with two babies while I finished school? What kind of father would my boyfriend be? Would he change once kids were in the picture? Would he be committed and support us? Would I be raising my children alone?* I pondered on these questions for weeks.

I was extremely sick on a daily basis but carried on, continuing my studies with my belly growing bigger and waddling around the school and my home. I found a nice, big, cozy house with lots of room and a huge backyard just for myself. Finally, I got a hold of my boyfriend on the phone, and we got into a big argument. I became distraught. I felt so frustrated and just wanted him to come home. He refused and said he was too busy. We didn't talk much in the last couple of months. I wondered if he was with someone else as I thought about breaking up with him, but I was carrying his children. Lost and uncertain, I kept trying to make it work. I just didn't know what to do.

Needing some support, I called my mom on the phone, and I mentioned that I had wet myself a few times. She laughed as a weak bladder is part of pregnancy, and I was only six months along. I was so big; I felt like a whale. I had felt slight cramping and told myself I would make a doctor's appointment the next day to get checked out. I felt something wasn't right. *What did I know? I had never been pregnant before!* That evening, I ended up going to bed. However, I did not sleep well and was very uncomfortable with cramps and leg spasms.

The following day, I had difficulty getting out of bed. After finally getting to the bathroom, I made some toast, making me nauseous. Something wasn't right, and I had to go to the hospital. I called everyone I knew, but everyone was busy at work or school and had no time to help me. Calling an ambulance was not an option as I didn't have the finances. I suddenly realized I had no one to lean on. *No one was there for me.*

In agonizing pain, I stayed in bed all day. Finally, around 4 PM, my friend picked me up and dropped me off at the emergency entrance, telling me she would return later to check on me. I was shocked that no nurse came to help as I struggled to walk to the desk. Realizing I had been having contractions, the doctor immediately hooked me up to monitors. An infection I was unaware of had caused my water to break the day before. I lay in the emergency room full of fear and confusion for a few hours, all alone, wondering what to do and what would happen next.

Suddenly, the doctor stood up, and as the words came pouring out of his mouth, my entire body trembled, and anxiety set in. "This is it; you're pushing these babies out. You're going into labor, and they need to come out now!" *Was this really happening?* I wasn't quite twenty-four weeks into my pregnancy. I called my family and boyfriend immediately to tell them the situation. Time seemed to flash before my eyes, and they were delivered. The babies were whisked away and flown to a NICU two hours away. Scared and confused, I was put to sleep for emergency surgery due to the infection.

Later that night, I woke up in the hospital without my babies, but my friend was standing at the foot of my bed. She was feeling ashamed and dismayed that she had not stayed with me. My boyfriend showed up briefly, drunk as always, and then left. I was so upset and discouraged; he just wanted to continue drinking and partying. I was going through so many emotions, feeling broken, confused, and rejected. My biggest questions: *Why am I still here, and my babies are two hours away? And why isn't their dad here with me?* That night, I rested and slept as much as I could. My parents went to the hospital to be with my babies. Even if I couldn't be there, I was relieved that my twins were not alone.

Against doctors' orders, less than twenty-four hours later, I checked myself out. I went home to pack my stuff, eager to see my twins. I wasn't supposed to be driving, but I did anyway. I wanted to see and hold my children for the first time. Although they were premature, I still expected magical moments as any first-time mom would. But that's not how things turned out.

When I got to the NICU, I was put up in a temporary wing until housing was available so I could be close to the twins. Over the next few days, Baby Girl got increasingly worse and eventually passed on day four. I was numb. That day also fell on my dad's birthday. The tears flowed like a waterfall. I ran into my father's arms, and our hearts were completely broken. Baby Boy continued to fight, gained strength over the next week, and was doing well. As the week went on, I became increasingly stressed from the control of my boyfriend, who was still hanging around. His every effort to keep me away from my sick child, not allowing me to hold or be with him when he needed me most, was incomprehensible. I felt devastated, powerless, and filled with so much anger, like my voice was not being heard. My parenting moments felt as if they were both ripped away and stifled. What should have been beautifully magical was agonizing and full of resentment.

On day ten, my boyfriend left with his family for the night so we could have some time apart. The grief and anger, among other things, were eating at the both of us. I asked the hospital staff if I could hold my boy for as long as I was able. I cuddled him the entire night, with the nurses constantly checking on him. I had not slept so peacefully like that in months. The following day, my boyfriend returned and immediately demanded to hold Baby Boy. Within a couple of hours, he passed away.

I was crushed; my heart felt like it was in a million pieces. Somehow, I found the courage to go home. While in the hospital, I missed all my final exams. I decided to pack up my things and said goodbye to the town that left me broken in pieces with no children or education. Two weeks later, I left the man who made me feel powerless and worthless.

A week after leaving him, I found work, got back on my feet, and rented my own place. I had a cute two-bedroom apartment that was cozy and set up how I liked. For company, I got myself a kitten so I wouldn't be coming home to an empty house. She was the cutest little thing with a lot of love and spunk.

Life was shifting in new ways. I was feeling free and more capable. I started fitting back into my clothes, meeting new friends, and feeling the waves of liberation and grief while establishing a normal life on my terms.

Four months had passed when the phone rang one evening, and without giving it any thought, I answered the strange number. A chill ran through my body as the person on the other end began speaking to me. "I need help. Can you come get me?" It was *him*. Little did I know I would fall into the trap again. He stayed a couple of days, making promises, acting like he wanted me back, and sweet-talking me into thinking he had changed and things would be different now. I thought to myself, *Maybe things would be different this time, now that I wasn't expecting.*

Within a few months after getting back together, I discovered I was pregnant...Again! Feeling brokenhearted, I realized I had let him weasel his way back into my life once more, and things had not changed. The psychological, emotional, and mental abuse was extreme this time. Abortion was brought up repeatedly, and even though it was not my wish, I stuck around for the remainder of my pregnancy because of the support I was receiving. I hoped this delivery would be wonderful since there was so much distress the last time. *Boy, was I wrong!*

My beautiful 'rainbow' baby was born within a year of losing his siblings. He was perfect in so many ways, but the delivery came with so much unnecessary stress and abusive behavior from my boyfriend. Unwilling to accept any more abuse, I moved back to the town where I grew up, and within weeks, I walked away from my boyfriend for the last time. He would not hurt me again, nor would he ever have the chance to hurt my son.

Filled with resilience, I returned to college one year later to further my education. I was determined to finish this time. Getting a career was the only way I knew that I could support us and raise my child independently. One year of school turned into five years.

In my last year of business school, on one winter day, I was scrolling on social media when I came across an old crush. I was wondering how he was doing and if, after all this time, we could connect. Shortly thereafter, he randomly messaged me. I was like a little schoolgirl again, never imagining we would get together after all these years. It didn't take long before he showed signs that he was not ready. With my emotions running high, the tension in my body increased, so I started focusing more on self-care. My body was constantly aching, and I knew booking myself a massage to release some of the tension was crucial.

Throughout my session, the therapist asked if she could do some Reiki on me. Not sure what it was or what it could do, I agreed. I had been to many different therapists over the years to heal from trauma, but nothing had worked. I just laid there and let her do her thing. Suddenly, tears began rolling down my face as she worked her magic. Then she said, "There are two people here that want to talk to you."

She was a Medium, but I didn't know it was possible to hear from those who had passed. Looking at her with what was probably a blank stare, I thought to myself, *Is this real? Do I believe this? What is happening here?* After all, she knew nothing except that I had lost my twins several years earlier. She asked me if she could say the message she was hearing. With complete curiosity, I said, "Yes." I was open to receiving anything at that point, just wanting to feel better and more grounded.

She shared one impactful sentence through her channeling: "Mom, we are doing good here. If we had survived, we would have been really sick all the time." Right there, as I heard those words, I started bawling uncontrollably, yet I also felt a sense of instant relief. I had so many unanswered questions that couldn't be explained, and I blamed the doctors for the babies' passing. The message was confusing as it was coming from the other side, but at the same time, the tears slowed down. Suddenly, I felt calmer and more at peace.

This was my Ignite moment. In the depths of my soul, I knew upon hearing those words they were from my children, my angels. At that moment, the healing began. I left my session calmer, in awe, trying to process what had happened. When I got home, I felt lighter. It was as if all the weight had been lifted off my shoulders. I felt connected, happier, and more compassionate. There was healing and trust, with less blame, more forgiveness for the situation, and even forgiveness toward myself. I knew it was God's plan, even though I didn't fully understand.

Seeking clarity, I called my old college friend, who was into energetics. I wanted to have a conversation about what I had experienced. She had been learning about energy healing and helped me understand more, as energy and spirituality were all new to me. She had tried talking to me about these topics, but it never clicked or made sense. After what had happened, I was now curious.

I began opening my heart and was inspired by my therapist to take a Reiki Certification and a mediumship course. This became a newfound love. Although trauma goes deep, it can be healed. I discovered that it doesn't matter what we go through; we can find our strengths and develop our abilities. We can overcome painful moments and turn them into personal triumphs. We all have the strength inside ourselves to make a change in our lives; it requires finding our voice, speaking our truth, and stepping up.

Today, I learned new things that help heal wounds and overcome trauma. I now know that hardships are the foundation of heroism. I also believe that angels can guide us and make it possible to connect with those who have crossed over. It wasn't until losing my precious angels that I realized there was a way to communicate with them and get answers.

Perseverance, self-care, and dedication can help you move through your grief and stay grounded within yourself. When feeling stressed, stay strong, forgive, and tap into the energies of potential opportunities and possibilities. You will become more at peace with your inner self and gain clarity. We learn at a young age that everything is energy, but throughout the years, we are conditioned to believe it is all nonsense and impossible. Use positive energy and your intuition to heal and create harmony. Reconnecting with ourselves is what matters. You have the strength inside you to make change in all situations; all it requires is *finding*, *using*, and *amplifying* your voice.

Ignite Action Steps

- Consider getting an emotional support animal. Having something to cuddle, cry on, and support me was wonderful. You can be emotional with them and even talk to them, and they won't judge you. Animals are so intelligent.

- Be open to trying different healing modalities like Reiki, Sound Healing, or Energy Healers. Even if it is new and you are skeptical, be open to new opportunities or possibilities. I was skeptical, but it ended up being a great tool to help me let go of anything that was no longer serving me and move on.

- Talk to someone who is out of your circle: someone who doesn't know you and will not judge but just be there to listen. It was so good talking to professionals who didn't know all the details of me or my circumstances.

Claire Valiquette — Canada
Author, Virtual Assistant & CEO of Claire's Remote Cubicle
✉ *clairesremotecubicle1@gmail.com*
clairesremotecubicle
clairesremotecubicle

Janice Gallant

Janice Gallant

*"Never underestimate the power of the Universe to
bring miracles through for you."*

**Watching your child journey down a dark path is not easy. We often hold
guilt and shame, blaming our parenting skills. Regardless of how we parent,
our children have their *own* paths to walk. I want you to know you can
achieve lightness, peace, and calm, allowing you to let go of the emotional
burden you have been holding and feel inner freedom.**

Clearing Debris Through Forgiveness

"Mom?" My son's voice came through the phone line. It was just after Christmas,
and I was painting the living room after putting the decorations away. "I'm in
jail," he stated, with fear in his voice.

The room began to spin, and my knees went weak. Instinctively, I knew
this was not a joke. I remember standing with a paint roller in my left hand
as I held the phone to my ear. Honestly, it is difficult to recall what happened
next. I believe an officer got on the line to give me the address of where my
son was being held.

My husband and I drove the hour-and-a-half distance to the jail in complete silence. Each of us was in shock, trying to process what was happening.

Questions rolled around in our heads, but neither of us could voice what we were thinking. I would open my mouth to say something but didn't even know what I *should* say.

Two years of turmoil followed, an emotional rollercoaster for our whole family.

My son had gotten mixed up with the wrong crowd, addicted to drugs, and in lots of trouble. We, as a family, were in trauma.

He was 19 years old and had left our family acreage to live in a big city. Having graduated high school, ambitious and excited, he loved being on his own. His life appeared to be off to a great start. Unknown to us, things were not headed in the best direction for him. We did not see this 'train wreck' coming. *How could this have happened? How did we miss this?* We had just spent a wonderful Christmas together as a family! I didn't see any of the signs.

There were charges, but the bail was set low, as this was his first encounter with the law. The days following brought many moments of anxiety, tears, and desperate prayers to the Universe for help. We had brought him home to our acreage, away from the city, but he resisted any help we tried to offer. He eventually found various reasons to return to the city, and we couldn't find him as time passed. Occasionally, he would call. We would try to convince him to come home. We all knew he was dodging imminent jail time. This was not the responsible, level-headed, outdoor enthusiast kid we had raised.

I showed up for his court date. He didn't. That was one of the hardest, most heart-wrenching days of my life. Day after day, we were tormented by worry about where he was, what he was doing, and who he was with. *Was he even still alive?* We didn't know what to do. And all the while, the pain and shame kept us in silence.

Finally, one early summer day, he called. I was exhausted, both emotionally and physically. When I picked up the phone and began talking, I knew it was time. I had to do it, the thing that every parent of an addict struggles to do. With fear thick in my throat, I told him, "We love you so much. When you are ready to come home and get help, we are here for you." And I hung up the phone. My tears flowed.

Every day, I envisioned light around him. Every day, I walked around with my cell phone in my hand, hopeful yet fearful of a call.

Then, about two months later, he reached out. He had gotten a job in construction and was working close by. He wanted to meet us for dinner. He was ready to embrace recovery. It wasn't all easy from then on, but each time I saw him, I could see he was more and more the person we knew, the real him. He was getting off the drugs and separating himself from the people who were influencing him. That December, he returned home, and we spent another Christmas together. We were healing as a family. His brother and sister navigated through it in their own way, and we needed each other.

The following spring, he turned himself in and bravely served his jail time. He kept saying, "It's okay, Mom, I have to do this." This was a difficult journey for all of us. My husband and I had both grown up watching loved ones with alcohol or drug addictions. We had worked hard to keep our kids away from addictions, warning them how easy it was to find yourself too far down that road. My heart ached, and I continually questioned how I missed the signs. I was a teacher, passionately guiding my students to stay away from drugs, and yet I couldn't even help my own son. The guilt and shame were getting deeply anchored into my core. I constantly relived moments through his childhood, thinking about where I may have gone wrong, what I missed, or what I did not bring enough attention to. *Was I not strict enough? Did I coddle him? How could this have happened?* All of these questions constantly rang through my mind.

As my daughter's 18th birthday arrived, my son was still in jail. We both felt the emptiness that he would not be around for her milestone birthday, so I took her shopping for a new outfit. As we walked around the mall, we passed a gallery of beautiful, vibrant artwork that showed such movement and flow it totally captivated me. I stopped, staring at the art as something deep within me stirred, and wistfully whispered to my daughter, "Oh, I love this! If I were to paint again, this is how I would love to paint." And she simply said, "Then why don't you?"

Ping! An epiphany! *Why don't I?*

The next day, I got my paints out of a box at the back of the closet, something I hadn't done in many years, and I painted *for myself.* I painted for my heart. I chose colors and shapes that brought joy and healing. I painted from my soul. Brushstrokes of vibrant colors moved on the canvas: purple and orange trees; bright, colorful skies with clouds that moved across the canvas, swirling around; and water that flowed with continuous currents. It felt so good! It was healing me at my very core, helping me rediscover a love that was missing from all the torture my mind had been putting me through. The flow of creativity brought me peace. The colors brought me joy. Creating something from my soul took me away from the guilt-ridden reality I was living in. Painting brought me back to me into my flow state!

My unique painting style was a gift I received from my journey through that darkness. I painted for hours a day, often forgetting to eat as I immersed myself in my canvas. After I had finished several paintings, I put them on Facebook™ to show my friends and family. Many sold within twenty-four hours! I felt uplifted like the rainbow appearing after the storm. I connected with my purpose; it was the gold beneath the darkness and impacted me profoundly.

When my son came home from jail, he was more grateful for his family than ever, wanting only to spend time with all of us. His underworld journey helped him become a man of solid integrity and more loyal to his loved ones. I don't know everything that happened to him in those years, but he had changed. He emerged from it as a stronger person and much clearer about who he wanted to be.

Life doesn't happen to us; it happens *for* us if we let it. But the story doesn't end here, not for a parent. Years passed, and we had all truly grown and gained wisdom from this experience. However, still buried deep down in me was shame and guilt as a mom. These buried feelings were affecting me in hidden ways I wasn't even aware of *yet*.

Many years passed, but the guilt and shame remained in the deeper layers, submerged in an undercurrent I wasn't conscious of.

At that time, I was growing my spiritually-based coaching business, *Soulfully Aligned Women*. I was doing well but definitely not where I wanted to be financially. It seemed I kept hitting those glass ceilings in my life. At the time, I also dreamed of receiving in-person training from entrepreneurial guru Gabby Bernstein. The program was very expensive and required me to travel to New York state alone, something I had never done before. I was immersed in my fears: scarcity, not being good enough, lacking a sense of belonging in a room with other powerful women, and the terror of flying alone.

Who am I to do this? Just a little country girl from the middle of Canada thinking she can be in the company of all these other, more accomplished women. *Who am I to spend that kind of money on myself?* I felt like a little girl with a big dream.

Determined to overcome those fears, I declared to the Universe, "Enough, we are doing this! We are breaking through these glass ceilings. I am ready! Let's go." Then, I hired a business coach. If I wanted to take Gabby's training, I would have to do the work in her book, *May Cause Miracles*. With the help of my coach, I hoped this would uncover whatever was blocking my ability to receive. As I began this work, old stories bubbled up to be forgiven. I had worked through a lot of trauma in my life. Through my continuous self-aware-ness, I reaped the growth and gold, but forgiveness is another layer I didn't understand. I saw all the blessings I received from all my underworld journeys, but I had not realized there was more work to do.

At first, I resisted rehashing those old feelings. I did not want to go back and relive all the darkness about my son that I was proud to have moved through and away from. My drive to break through the energetic barriers holding me back kept me going. I diligently worked through the steps of deeper inner for-giveness. Each day, I began by writing in my journal: "Universe, I am ready to forgive myself for…" I stayed open, holding myself in an energy of surrender. I didn't know what to expect; I simply followed the day-by-day guidance in the book. And suddenly, on Day 5, something happened.

I sat down with my journal and wrote…

"Today, I let myself off the hook; I look upon my life's experience with a loving eye…today, self-forgiveness is my primary function. I forgive myself for holding myself in this pattern. I forgive myself for the lack mentality I have created…I forgive myself….."

Suddenly, my son and his experience came to mind.

I forgive myself for all the shame and guilt I felt and have been holding for my son's addiction and his experience of going to jail. I forgive myself for any way that I didn't handle it in the way I thought a perfect parent would. I forgive myself for blaming myself that this happened to him."

As I finished writing that last sentence, tears came to my eyes. They welled up from deep within me, and I released them, crying, "Why, why did this have to happen to him? Why couldn't I have saved him from this?"

The emotions came up from the very depths, retching from my body as I had never felt before. I let the anguish flow. I felt so many emotions rising up, expelling feelings of shame, blame, and guilt out of my body. Years of buried agony, grief, and pain were released. I was finally clearing all the debris. It was the first time I gave voice to my sorrow and, in doing so, freed myself from decades of silence; I let myself wail and pushed all the pain out. *Why? Why? Why did he have to go through this? Why couldn't I have saved him? What did I miss? What did I do wrong?* Each question cracked open my heart, breaking down the walls and purging the sludge from my soul.

With the tears subsiding, I lay with my head in my arms, exhausted. I felt like I had released a heavy weight. I felt clearer. I went to the washroom, splashing cold water on my face and feeling like I had surrendered so much dark energy that had been held down for far too many years. I envisioned laying all my shame at the altar and relinquishing what I didn't need to carry any longer. Finally! I had completely surrendered those debilitating feelings all to my Higher Power, to Source.

I sat down at my journal once again, and to my surprise, words flooded through me and onto my page:

"Dear one, it is not for you to see the gifts that he has reaped through his journey. Each has their own perspective. You will see in time the gifts you have gained through your sacrifices. Stay in the light. Rest in the arms of ours. We hold you closely; we love you. You are our child, and we love you as you love your own children. There is always light in every dark corner. You are cleaning house, and this will lead you to wonderful new beginnings. The messages you bring forth are needed for all. Stay on the path. Bask in love. We trusted you with this blessed soul, and you never did anything that was wrong. Your love carried him through his darkness. You gave him the strength to come back to the light. Your children continue to follow your lead. You are a divine light, illuminating the way for so many. You give strength and hope.

You were not the cause but were the lighthouse to find his way home.

It is safe to release now. Let it all go. Let go of all the blocks that blind your way to fully absorb the light."

Those words! They were not from me, but what an impact they had! I had never thought of this before. They came from angels, from the Universe, God, Goddess, and Source; call it what you want, but I had never thought about this whole situation from this perspective before! That message was a higher perspective. That sentiment was a miracle moment, a shift into grace.

Working through the debris of feelings that we hold within us can be some of the hardest work we've ever done. We shy away from it. Turn away. Ignore it when it peeks its heavy head out once in a while. But the real courage comes when you consciously choose to clear the canvas of your own life, whitewash the old paint, and begin again with a fresh palette of colors. This desire to live in your artistry requires pulling the remnants out of the dark corner and forcing them into the light. This is where freedom and peace come through, transforming old wounds into your strength and power. *Your underworld journey becomes your superpower.*

I realized that my hidden feelings had been holding me stuck in an undercurrent of debris in the muddy colors of my life canvas. I had been hitting a glass ceiling because my underlying shame was secretly telling the Universe to paint a different picture than what I was trying to create. The negative feelings kept me in a holding pattern. I had finally found the root of the dark emotions from many years ago that were keeping me small. Living with them felt normal. It was only after I cleared the debris that I realized how heavy it all had been! I had had enough of the guilt and shame hiding in the shadows of my life. I found that underneath all the muck was a place where I could begin a newly painted life with bright colors and a beautiful, light-filled canvas of truth. I forgave myself for all the years of self-blame. I felt empowered! With more space for love. At the end of that momentous journaling session, forgiving myself brought me into a place of divine self-love.

With self-forgiveness, the light crumbled the walls and glass ceilings, and I was able to expand my voice and business. I forgave myself for feeling fear and released it *all* to the Universe, choosing to wrap myself in love instead. I was freed to create a bigger impact in my life and see myself as courageous, empowered, and could begin honoring my journey and growth.

Today, I walk others through these fears and back into loving themselves again. In my program, *Clearing Debris Through Forgiveness*, we courageously navigate through the blocks that hold you back from receiving and into loving relationships, stronger health, abundance, and deeper self-love.

Never underestimate the power of the Universe to bring miracles through for you.

Scarcity and limitations are always rooted in an old story that you believe is true. By choosing a more loving perspective, you can remove the old debris that is weighing you down and become the artist of your life, creating your new painting. This new loving perspective is already inherent within you, and by clearing the old heavy emotions, you gain the clarity to embrace forgiveness and self-love. Whatever your past story was, you were never meant to hold on to all the heavy burden for so long. For an artist, the underlayers of a painting create contrast, richness, and beauty in the work of art. The same is true for you as the artist of your life.

There are many bright new layers ready to be added to your canvas. Decide to step forward and begin choosing a new color for your life.

Ignite Action Steps:

Ask - You can lean into help by simply asking. You don't have to do it all alone. Regardless of your beliefs, these overwhelming journeys often bring you to your knees begging for mercy from the Universe, God, Creator, Source, whoever is there to *please help*! Recognizing you can't do it alone and asking will quickly bring in the forces. Your heart-centered willingness to surrender, instead of trying to control everything, is key here. Love will swoop in when your prayer comes from the depths of your heart.

Let Go - Be willing to step back, let go, and just listen. Don't try to figure it out. Trust you will be shown. The solution isn't in searching for more answers because you've already tried everything. Be an empty vessel, ready to receive. Lay your problem in the arms of the angels; you no longer need to hold this weight. I did this with my son during his struggles. I let him go. I laid all the problems in the arms of the Universe and said, "This is too big for me, Universe; please take this. Show me the way." I also did it when I released all the pain I was holding within me and asked to be shown how to forgive myself for my perceived parenting failures. Your free will in this life means nothing will change until you ask. Ask through writing, prayer, or just having a heart-to-heart conversation with your Higher Power.

Trust - Once you ask, now it is done. It is time for you to lean into your faith and trust that your prayers have been heard and the Universe is working on it. Sometimes prayers take time to be answered, and your job is to stay in the faith that help is coming, even when you don't observe it happening around you. This is not always easy, but lean back into trust each time you feel yourself trying to control the situation. Breathe. Do something creative that brings you joy, like painting, hiking up a mountain, playing with your pets, or trying out a new recipe. Know that you have a team working on the problem.

Listen and Receive - As you stay in your trust, answers from the Universe will come through, often in miraculous ways. You will receive a moment of awareness, a new idea, inspiration, or an inspired action, perhaps a strong feeling to call someone and share what you are going through. Miracles often come through the angels disguised as people around you. Be open to these miracles.

Take Action - Whatever subtle or big messages you are receiving, you must follow through with action. We are not helpless beings; we co-create with the Universe. When you surrender your desire to the Universe, asking for support, you will be shown the way. In your internal shift, you allow more love to enter the situation and are open to forgiveness. In your external action, you reclaim your personal power. Your willingness to see yourself through the eyes of love opens you to beautiful miracles. Remember, you are ultimately the creator of your life, with a beautiful divine force of support at your back. Your part is to take steps from the inspired guidance.

As you navigate through your miraculous shifts, you will discover an inner peace and a deeper calm blanketing your life and witness a grander impact on those around you. With this lightness emerging from within, life around you shifts as you create from the full spectrum of color now available to you.

Janice Gallant — Canada
Author, Speaker, Artist, Women's Empowerment Mentor
janicegallant.com
soulfullyalignedwomen / janicegallantart
soulfullyalignedwomen / janicegallantart

Anita Adrain & Cheryl Viczko

ANITA ADRAIN &
CHERYL VICZKO

*"The life you deserve is waiting. Sometimes, all it takes is a single step,
a moment of trust to set everything in motion."*

Reflect on the times intuition has steered you and consider how those moments have gently guided your choices. In a world filled with noise and distraction, your inner voice, soft yet profoundly wise, is a compass that knows the way. By leaning into its guidance, you will have the courage to embrace the opportunities, knowing that your inner wisdom is always there to illuminate the way. Our desire is for you to honor those subtle whispers, opening yourself to deeper connections, profound growth, and transformative impact.

DIVINELY GUIDED ENCOUNTERS: HOW ONE MOMENT CHANGED EVERYTHING

Her Inspired Journey: Holy Shift Moments
One impactful moment occurred during a class when a student had a sudden realization and exclaimed, "Holy…'" To which Anita quickly responded, "Shift!" That moment gave birth to the term 'Holy Shift,' which has since come to symbolize those powerful breakthroughs in awareness. The following stories will

share the 'Holy Shift' moments that have shaped the lives of Anita and Cheryl, allowing them to step into their purpose of impacting others and experiencing their own powerful shifts.

A Life-Altering Weekend in Banff

The suitcase was packed. It had been an exhausting week for Anita, juggling the demands of three small children, managing a business, and navigating the usual chaos of life. Yet, somehow, everything had magically aligned. She was ready for a weekend away in the majestic Rocky Mountains of Alberta. To anyone who has ever stood beneath those eternal, snow-capped giants, a mystical stirring of the soul beyond explanation awaits them. It was more than a getaway for Anita; it was a chance to escape everyday life, discover more about herself, recharge, and reconnect.

Late at night, after her children were asleep, she would immerse herself in the pages of books about self-help, or what is now known as 'New Age.' Expanding her consciousness, every word resonated with and awakened something within her she hadn't realized was dormant. One author who she adored, Lee Carroll, was making his first appearance in Canada. His personality and humor shone through the words on the pages of the book she was reading. The book embodied the Source Energy of God and the Divine and how channeling messages were transcribed for those to glean timeless truths from.

Without the logistics in place, Anita followed that gentle nudge, that inner voice that said, "You should go; it's the chance of a lifetime." "Everything happens for a reason," she reassured herself when her decision to attend was being questioned by her practical mind and the good opinion of others. Without the logistics, Anita purchased the tickets months in advance, as she trusted it would all work out if it was meant to be.

Anita's husband met her excitement with skepticism as the weekend approached… he is not much of a reader himself. He struggled to understand why she was so eager to invest both time and money to see an author speak. "If it were Mick Jagger, I'd get it," he joked, trying to relate. But when it came to Lee Carroll's teachings, he found them to be 'out there.' His concerns about her getting involved in something 'cult-like' added a quiet undercurrent of tension to their relationship. To reassure him, she attempted to define what *channeling* was. Many religions originally channeled sacred scriptures, and most music and artwork are also channeled. Receiving messages from a Higher Place is not unusual, but like many other modalities in the New Age, channeling has a stigma associated with it.

Anita's heart raced with a mix of excitement and nervous anticipation as she kissed her family goodbye. Imparting the last instructions of 'remember to…,' it was hard to leave them behind, even for just two days. As she hugged each of them, a brief moment of trepidation crept in. *Was she being selfish? Shouldn't she be spending the weekend with her family instead of venturing off on this spiritual adventure?* That nagging doubt slowly faded into the background as the car pulled away. Anita, Anita's mom Aldia, and her friend Trudy, giddy as teenagers, embarked on the three-and-a-half-hour drive to Banff. Aldia introduced both Anita and Trudy to many spiritual authors and self-help books, and the three of them gained insights into the consciousness of the human spirit. As they set out, they eagerly chatted about the upcoming weekend and the excitement of finally meeting the author whose words had touched them so deeply.

For Anita, this trip wasn't just a getaway; it was a calling. Deep inside her, there was a quiet, powerful knowing that she was stepping into something significant. As the miles passed, the glorious foothills emerged, signaling the way to the majestic Rocky Mountains ahead. The landscape was breathtaking, but the growing excitement within the car truly filled the space. This was the first self-development conference that Anita had ever had the privilege or courage to attend.

The trio checked into a cozy bed-and-breakfast and then headed off to explore the enchanting town of Banff, its breathtaking landscapes and vibrant charm. As they wandered the picturesque streets, they inhaled the clean, crisp mountain air and admired the blend of historic architecture and stunning natural backdrops. Though they had often visited this iconic mountain town, this trip felt different.

The Energy of Feng Shui

The next day, Anita entered a spacious conference room meticulously prepared to hold over 500 attendees, magnetically drawn together by some higher force. Rows of chairs stretched across the room, each neatly arranged to face a raised stage illuminated by soft, warm lighting. Floor-to-ceiling windows along one wall allowed the grandeur of the Rocky Mountains to serve as a breathtaking canvas, a reminder of the beauty and vastness that mirrored the energy in the room. The air was charged with quiet chatter, laughter, and the hum of anticipation as people settled in and exchanged stories of what had brought them there. It wasn't just a conference; it was a convergence of souls, each carrying a unique story of awakening to a new perspective.

When the hostess stepped onto the stage to open the weekend and introduce Lee Carroll, the room fell silent, and the energy shifted. She was elegantly dressed in a delicately layered soft pink chiffon dress adorned with exquisite gemstone jewelry that seemed to catch and reflect the light. With her pure and melodic voice enveloping the room, she invited everyone to relax into a collective meditation that would anchor the weekend for receptivity. The room became a sanctuary, offering Anita a rare opportunity to be free from worries about children, meals, and daily responsibilities.

The morning continued with Lee recounting his personal story of 'awakening' from his life as an engineer to becoming a well-known channel and a sought-after spiritual teacher.

Preparing to deliver the first channeled message of the weekend, Lee sat on his chair and closed his eyes, holding the microphone in one hand. The other one gestured as his conscious mind stepped aside to allow the angelic presence to come through. The tone of voice shifted as the one in the chair said, *"Greetings, dear ones, I am Kryon of Magnetic Service. In the energy of these mountains, I invite you to sit in the golden chair as we talk about a subject we have never opened before regarding partnering with God. Of the great golden one that sits on the chair in your heart. Inside, there is something you call the 'higher self.' We've told you of the self-worth issue that you can grab hold of and claim. We invite you to metaphorically sit in the chair with the golden one to see who you are and feel the love permeate every cell. To see the concept of the partnership with God that is available in this New Age, the marriage to the higher self, and we told you that it was the beginning step for many."*

The channeling ended with a wash of unconditional love that encircled the room, leaving some, including Anita, with tears of remembrance gently flowing down their cheeks. That event catalyzed Anita to remember the angelic being that lives within. Anita felt a glimpse of her inner knowing and that there was more in the world than just *being* human. It was an impactful confirmation for Anita that she was on the right path, and so much was before her.

After lunch, conversations hushed as the soul reunion resumed with the afternoon agenda. Anita listened intently as the next speaker, Jan Tober, explained Feng Shui, the ancient art of creating harmony by aligning your environment with the natural flow of energy. She shared how every space holds *chi,* and when we honor it, we open the door to abundance, health, and peace. She held up a small, beautifully designed handbook, the cover gleaming with the image of a shimmering water bowl. It was a book she had authored as a do-it-yourself guide, making your own Bubble Bowl, a tool to enhance and activate the flow of *chi in your home.* She continued her presentation, saying, "A bubble bowl invites movement, flow, and balance, helping stagnant energy transform into vitality."

The words *Feng Shui* resonated in every cell of her being. For the first time, Anita had a name for what she had instinctively been practicing her entire life. Now, it all made sense. It was as though the Universe whispered directly to her: *This is it. This is what you've been searching for.* Her heart raced with delight. It was more than an introduction to an ancient practice; it was a 'Holy Shift' moment. Energy surged through her body, and all the hairs on her arms stood up, confirming the insights.

When the session ended, Anita felt an undeniable pull to speak with Jan. As the room filled with chatter and movement; she swiftly made her way to the left of the stage, her steps fueled with determination. Anita expressed her gratitude, sharing how deeply Jan's talk resonated. Graciously, Jan smiled and offered a next step. "If this feels aligned for you, I recommend *The Western Guide to Feng Shui* by Terah Kathryn Collins. It's a brilliantly written yet easy-to-understand guide on how to apply Feng Shui principles to your home, a great place to start."

The synchronicity, the clarity, the newfound term, it was as if the universe had orchestrated everything to lead Anita to this moment. As she left the conversation, a spark ignited within her, one that would grow into a guiding flame, illuminating an exploration of ancient wisdom.

The weekend ended far too soon, and Anita left with a heart full of gratitude and awe. The connections she made with so many kindred spirits, individuals walking the same spiritual path, who she knew would become lifelong friends, felt nothing short of miraculous. Witnessing the unraveling of science as it relates to spirituality during moments of profound 'channeling' left her spellbound as if she had been privy to a sacred unveiling of universal truths. Driving home, it was as though time itself had paused, allowing Anita to savor the transformation unfolding within. Her soul tingled with remembrance, her mind brimming with possibilities. That single event and trusting her intuition was the launching point, unveiling her destiny.

A Leap of Faith

Back home, resources on Feng Shui were scarce, and very few people had heard the term. Months later, Anita's friend returned from a trip to the United States with *The Western Guide to Feng Shui* as a gift. Anita devoured every word, feeling as though the book had been written just for her. In the end, an invitation to become a Certified Essential Feng Shui® Practitioner in San Diego leaped off the page. It felt like the universe had placed the opportunity directly in her hands. The logistics of attending, however, were daunting. *How could she leave her three young children, business, and home for an entire week?* It seemed impossible, yet she knew the seed had been planted. Her intuition, that little voice inside, confirmed her heart's desire to trust this was her soul's calling.

Divinely, the mosaic of pieces finally fell into place. Sitting on a plane bound for San Diego, Anita reflected on how that weekend in Banff had set her life on a different trajectory. That one event led to dreaming of what was possible. Once immersed in the teachings at The Western School of Feng Shui, Anita felt her soul had been waiting for this moment all her life. By the end of the week, she had not only gained knowledge but experienced a profound personal breakthrough in how powerful the environment is in every aspect of one's life. It was another 'Holy Shift.'

Anita returned home lighter, more present, and filled with confidence her husband couldn't ignore. He slowly began to accept that this quest wasn't about leaving their life behind but creating a better one. Anita's leap of faith blossomed into a passion and purpose beyond her imagination. Her life became infused with Feng Shui as she embraced its wisdom. She discovered the power of decluttering, not just physical spaces but also the mental and emotional clutter that weighs people down. She became the facilitator of The Western School of Feng Shui® curriculum and introduced people to Feng Shui in Canada.

Feng Shui wasn't readily accepted in the late 90s in rural Alberta, Canada. People didn't understand the word, and Anita struggled to share the concept, doing her utmost to explain how beneficial it was to look at your environment energetically and live in a state of harmony. She followed her intuition, embraced every opportunity to attend networking events, and inspired that 'Holy Shift' feeling in others. Divine intervention was on her side one day, years later, in April 2009.

Meeting Cheryl: A Connection of Collaboration
Cheryl's path first crossed with Anita at a business coaching function, which Cheryl attended every quarter. Unbeknownst to Cheryl, that day would significantly alter her life. Walking into the conference room, she joined over a hundred entrepreneurs, all eager to learn from an internationally respected business coach.

That workshop stood out from others Cheryl had attended, as vendors were also present. Like many attendees, the aroma of coffee beckoned, leading her to the far side of the room where a line had formed. Along a wall of vendor tables, Cheryl noticed a delightful woman introducing attendees to 'healthy coffee' and offering samples. Before the session began, Cheryl exchanged pleasantries with the lady, who passed out cups of the dark, aromatic brew. That simple act of connection sparked something in Cheryl. She felt a knock on her energetic field and remembered feeling a synchronistic pull. Liking the coffee, Cheryl grabbed a business card and saw the name read: Anita Adrain. That was a pivotal moment, marking the first in-person meeting between them.

Years passed before their next momentous meeting. Recovering from an accident, Cheryl found herself with time to reflect on her life and make decisions for the future. She decided it was the perfect opportunity to declutter her home and part with unwanted possessions by hosting a garage sale. On a sunny spring morning, ideal for propping the garage door wide open, Cheryl showcased an array of items she was letting go of. The morning shoppers came and went, haggling and chatting. Cheryl found joy in the lively conversations that accompanied the day's exchanges.

As the afternoon sun warmed the driveway, Anita strolled up, instantly recognizing Cheryl. She had spotted the vibrant red 'Garage Sale' sign; obviously, it had been carefully designed, and its cheerful invitation was hard to miss. The two women greeted each other warmly, reconnecting amid the treasures scattered across the garage. Among the items, Anita discovered two paintings she later remarked would be 'perfect Feng Shui' examples for her upcoming Introduction to Feng Shui class.

The mention of Feng Shui piqued Cheryl's interest. Twenty-three years earlier, when she and her husband first moved into their home, she had attempted to incorporate Feng Shui principles. Armed with a basic understanding gleaned from two books and her landscaping background, Cheryl had designed the exterior, interior, and garden with intention. However, despite her efforts, she found Feng Shui confusing. Some of the guidance she received was rooted in traditional practices centered on the home patriarch, an approach that felt misaligned with her personality and way of life. This mismatch left her uncertain about how to fully apply the principles in a way that resonated with her.

That divinely guided reunion led Cheryl to invite Anita for coffee. Weeks later, the two sat at Cheryl's kitchen island; their conversation meandered through topics like Feng Shui, color, their joint love of horticulture, and energy. During their discussion, Anita introduced The Western School of Feng Shui, explaining how it honors the Eastern heritage of Form School Feng Shui while adapting its principles for practical use in Western lifestyles and homes.

Excited by Anita's client stories and the thrill of discovering new insights, Cheryl eagerly signed up for the introductory classes, embarking on a path of self-discovery. It was a revelation, an immediate 'Holy Shift' moment, as she recognized that her natural decorating skills and intuitive energy alignment had already contributed to the calm, welcoming atmosphere her friends and family admired. Cheryl laughed, recalling how her husband often shook his head when he caught her adjusting the furniture by a fraction of an inch and explaining to him, "It just didn't feel right."

Guided by her facilitator, mentor, and friend, Anita, Cheryl, who was in her fifties, followed her intuition and felt a newfound passion for Feng Shui. With renewed optimism, Cheryl immersed herself in the practice, quickly completing the Essential Feng Shui® Practitioner Certification training. Energized by her studies, she ignited an exciting new chapter in her life and began transforming various areas of her home. Recognizing her enthusiasm and dedication, Anita invited Cheryl to co-facilitate her Feng Shui classes, sparking a dynamic and powerful collaboration. With Divine Guidance and trust in their inner wisdom, the two women's paths synchronized at the perfect time, opening into the flow of life and setting these events into motion.

The Bond Strengthens

Their bond deepened when Anita introduced Cheryl to her spiritual community and enlightened thought leaders. After completing The Western School of Feng Shui® certification program, an invitation from Anita led to Cheryl's first New Age gathering. Though Cheryl had never taken part in anything like this before, a mix of intrigue and uncertainty stirred within her. Initially hesitant about what the encounter might bring, an undeniable call to attend eventually overcame the doubt.

Guided by a sense of commitment and integrity, Cheryl chose to step into the unknown, a decision that would radically shape her future. It was at that event that she witnessed Adironnda, a seventeenth-dimensional being, channeled through Marilyn Harper. The way Adironnda spoke, with her blue eyes wide open, her gaze seeming to penetrate every cell of her body, filled Cheryl with a soul-felt sense of love. It was unlike anything she had ever felt before. The interaction left Cheryl with a sense of comfort and power. Adironnda's presence stirred something deep within her, expanding her understanding of the vastness of the universe and awakening Cheryl to a deeper connection with the spiritual realm.

A few months later, Anita invited Cheryl to another function in the nearby city, Calgary. Though financial constraints were an obstacle, Anita found a way for her to attend by offering the opportunity to volunteer for setup, teardown, and managing the sales table. A week prior to her departure, Cheryl found herself hesitating once again. *Could she afford to go? Where would she stay?* She fell asleep with these questions swirling in her mind. Then, in the middle of the night, Cheryl was jolted awake by a loud, clear voice: *GO TO CALGARY.* She sat up in bed, heart racing, and scanned the darkened room. Her husband and puppy were sound asleep, and it became instantly clear that the message wasn't meant for either of them—it was unmistakably for her. It was time to listen to that voice, that demanding *yes*, even though her ego was reciting one hundred reasons why she should stay home.

Though Cheryl wasn't sure what to expect, the memory of her first encounter with Adironnda had left a lasting impression. The channeling had been infused with lightness, humor, and deep wisdom. As Cheryl reflected, she wondered how the upcoming event with the headliner, Lee Carroll, would compare. Known for emanating a powerful 'love-wash' energy, *Kryon* promised to offer an equally moving exploration of self-discovery.

When Cheryl arrived, the conference room was alive with energy as hundreds of attendees filled the space, an unequivocal feeling of their united purpose triggering goosebumps. People embraced one another like long-lost friends, exchanging smiles, hugs, and laughter. Attendees had traveled from miles and even provinces away to hear the messages of enlightenment.

The weekend became a pivotal moment in Cheryl's life. Over two days, she witnessed the brilliance of numerous speakers and channels, deeply appreciating their wisdom. When the invitation came to join the team on stage for a group photo, she accepted with gratitude. Surrounded by an atmosphere of love and warmth, that moment symbolized her official welcome into the spiritual community. It was a benevolent 'Holy Shift' moment. Cheryl was feeling fully embraced, included, and connected to something far greater than herself. Cheryl's soul began to sing. The unquestionable acceptance, matched with the unconditional love, left her feeling like she had arrived home.

Nourishing relationships with Anita's life-long connections in Banff decades ago sparked a wave of opportunities for both women. As the duo traveled across North America, they began sketching ideas for their own unique, highly experiential events that would blend their skills and passions. Within these international gatherings, they forged meaningful connections with renowned thought leaders and attendees, inevitably shaping their destinies as impactful, empowered women.

Creating Impact Together

Through their in-person and online experiences, Anita and Cheryl discovered that the deepest impacts often remain hidden until stories are shared. Energized by these revelations, they envisioned a live function holistically supporting women. Finding the right venue proved challenging, but they had faith the perfect space would appear.

Cheryl received an intuitive message during a celebration of life: *it belonged there.* Miraculously, the venue had one open weekend, aligning perfectly with their key speakers and their four pillars: *Home, Heart, Health,* and *HarMoney.* With the venue secured, Anita and Cheryl dove into organizing their first two-day function. They signed contracts, coordinated logistics, and rallied speakers, volunteers, and local sponsors, all within a tight three-month timeline. Moments of doubt arose, but the word 'unstoppable' fueled their determination. Long days of marketing, ticket sales, and fine-tuning details often stretched into late nights, but their vision kept them focused. They knew their event would impact others the same way the events they attended had directed the flow of their lives.

When the day had arrived, early morning activity buzzed as volunteers and vendors filled the space. Anita and Cheryl orchestrated every detail, from sound checks to last-minute adjustments, ensuring everything ran smoothly. As the doors opened, they stood together, sharing a deep breath and a victorious high-five. Their vision had come to life, ready to touch lives in ways they could only imagine.

The inaugural conference appeared successful, but its true impact unfolded over time. One attendee (who was initially hesitant to attend) in the months following, co-authored a best-selling book, spoke internationally, and launched a business. A 'Holy Shift' had transpired. Returning the next year to build on her momentum, she embodied the transformative power of Anita and Cheryl's inspiration.

Moved by the powerful impact of testimonials, Anita and Cheryl reimagined the event's identity and created Her Inspired Journey ~ Women's Wellness Weekend (HIJ). The rebrand reflected the weekend's transformative growth and authentic connections. Every presenter had a story of 'Her Inspired Journey' that was motivational, uplifting, and heartfelt by everyone who had experienced it. The ripple of impact was expanding just as they envisioned. Just as they had dreamed, their event profoundly changed their lives.

As with any firsts, there are lessons learned and the promise to expand, elevate, and improve any subsequent undertaking. Dedicated to empowering women, Anita and Cheryl poured their hearts into the second year, refining every detail and exploring new possibilities to create an even more profound and personal experience than before.

Feng Shui principles were woven into executing the venue design, creating a harmonious space that embraced attendees, speakers, vendors, and sponsors alike. At the heart of the venue was a stage alive with lush greenery and natural elements, symbolizing growth and renewal. Intentional seating and vendor placements encouraged connection and cooperation. Every element reflected a commitment to environmental consciousness and a nurturing discovery for all involved.

The impact was immediate. Attendees felt embraced by the calming yet invigorating atmosphere, sparking moments of clarity and renewal. Each person there deepened their connections to themself and others. When the doors opened, souls were drawn together, and the collective energy of Anita and Cheryl guiding, amplifying, and supporting everyone sparked a profound 'Holy Shift' that united them all.

By blending Feng Shui, mindful design, and heartfelt intention, *HIJ* exceeded all expectations, leaving a legacy of inspiration, connection, and growth. During the first day at *HIJ*, Lady JB Owen, an international speaker, graced the stage and conveyed a deeply personal story, showcasing the significant impact of vulnerability and how sharing our truths can spark meaningful change. Her session concluded with an exercise: participants paired with strangers to share a recent personal insight.

Feeling apprehensive and engaged, Cheryl partnered with a woman she'd never met. As the stranger communicated her raw and heartfelt story, Cheryl was deeply moved and felt compelled to reciprocate. Overwhelmed with emotion, Cheryl confessed a recent realization that had consumed her weeks earlier while reviewing the attendance numbers. Cheryl admitted that she had asked herself, *Where am I blocking the flow of trusting this event will be a success?*

This question lingered in her mind until an unexpected moment of clarity shifted her perspective entirely. Thinking about the friends who had traveled long distances to stand by them, Cheryl was struck by the magnitude of their gestures and the profound acts of kindness she had overlooked. It was a transformative 'Holy Shift' moment, exposing and releasing a hidden fear she hadn't realized she was carrying.

For years, Cheryl had kept people at a distance, convinced they wouldn't show up for her. This protective narrative, born of insecurities and self-reliance, shattered under the weight of her friends' unwavering commitment. Standing vulnerable on stage as the co-host, Cheryl felt both embarrassed and liberated. She realized her resistance to receiving help was rooted in a fear of disappointment and shaped by childhood memories of loss and responsibility. This newfound awareness stayed with her, surfacing in quiet moments and challenging her long-held beliefs.

Days later, Cheryl couldn't shake the impact of her recent revelation. For years, she had been operating under an unspoken rule: if it had to be done, it had to be done by her. "When did I decide I needed to control everything?" she asked herself. The question burrowed into her mind, a constant irritant, like a pebble trapped in her shoe, forcing her to pause and examine the burden she had unknowingly chosen to carry. That 'Holy Shift' moment sparked a cascade of insights for Cheryl and illuminated a universal truth: one story, one act of vulnerability, can ripple outward, creating meaningful changes in ways we can't fully comprehend.

As Cheryl and Anita reflected on the evolution that led to HIJ, they felt immense gratitude for the women who had walked alongside them. Their vision was always to create a safe, sacred space where women could be seen, heard, and celebrated, a place to embrace their fullest potential.

Her Inspired Journey was more than a two-day highly experiential event; it was a catalyst for healing, growth, and connection. It united women, enabling them to forge new friendships, discover inner strength, and empower one another to live uplifted lives. It was also a deep confirmation of the amazing friendship and powerful admiration that Cheryl and Anita had formed for one another.

The Path to *AllIn Alignment*

As hosts of *Her Inspired Journey ~ Women's Wellness Weekend*, Anita and Cheryl have come full circle, honoring the in-person conferences' impact on their lives. For Anita, the pilgrimage from Banff to San Diego proved the power of acknowledging her inner knowing. For Cheryl, it began with a chance conversation over coffee, sparking endless possibilities. Together, they know the magnitude of a supportive community and the clarity that comes from believing in that inner voice. These interactions shaped their mission, the belief that every woman deserves to feel seen, heard, and aligned with her potential.

Looking back, Anita and Cheryl realized their choices to embrace opportunity weren't just for themselves. They were for every woman they would serve, the homes that would be healed, the lives uplifted, and the ripples of peace and joy extending far beyond their reach. The evolution of '*All In Alignment,*' their business, was both intentional and natural. What began as *Feng Shui with*

Anita & Cheryl evolved into a name that perfectly expresses their passion for helping women balance their homes and lives.

To the woman who feels the pull of something greater: You are not alone. The life you deserve is waiting, and it starts with a single step: a moment of belief. It takes courage to leave the familiar, but when you do, the universe will meet you there, and your impact will be felt. When you say *yes* to your intuition and follow your inner voice, Anita and Cheryl will be there, cheering you on. Together, they are devoted to *creating sacred spaces* where women can embrace their next steps, one 'Holy Shift' moment at a time.

Ignite Action Steps

- **Tune Into Your Body - Listen to your physical sensations:** Often, intuition speaks through bodily sensations. Pay attention to how your body feels in different situations: tightness, relaxation, or even a gut feeling. These are your body's way of communicating with you.

- **Ask for Guidance - Seek clarity through questions:** If you're unsure, ask your inner voice for guidance. For example, *"What should I do in this situation?" or "What feels right for me?"* Rely on the first answer that comes, even if it doesn't seem logical at first.

- **Start Small - Practice with everyday decisions:** Begin by trusting your intuition on smaller, low-stakes decisions, like choosing a route to drive, what to eat, or which book to read. This helps build confidence and trust in your inner guidance.

- **Pay Attention to Repeating Signs - Look for synchronicities:** Often, intuition sends messages in the form of repeating signs, symbols, or encounters. These can be dreams, a book, or the same advice from different sources. Recognizing these patterns can strengthen your belief.

- **Reflect and Celebrate - Acknowledge the moments when it works:** Celebrate when your intuition leads you in the right direction. Reflect on how it felt when you followed your gut, and reinforce the connection by recognizing those moments.

- **Release the Need for Perfection - Let go of self-doubt:** Listening to your intuition requires releasing the need to be perfect or always right. Intuition is not about having all the answers; it's about believing that you are guided toward what you need to know.

If you're ready to reclaim your power, create a life that's truly yours, and find the support you deserve, we invite you to connect with us. Let's build a life of clarity, purpose, and peace together.

Anita Adrain & Cheryl Viczko — Canada
Stress Reduction Gurus, Feng Shui Practitioners,
Speakers, Teachers, Event Hosts, Authors
holyshiftmoment.com
allinalignment.com
herinspiredjourney.com
groups/allinalignmentwithanitaandcheryl
allinalignment88
@allinalignment

Your Impact Starts Now

You have been on a journey through the pages of this book, learning from the experiences of others, reflecting on your impact, and recognizing the power of your story. But transformation does not happen just by reading; it happens when we take action.

Now, it is your turn. Your story has the power to change someone's life. The lessons you have learned, the growth you have experienced, and the challenges you have overcome can be a beacon for someone else who is searching for guidance, hope, or inspiration.

The world is waiting for the impact only you can make. Your experiences, your voice, and your journey hold the power to uplift, inspire, and ignite change in ways you may not even realize. The authors in this book once stood where you are, having lived stories that shaped their lives. By sharing their journey, they have touched lives, shifted perspectives, and made a lasting impact on the world.

Stories transcend barriers, break down walls, and connect us in ways nothing else can. They have the power to heal, inspire, and ignite change across generations and cultures. The authors in this book have shared their journeys to spark transformation, and now the world is waiting for yours. Your story holds the ability to uplift, empower, and remind others that they are not alone. If you feel called to share it, we are here to support you. We believe that every person's story has the potential to impact thousands. And we know that together, we can use the power of storytelling to Ignite Humanity™ and raise the consciousness of what is possible for everyone.

When we tell our story, we transform our own lives and the lives of countless others.

Take a moment to write out some of your story, highlight your Ignite Moment, and discover how your story can make a difference in the lives of so many.

Once you are done, reach out. Visit www.igniteyou.life and let us help you share your story with the world.

My Ignite Moment is...

____

____

____

____

____

IMPACTFUL AFFIRMATIONS FOR YOU TO USE IN YOUR LIFE.

Words carry power. The thoughts we repeat shape our actions, influence our mindset, and create the reality we live in. To continue the ripple effect of this book, each author has shared an affirmation that has had a profound impact on their own journey.

These affirmations are here for you to use, embody, and integrate into your daily life. Speak them aloud, write them down, and let them serve as reminders of your strength, purpose, and ability to create impact in the world around you.

Choose the ones that resonate most and let them ignite something powerful within you.

ANDONIA REYNOLDS

I trust the journey, knowing that every step, whether smooth or challenging, brings me closer to my true self. I am grounded, resilient, and open to the wisdom that life offers me today.
Breathe deeply, embrace the moment, and move forward with confidence.

ANGELA H. ROBINETTE

Love God; love others.

ANITA ADRAIN

I honor, respect, and care for my surroundings as a reflection of how I honor, respect, and care for myself. With every choice I make, I affirm my self-worth, creating a space that nurtures and uplifts me.

ANN M. B. McINTYRE

Finding someone else's truth is the dawn of finding your own.

BRENDA GERLING

I love Life, and life loves me!

Chantelle McFarland

When I choose gratitude for the uncomfortable lessons, the blessings within the experience are revealed.

Cheryl Viczko

I trust I'm always in the right place at the right time. I embody joy, peace, gratitude, and kindness. With an open heart, I welcome abundance in all areas of life. And so it is.

Christine Lang

Never, never, never give up because you don't know how close you are to getting what you want.

Ciara Caston Finley

Every wound is healing, every chain is breaking, and I stand in my POWER, whole and unshaken.

Claire Valiquette

My voice matters and is valuable.

Dave August

Life's a journey, and you choose what you make out of it. If you are given an opportunity, run with it. Don't ever stop dreaming.

Dee Taggart

I am worthy of the highest quality of life.

Doreen Kilbreath

I am living each and every day being the best version of myself and trust I am always safe and supported.

Elaine Valerie Thompson

*I am observing; I observe thoughts that come and go. I am not my thoughts;
I am the unattached observer.*

Janice Gallant

Ask, let go, and receive.

Lady JB Owen

*Anything and everything is possible. The Universe wants you to succeed
because what you want, wants you.*

Jennifer Pascoa

*God knows what He is doing. He is always working, even when I don't see it.
He's got me.*

Jessica Sinclair

Everything is leading me to my highest path and greatest purpose.

Joe Kavanagh

Listen to relate, not to respond.

Karla VandenBerg

*Sometimes, it might seem as if one is walking through quicksand when the
rainbow is only one step away.*

Kerstin Pelletier

*With every breath, I return to my true self, knowing I am worthy of love,
wholeness, and joy exactly as I am. Every challenge I have faced has led me
closer to my truth, and I now choose to stand in my power, embrace my worth,
and breathe in the freedom of self-love.*

Kimberly E. Beaudoin
Dreams do come true
Just believe in yourself and trust.

Marion Andrews
I am grateful for the love and light I have in my life.

Matthew A. Swierk
I embody expansion, alignment, and infinite possibility. I lead with purpose, connect with power, and create with divine energy. I elevate those around me as I rise, forging a world of abundance, love, and transformation.

Melody J. Carberry
The beautiful thing about life is that we have choices.
The choice to improve, the choice to change what is, and the choice to stand in our truth and be authentic and courageous. Shine your light, and empower others to shine theirs. Leave the world better than you came to it.
It's all about Love ♥.

Mickey Forsyth
Take care of yourself, you matter.

Peter Giesin
My story is still being written. With each new chapter, I can deepen into courage, compassion, and purposeful living. My journey is a gift, and I share it to inspire others.

Summer Bozohora
You can't think your way out of something you felt your way into.

Yun Rhee
I am all that I am.

IMPACTFUL BOOKS RECOMMENDATIONS

Stories have the power to transform, inspire, and shift perspectives. The authors of Ignite Impact have come together to share books that have deeply influenced their journeys. These are the titles that sparked new ways of thinking, provided clarity, and fueled their passion for growth and change.

As you explore these recommendations, trust that the right book will find you at the right time. Whether you seek personal growth, professional transformation, or a fresh perspective, may these books continue to ignite impact in your life.

Andonia Reynolds
- *Half Broke Horses* by Jeannette Walls

Angela H. Robinette
- *Ignite Your Courage* by Ignite Publishing

Anita Adrain
- *The Journey Home* by Lee Carroll

Ann M. B. McIntyre
- *Start With Why* by Simon Sinek

Brenda Gerling
- *Dying to Be Me* by Anita Moorjani

Chantelle McFarland
- *The Glass Castle* by Jeannette Walls

Cheryl Viczko
- *Return of the Bird Tribes* by Ken Carey

Christine Lang
- *Worthy* by Jamie Kern Lima

Ciara Caston Finley
- *The Garden Within* by Dr. Anita Phillips

Claire Valiquette
- *Atomic Habits* by James Clear

Dee Taggart
- *Good Vibes Good Life* by Vex King

Doreen Kilbreath
- *The Four Agreements* by Don Miguel Ruiz

Elaine Valerie Thompson
- *You Can Heal Your Life* by Louise L. Hay

Janice Gallant
- *The Creation Guild* by Janice Gallant

Lady JB Owen
- *The Science of Getting Rich* by Wallace D. Wattles

Jennifer Pascoa
- *The Gifts of Imperfection* by Brene Brown

Jessica Sinclair
- *Metaphysical Anatomy* by Yvette Rose

Joe Kavanagh
- *Don't Die with Your Music Still In You* by Wayne Dyer and Serena J Dyer

Kerstin Pelletier
- *I Love You, Me* by Tara Love Perry

Kimberly E. Beaudoin
- *When the Body Says No* by Gamer Maté

Marion Andrews
- *Psycho-Cybernetics* by Maxwell Maltz

Matthew A. Swierk
- *Power of Awareness* by Neville Goddard

Melody J. Carberry
- *The Heart's Code* by Paul Pearsall

Mickey Forsyth
- *Lean In* by Sheryl Sandberg

Peter Giesin
- *The Other Talent* by Matt Fitzgerald

Summer Bozohora
- *Ex the Spiritual Roots of Disease* by Dr. Henry Wright

Yun Rhee
- *Oneness* by Rasha

RESOURCES

Andonia Reynolds
Websites:
- www.a.co/d/3quRyNU

Anita Adrain & Cheryl Viczko
Websites:
- www.herinspiredjourney.com
- www.wsfs.com (The Western School of Feng Shui)
- www.kryon.com (Lee Carroll)
- www.holyshiftmoment.com

Brenda Gerling
Websites:
- www.inspiredwellnessandwisdom.com

Books:
- *Change Your Thoughts, Change Your Life* by Wayne Dyer
- *You Can Heal Your Life* by Louise Hay
- *Dying to Be Me* by Anita Moorjani
- *A New Earth* by Eckhart Tolle
- *The Biology of Belief* by Bruce Lipton
- *Conversations with God* by Neale Donald Walsch

Christine Lang
Websites:
- www.liveabiglife.ca
- www.liveabiglife-books.ca

Ciara Caston Finley
Books:
- *The Bible* (various scriptures)
- *The Garden Within* by Dr. Anita Phillips
- *The Body Keeps the Score* by Bessel van der Kolk
- *Healing the Wounded Heart* by Dan Allender

Elaine Valerie Thompson
Websites:
- www.thewellwishershaven.com
- www.crackmycode.com/Wellwish (Personality Science Test)
- https://bit.ly/Wellwish7DaysofFLow (7 Days to Live Your Life in Flow)

Janice Gallant
Websites:
- www.thecreationguild.com/clearingdebristhroughforgivenesscourse/ (Clearing Debris Through Forgiveness Course)
- https://mailchi.mp/9b65e311b382/8-days-of-painting (8 Days of Painting)

Joe Kavanagh
Websites:
- www.codebreakerglobal.com/crackyourcode?code=kavanagh (Crack Your Code)

Lynda L. Sullivan
Websites:
- www.elevatedhumanexperience.com

Books:
- *Thinking into Results* by PGI
- *The Strangest Secret* by Earl Nightingale

Marion Andrews
Books:
- *Gloriously Grateful* by Marion Andrews

Matthew A. Swierk
Websites:
- www.ElevatedHumanExperience.com
- www.ElevatedSafariExperience.com
- www.MattSwierk.com

Summer Bozohora

Websites:

- www.courses.mindbodymedicinetherapy.com
- www.tinyurl.com/ConflictConnection (Conflict to Connection Course)
- www.achievingliberty.com/innerstrengthoutercalm (Inner Strength, Outer Calm)

Books:

- *Speak Peace in a World of Conflict* by Marshall Rosenberg
- *Soul-Side Out* by Summer Bozohora
- *Getting to Zero* by Jayson Gaddis

Podcast:

- *The Estranged Heart with Creed Revere*

Yun Rhee

Websites:

- www.linktr.ee/yunrhee
- www.elevatedhumanexperience.com

PROJECT LEADERS

LADY JB OWEN - EDITOR-IN-CHIEF

Lady JB Owen is a visionary entrepreneur, global speaker, and the founder of *Ignite Publishing*™ and the *Ignite Humanity*™ movement. She is dedicated to helping individuals around the world discover their unique greatness and live their best lives. Her humanitarian project Inspiration Classrooms is empowering education around the world. She is a world-class speaker, 25-time bestselling author, and powerful business owner who is committed to raising the vibration of the planet and igniting a billion lives. She combines purpose, passion, and possibilities in everything she does. Exemplifying a new paradigm of what's possible, Lady JB motivates and inspires her clients to impact others and IGNITE humanity.

ELAINE VALERIE THOMPSON - PROJECT COORDINATOR

Elaine Thompson, founder of *Yes You Can* and *The Wellwishers Haven*, is an International Best-Selling Author, Speaker, Reiki Master Teacher, Intuitive Healer, and Certified *FlowCode Coach*™. She blends neuroscience, cellular health, and intuitive healing to create lasting transformation; empowering women to shift their frequency, silence inner doubt, and step into a life of authenticity, flow, and divine purpose. Having overcome 33 years of chronic pain and self-doubt, Elaine chose faith over fear, deepened her intuition, and embraced a life of "being" over "doing". She champions living life in flow, guiding women to their most empowered path through workshops, one-on-one guidance, and inspirational talks.

CIARA CASTON FINLEY - PROJECT LEADER

Ciara Finley is a chef, innovator, and changemaker who uses her culinary gifts and personal journey to uplift, inspire, and impact others. As the Desiderata Kitchen Catering & Events owner, she blends leadership, generosity, and creativity to craft unforgettable culinary experiences. Deeply committed to giving back, she serves her community through shared meals and donations, using food as a vehicle for healing and support. Through her heartfelt storytelling, she empowers women who have battled self-doubt, encouraging them to embrace their worth. A devoted wife and mother, she believes food is more than nourishment; it's a bridge for connection, healing, and joy.

ANDONIA REYNOLDS - PROJECT LEADER

Andonia Reynolds is an equine specialist and cognitive behavior life coach with over 25 years of experience in the field. She harnesses the wisdom of horses to guide individuals through personal transformation, blending equine science, personal development, and emotional resilience. Growing up, Andonia found strength and clarity through her deep connection with horses, which empowered her to defy expectations and create a life of purpose. Today, through Mustang Wisdom, she offers transformative coaching experiences that merge nature, adventure, and self-discovery, inspiring others to overcome limiting beliefs and embrace their true potential.

FORBES RILEY - FOREWORD WRITER

Forbes is an author, award winning television personality, entrepreneur, creator of the SpinGym fitness sensation and one of the most sought after female keynote speakers. As a motivator and role model, Forbes has a unique connection with her audience that stems from her own personal journey.

Before becoming a media success, host of more than 100 infomercials and 20 years marketing products on home shopping channels worldwide, Forbes struggled with her own weight. Crowned by the press as the $2 Billion Dollar Host, she was determined to reach her goals — and through dedication, never ending passion and hard work, she has.

Dream It. Believe It. Achieve It. Forbes Riley has created a trusted brand name for herself and is recognized internationally as an award-winning TV host, spokesperson, celebrity fitness and lifestyle expert, professional coach, keynote speaker, actress and author. By sharing a unique and inspiring philosophy that stresses the integration of fitness, nutrition, and behavioral changes, Forbes empowers people everywhere to define and reach their personal goals, both physical and psychological and she is the true embodiment of dreaming it, believing it and achieving it.

PHOTO CREDITS

Andonia Reynolds - *Portraits by Rachelle*

Angela Robinette - *Roscoe Griffin*

Anita Adrain & Cheryl Viczko - *Kim Mortimer, SnapHappy Photographer*

Ann M. B. McIntyre - *Kathy Strauss*

Brenda Gerling - *Prairie Girl Photography*

Chantelle McFarland - *Natalia Wells with Affordable & Adorable Photography and Design*

Christine Lang - *Charlene Woodman*

Ciara Caston Finley - *Brandon Gilmore of Gilmore Photography & Design*

Claire Valiquette - *Natalia Wells with Affordable & Adorable - Photography and Design*

Dave August - *Sabrina Mounkes*

Doreen Kilbreath - *Natalia Wells with Affordable & Adorable - Photography*

Elaine Valerie Thompson - *Chanthavee Samountry - Chanthavee Photography*

Janice Gallant - *Mallory Todd Photography*

Lady JB Owen - *Stacey Thompkins Photography*

Jessica Sinclair - *Natalia Wells ~ Affordable and Adorable Photography*

Joe Kavanagh - *Matt Parker*

Karla VandenBerg - *Elizabeth Trujillo, Blushpiz Photography*

Kerstin Pelletier - *Pauline Valberg*

Kimberly E. Beaudoin - *Jodie Eljoke, Urban Flare Photography*

Lynda L. Sullivan - *Ashley Lucente*

Marion Andrews - *Michelle Frechette at https://clickhappydesigns.com*

Matthew A. Swierk - *Ashley Lucente*

Melody Carberry - *Mallory Todd Photography*

Mickey Forsyth - *Michelle Frechette*

Summer Bozohora - *Kayla HiddenSalt Studios*

Yun Rhee - *Ashley Lucente*

THANK YOU

To You, the Reader

Thank you for being here. Thank you for spending time with this book, opening your heart to these stories, and allowing yourself to be moved, inspired, and ignited. Your presence and enjoyment of these pages matter more than you will ever know.

By reading *Ignite Impact*, you are not just absorbing words. You are stepping into a shared experience, connecting with the voices of authors who have poured their hearts into their stories. You are engaging in something greater, a movement of transformation, expansion, and human connection. The lessons, insights, and emotions within these pages are now yours to carry forward in your own unique way.

Every book has the power to change a life, and every reader plays a role in that change. Whether this book has given you clarity, strength, a new perspective, or simply a moment of reflection, you are now part of its impact. Your willingness to engage with these stories keeps their impactful effect continuing for years to come.

By reading *Ignite Impact*, you are not just experiencing the journeys of others. You are engaging in a movement of transformation, connection, and possibility. These stories are reminders that impact is not reserved for the few; it lives within all of us. Every lesson, breakthrough, and act of impact shared in this book is now part of your journey also.

We hope these stories spark something within you. Whether they remind you of your own strength, encourage you to take action, or simply offer a new perspective, know that your engagement with this book creates an impact on you. By reading, reflecting, and sharing, you are already igniting impact in ways you may not even realize.

On behalf of our authors, our team, and storytellers around the world, we thank you for choosing to make *Ignite Impact* part of your book collection. Your appreciation for storytelling, personal growth, and the power of shared experiences makes books like this a force for connection and community.

To the Authors

A heartfelt thank you to every author who courageously shared their story in this book. Your words are more than just stories; they are sparks that have the potential to ignite hope, transformation, and limitless possibilities in others.

It takes bravery to be vulnerable, share a personal journey, and trust that your experiences will resonate with those who need them most. Your story's impact will travel far beyond these pages, reaching people in unexpected ways at precisely the right time. That is the true gift of sharing your story.

We deeply admire each author's voice's raw, unfiltered essence, recognizing that true impact comes from authenticity. Every story in this book was written from the heart, shaped by real experiences, and shared with the courage to be seen exactly as one is. Rather than polishing these stories into conventional perfection, we chose to preserve their individuality, the unique expressions, emotions, and truths that make them powerful.

The voices within these pages are not just words; they are lived experiences, moments of transformation, and deeply personal reflections that carry the ability to inspire, uplift, and ignite change. By staying true to each author's perspective, this book becomes more than a collection of stories. It becomes a testament to the strength in vulnerability, the wisdom in lived experience, and the undeniable power of storytelling in its purest form.

Ignite Impact is not about presenting a perfect narrative. It is about sharing real, raw, and resonant truths that remind us that **our stories, just as they are, hold the power to transform lives**.

To the Team

Behind every Ignite book is a dedicated team of individuals who believe in the power of storytelling and the limitless potential of human connection. To the *Ignite Publishing*™ team, we extend our deepest gratitude.

Your commitment, expertise, and unwavering support have shaped this book into something truly special. From the first draft to the final pages, every detail has been handled with care, intention, and love. This book exists because of your passion, your precision, and your belief in the power of every voice.

Your work does not just produce books. It ignites transformation that will Ignite Humanity™. Thank you for your dedication, your heart, and your vision.

Together, we Ignite.

Production Team: JB Owen, Kristine Joy Magno, Peter Giesin, Mimi Safiyah, Carolina Gold, and Brent Casteling

Editing Team: JB Owen, Mimi Safiyah, Jenette Longoria, Sarah Cross, Carissa Simpson, and Steph Elliott

Project Coordinator: Elaine Thompson

Project Leaders: Andonia Reynolds and Ciara Finley

WRITE YOUR STORY IN AN IGN|TE BOOK!!

THE ROAD TO SHARING YOUR MESSAGE AND BECOMING A BEST-SELLING AUTHOR BEGINS RIGHT HERE.

We make YOU a best-selling author in just four months!

If you have a story of perseverance, determination, growth, awakening, and change... and you've felt the power of your Ignite Moment, we'd love to hear from you.

We are always looking for motivating stories that will make a difference in someone's life. Our fun, enjoyable, four-month writing process is like no other—and the best thing about IGNITE is the community of outstanding, like-minded individuals dedicated to helping others.

With over 700 amazing individuals to date writing their stories and sharing their Ignite Moment, we are positively impacting the planet and raising the vibration of HUMANITY. Our stories inspire and empower others and we want to add your story to one of our upcoming books!

Go to our website, click How To Get Started, and share a bit of your Ignite transformation.

JOIN US TO IGNITE A BILLION LIVES WITH A BILLION WORDS.

Apply at: www.igniteyou.life/apply   Find out more at: www.igniteyou.life

Inquire at: info@igniteyou.life